MARIE STOPES AND THE SEXUAL REVOLUTION

'I am writing a book which will electrify England,' Marie Stopes told a friend, 'a book about the plain facts of marriage.' *Married Love* was published in 1918, sold over a million copies and was translated into 13 languages. Yet its thirty-seven-year-old author, a lecturer in fossil plants, was, she insisted, still a virgin.

Marie Stopes went on to open the first free birth control clinic in the British Empire and to win international fame for her work. But while admired by Bernard Shaw, the Duke of Windsor and much of the general public, her crusades aroused the violent opposition of the Roman Catholic Church, and she became enmeshed in a series of sensational libel suits. Orderly and brilliant as a scientist, Marie Stopes's emotional life reigned chaotic. She followed a married Japanese professor to Japan, declared her Canadian husband impotent, and so exhausted her second husband that he consented, in writing, to allow her to take any lover she pleased.

Drawing on hitherto unpublished family and personal letters and papers, a diary and Marie Stopes's unpublished novel, June Rose throws new light on the interweaving of the public and personal life of a fascinating and formidable woman.

June Rose is the author of several biographies: *The Perfect Gentleman*, the story of a Victorian woman who masquaraded as a man in the British Army; *Elizabeth Fry*, the nineteenth-century prison reformer; and *Modigliani*, the twentieth-century Italian painter. She lives in Highgate, London.

D0618509

"Marie Stopes, lady!—we ain't never 'eard of 'er!"

Marie Stopes and the Sexual Revolution

JUNE ROSE

faber and faber

LONDON · BOSTON

First published in 1992
by Faber and Faber Limited
3 Queen Square London WC1N 3AU
This paperback edition first published in 1993

Printed in England by Clays Ltd, St Ives Plc

A CIP record for this book is available from the British Library
ISBN 0–571–16970–8

2 4 6 8 10 9 7 5 3 1

To Ann and Neil

Contents

	List of Illustrations	x
	Acknowledgements	xi
	Preface	xiii
1	Growing Pains	1
2	Scholarly Pursuits	21
3	Japan	46
4	Independence	58
5	Breaking Out	83
6	Fulfilment	105
7	The Turning Point	130
8	Conflict	151
9	Private Life?	176
10	Late Blooms	197
11	Surviving	221
	Notes	247
	Chronology	262
	Select Bibliography	265
	Index	268

Illustrations

(All photographs courtesy of Harry Stopes-Roe, except where otherwise specified.)

1 Marie with her nurses at the Mother's Clinic, Holloway, in the early 1920s
2 Charlotte Carmichael Stopes, Marie's mother
3 Henry Stopes, Marie's father
4 The Stopes sisters
5 Marie's enrolment to the North London Collegiate. (Courtesy of the North London Collegiate School.)
6 Clothilde Von Wyss, pupil–teacher at the North London Collegiate
7 On a field trip from London University, c. 1902–3
8 Marie as a student in Munich c. 1903–4
9 Marie in her laboratory
10 Professor Fujii in Munich, 1904
11 Reginald Ruggles Gates
12 Aylmer Maude
13 Marie's second wedding, 1918
14 The National Birth Rate Commission's Deputation to the Home Office, 1919
15 Humphrey and Marie gardening at their home in Leatherhead
16 Marie with her son, June 1924
17 Marie and family
18 With Keith Briant, Humphrey Roe and Lord Alfred Douglas at Norbury Park, 1939
19 Off Portland Island with Avro Manhattan in 1957

Acknowledgements

Many people have helped me in the making of this book and I am most grateful for all the advice and encouragement I have received. In particular I would like to thank Marie Stopes's son, Dr Harry Stopes-Roe, and his wife Mary for generously inviting me to visit their home, granting me access to their collection of family papers and photographs and discussing the subject of my biography so openly and honestly.

No one could have been more helpful than Professor William G. Chaloner, FRS, of Royal Holloway and Bedford New College, who patiently explained the ABC of Paleobotany to me. I am grateful also to Mrs Joan Clanchy, Headmistress of North London Collegiate, and her archivist, Mrs Robin Townley, for allowing me to browse in the school's archives. Special thanks too to Ruth Dixon who permitted me to reproduce an unpublished letter from Marie Stopes to Frances Stevenson. James McGibbon, one of Marie's former publishers, kindly gave me his insight into her character; Mrs G. Gower contributed her memories of her stay with Marie Stopes as a child; and Lady Helen Brook was most helpful in her reminiscences of the early days of birth control.

To the staff of the British Library, particularly of the Manuscript Room, I owe a debt of gratitude for their unfailing courtesy. My particular thanks to Dr Lesley Hall, archivist at the Wellcome Institute for the History of Medicine, for helpful suggestions as to further reading. I would also like to thank David Doughan of the Fawcett Library and Susie Donat of Camden Libraries for their kind help.

I do appreciate the personal friends who gave me so much support: Renate Koenigsberger who read the manuscript and improved it with her suggestions; Miryana Vidakovic who delved into the immense manuscript collection on my behalf; and, not least, Gabrielle Morrison who typed the manuscript meticulously and made many valuable suggestions.

Finally I would like to thank my editor, Susanne McDadd, for her patience, encouragement and perceptive comments.

J.R., March 1992

Preface

'. . . there is nothing that helps so much with the economic emancipation of woman as a knowledge of how to control her maternity,' Marie Stopes wrote sixty years ago, a reformer with a vision of ideal marriage so radical that it threw her personal life into chaos.

Her famous book, *Married Love*, clarified the conduct and language of sexual intercourse after the First World War. Her name and her influence helped to boost birth control all over the world.

In 1921, with her husband, Humphrey Roe, she founded the first free birth control clinic in the British Empire, with the aim of enabling all women, particularly the poorest, to have their children when they chose.

With her vivid and complex personality, Marie Stopes fascinated both men and women. Yet although she forged a blueprint for ideal marriage and helped thousands of couples to attain sexual satisfaction, her own emotional life remained entangled. Her outstanding intellectual gifts, as paleobotanist, sexologist and later prolific, if indifferent, poet, left her elevated and isolated.

In the end Marie Stopes's career suffered because of her inability to co-operate with others in the field. Yet only a woman possessed of a passionate belief in herself could have torn away the twin veils of prudery and pornography to reveal a new vision of sexual love in marriage.

I

Growing Pains

Marie Stopes did not think so, but as a social reformer she was remarkably fortunate in her mother. Scholarly, neglectful of household duties and hypercritical of her daughter, Charlotte Carmichael Stopes fought for Women's Rights as Marie was growing up. Almost a hundred years ago, she analysed the plight of women: 'The lawyers of the nineteenth century have decided that the word "man" always includes "woman" when there is a penalty to be incurred but never includes "woman" when there is a privilege to be conferred.'[1] Her mother's example gave Marie the confidence and freedom to take women's emancipation for granted and to effect a sexual revolution in her turn.

Charlotte Carmichael was born in Edinburgh on 6 February 1841, shortly after Queen Victoria's accession to the throne. Charlotte retained a fierce pride in her Scottish ancestry: she could trace her lineage back to the eleventh century. A great-grandfather, an architect, had helped to design Edinburgh's elegant New Town, and Charlotte's grandfather was a friend and colleague of Sir Walter Scott, a partner and successor in his legal business. The family heirlooms that Charlotte handed down to Marie included a silver inkwell used by the novelist and a small, round oak table, said by the family to have belonged to Mary Queen of Scots.[2]

Eminently respectable as the family was, however, Charlotte's childhood was depressed by genteel poverty. She was the youngest of five children and was only thirteen when her father, the landscape painter James Ferrier Carmichael, died of tuberculosis. Sacrifices were made to give Charlotte an education at the best schools in Edinburgh but she spent a final session at a school for teacher training, for it was now clear that unless she could find a wealthy husband, Charlotte must support herself.

In the 1850s, opportunities for women's employment were bleak but pioneers had begun to address the deplorable state of girls' education. By the time Charlotte reached her teens there were four progressive schools in England offering girls a proper secondary education: Queen's College, Harley Street, Bedford College, the North London Collegiate School and Cheltenham Ladies' College. In London and Edinburgh progressive people began to discuss the need for a higher education for girls. Charlotte, a clever and studious child, listened intently to some of these discussions and began to long to enter university. She bitterly resented her idle elder brother William, who could easily take a degree at Edinburgh University yet cared nothing for his books. (He subsequently became a wholesale fruiterer.)

Charlotte refused to allow herself to be discouraged. In her teens she began to write stories for young people; *Alice Errol and other Tales* was published by Chambers when Charlotte was twenty.[3] She taught for a living, first in Miss Brodie's school; later she was employed with great success as a governess to Professor George Lawson's children. Lawson regarded Charlotte as an asset to his family and described her in a reference as a 'very intelligent and accomplished young lady'. Meantime she continued her cultural pilgrimage, joined an Edinburgh Literary Society and contributed frequently under the pen-name 'Lutea Reseda' to a literary magazine, *The Attempt*. The range of subjects she tackled reflects wide interests. They included medieval chivalry, George Eliot's characters, and Murillo's 'Holy Family'.

In 1867, when Charlotte was twenty-six, her yearning for a higher education was fulfilled, at least partially. A Society for the University Education of Women was founded in Edinburgh. Sympathetic professors offered extra-mural courses of lectures for clever young women. Charlotte was among the first to enrol and was, of course, an ideal candidate. She distinguished herself in English Literature, Logic and Psychology, her essays always singled out for praise, and she became the first woman in Scotland to gain a certificate for Arts to M.A. standard in three subjects. She also studied Experimental Physics and later took a diploma in seven subjects, the nearest equivalent to a degree that a female could attain.

As a young woman Charlotte had allowed herself little time for feminine pursuits, although it comes as a relief to learn that she did enjoy dancing. Her struggle to gain an education had taken up all of her energy. By her thirties she was a powerful and courageous woman with a probing brain and a sharp tongue which belied her demure, neat-featured appearance. Brought up in a Presbyterian home, Charlotte was a devout Christian but, like many Victorian intellectuals of the period, she had been shaken to the core by advances in science and believed that in the future science and scientists would play an influential part in the reform of society.

Marie Stopes said, years later, that she was a child of the British Association for the Advancement of Science. Her parents met through the Association and during Marie's childhood, one or the other or all of the family attended the meetings. The BAAS, founded in York in 1831 to promote interest in all the sciences, met annually in a provincial city in late August or early September. In 1876 the Annual Meeting was held in Glasgow, and it seems most likely that Charlotte met her future husband there, in an atmosphere of earnest and erudite discussion.

The couple were extraordinarily reticent about the courtship. Later, Charlotte said that it was Henry Stopes's spiritual qualities that had attracted her to him. He came from Quaker stock and often attended Friends' Meetings, although he was now a pillar of the Congregational Church, a deeply and quietly religious man. The first present he gave to Charlotte was a book with text, hymn and address for every day of the year. The attraction must, however, have been based on more earthly qualities, one suspects, especially since a friend of Charlotte's described her before her marriage as a 'born old maid who should never have married'.

The feeling between them, admiration and delight in a personable and educated woman on Henry's part and the attraction of a handsome husband with good prospects on Charlotte's, was strong enough to defy convention and overcome an unusual disparity in their ages. Henry looked older than his twenty-four years, with serious dark eyes, high forehead and a wealth of chestnut hair which merged into a moustache and beard almost covering the lower part of his face, while, at thirty-five, Charlotte had an exceptionally sturdy constitution and a trim figure and was a stimulating and challenging companion.

Most of the intellectuals who attended the British Association meetings to hear scientists of the stature of T. H. Huxley or Francis Galton (Darwin's cousin) were freethinkers. The challenge of Darwin's theory was stark. To many people it seemed to be a choice between 'a world with God and a world without God.'[4] Charlotte and Henry clung to each other in the face of the new knowledge and clung to God. That was particularly remarkable in Henry's case, because he was deeply absorbed by prehistoric science, and his inquiring nature could not be confined by the bounds of orthodoxy.

From boyhood Henry had been stirred and excited by the publication of Darwin's *The Origin of Species* and his imagination marvelled at the notion that beneath the earth's surface lay evidence of man's life millions of years before the Biblical accounts. When he was eight, Henry was whipped for hiding fossil stones in his bed but he was undeterred and grew up to become a knowledgeable amateur archaeologist and anthropologist. His 'real' profession was architecture and he had graduated as a civil engineer and architect. As the son of a wealthy brewing family in Colchester, Henry had built a brewery and had considerable expert knowledge of malt and barley. But his heart was not in it.

After their wedding in Edinburgh in June 1879, the couple settled at first in Langham Moor, a village some five miles from Colchester, while Henry concentrated on business affairs. Every Sunday if it was fine, he drove Charlotte in a dog cart to the Congregational Church in Colchester where he had his own pew. If the weather was wet, the couple attended the parish church instead. To make up for a delayed honeymoon the couple set off on an extensive tour of Europe and the Near East, travelling by train and by steamer. Henry mapped out the itinerary carefully to include sites of potential importance to prehistoric science. Charlotte had sensibly taken a course in Field Geology before her marriage, to equip herself for life with a man obsessed by archaeology. In Egypt, Asia Minor and Palestine Henry and, at first, Charlotte spent whole days digging in likely sites for flint implements and evidence of man's early settlement and, in Egypt, Henry uncovered the first stone axe ever found.

During the honeymoon Charlotte became pregnant, though from Henry's detailed account it would be difficult to deduce that he was a newly married husband with a pregnant wife. Charlotte's name does not occur once. In a microscopic hand he wrote on the left-hand side of a small diary detailed expenses for items such as hotel bills, cakes, wine, taxis, tips, etc., and on the right he gave a matter-of-fact report on his excursions. The visits to Pompeii, the Naples Museum, climbing Vesuvius, and so on are all noted meticulously and, occasionally, even the names of their travelling companions are mentioned, but Henry never once said 'we' or referred to his new wife.

Charlotte later wrote articles about their extensive honeymoon. She described a meal in an Egyptian harem when she had to eat lamb with her fingers and confessed that she was more thrilled by the performance of a Passion Play in Oberammergau than by visiting Jerusalem.

The tour was obviously of great cultural interest but the only clue to the couple's personal lives lay in the fact that when they came home in late July 1880, with Charlotte at thirty-nine over six months pregnant, Henry travelled enthusiastically to Swansea to present the evidence of the flint tools he had found to the British Association while Charlotte was left to journey up to Edinburgh, where she always felt more at home, to take long walks and wait for the baby.

The first positive hint that all might not be well in the marriage came in a letter from Henry while he was at Swansea: 'My darling,' he wrote, 'tell me what is the other danger that may make you care less for me than you even now do? . . . God bless you, my darling. Ever with fond love, Your Harry.'[5] The danger, never explained, might have come partly from a pamphlet Charlotte read that year. In 1879, Sydney Smith wrote a thirty-page tract on *The Enfranchisement of Women, the Law of the Land*.[6] Charlotte was deeply affected by his arguments and brooded on them for years. Later she was to study old records, law books and parliamentary journals in order to write and lecture on the inequalities and injustices of women's status in society. A year of marriage had done nothing to dissuade her from the view that men possessed an unfair advantage in life.

The couple had bought a house in Cintra Grove, Upper Norwood, near the Crystal Palace, conveniently close to Henry's offices in 24 Southwark Street in south-east London, but Charlotte stayed up in Edinburgh until the baby was born on 15 October.

'Is it a girl?' was her first question to the doctor. When she received the right answer she sighed: 'Thank the Lord', and lay back on the pillow. Both parents were delighted and the birth of their first child drew them together. Charlotte's attitude to her new baby was typically analytical. In her black diary she wrote:

Marie Stopes born on October 15 1880: Course of intellectual development. End of first month, November 15th: the baby has been christened Marie Charlotte Carmichael Stopes. She has shewn considerable enjoyment in life, rarely objecting to its manifestations. She loves to toast her feet at the fire, to be bathed, to be chucked under the chin and sung to. She shews this approbation by smiles.

At the end of November the proud mother added: 'Baby has shewn great intellectual development. No wonder, she has travelled far. At six weeks she has travelled by night from Edinburgh to London and was sublimely content with the rattle of the railway wheels.'[7]

Both Charlotte and Henry believed firmly in the benefit of calisthenics and the outdoor life, and when they took the ten-month-old baby to Shanklin on the Isle of Wight for her first summer holiday, Charlotte prided herself on dipping the baby into the sea every day, despite large waves and bitter winds.

At home, after living for almost forty years as a single woman, Charlotte found the running of a household a trial. She had Annie in the kitchen to cook and Bessie, Marie's nurse, who also waited at table to help her. But Bessie succeeded in setting the nursery curtains on fire and had to be discharged. Then Henry insisted on having his say in choosing the next nurse, Miss Ellsworth. And although Charlotte wanted desperately to be a model mother, when she made baby clothes for Marie they never seemed to fit properly.

Living in a south London suburb Charlotte missed her friends and tried to re-create in her Norwood drawing-room the stimulus of intellectual life in Edinburgh. Within months of settling in London she had founded a Logic Class, a Discussion Society and a Shakespeare Reading Society for the ladies of the district. Too often the discussions turned into lectures. Charlotte was so much more knowledgeable than the others and naturally didactic. Passionately interested in Shakespeare and Bacon, she was to write erudite books and papers on the subject.

That year, 1881, Henry decided not to attend the Annual Meeting of the British Association, a real sacrifice for him since Professor Huxley was speaking on 'The Rise and Progress of Palaeontology'. But, by March 1882, the urge to join an archaeological expedition gripped him again and he told Charlotte that he had to go to Greece for a month. 'Not feeling well and not being inclined to spend a month in dull loneliness, I suggested I should go to Scotland which was settled',[8] Charlotte wrote wearily. She took her eighteen-month-old baby back to Edinburgh where they stayed for a fortnight with Charlotte's Aunt Anne before coming home dutifully to prepare the house for Henry's homecoming.

Two years later, on 13 March 1884, another child, thankfully a girl, was born, three-and-a-half years after Marie. No separate diary was opened for Marie's younger sister Winnie, nor does her name crop up often in family letters or diaries. All the hopes were centred on Marie. Henry built a wing on the house and a veranda at the back where the little girls could play when it was too wet to go into the large garden. Marie loved the garden with its long flowerbeds, in particular an old quince tree, where as soon as she could scramble she would perch in its branches and watch her father's horses being groomed in the stable yard.

Marie was a solitary child and found the atmosphere of the home with its clutter of books, boxes of stone and heavy Victorian furniture somewhat oppressive. As a grown woman she vividly remembered the stern Presbyterian teachings of her mother. For Charlotte's family belonged to the Free Church of Scotland, the extreme Protestant sect. The Bible was law in the household in Edinburgh and Marie's Scottish grandmother read from it daily. As a small girl Marie was threatened with the torments of hellfire, which were 'an absolute reality' yet promised the protection and mercy of an all-loving God. The contradiction left her confused and anxious.

The girls dreaded Sundays, when the family attended the local Baptist church three times, and, after a traditionally heavy luncheon of roast beef, Yorkshire pudding, custard, fruit, walnuts and wine, their mother would retire to her bedroom to rest, while father read Carlisle on the dining room sofa. Marie and Winnie had to speak in whispers, were allowed no toys and given only improving Sunday books to read. Once, as Marie tiptoed past Charlotte's bedroom she was shocked to see her mother sewing but Charlotte explained hastily that it was to save the servants from sinning. The sense of sin was strong in the home and played upon Marie's imagination. Years later she recalled yearning for the Blood of Jesus to cleanse her from her sins: 'I remember placing myself at the foot of a long flight of stairs, the bottom of which was a sheepskin mat dyed crimson and I rubbed myself in the crimson wool of the mat and tried to picture the stream of the Blood of the Lamb cascading down the stairs and over me, purifying me and taking away my manifold sins.'[9] Marie's feelings of guilt and longing for attention led her to imagine herself at the centre of catastrophic events. One day when the family were staying with friends, their hostess read out a paragraph in the paper about an earthquake. To her astonishment Marie burst out crying: 'Oh, but I can't help it. It is really not my fault.'[10]

Despite Charlotte's best efforts to bring up her daughters, the religiosity of her background, combined with her dour temperament, cast a shadow on their childhood. Henry was content to allow his wife to supervise the children's religious education. He brought a much needed playfulness into the home with his passion for animals. Henry trained Fluff, the family cat and the girls' 'brother' to sit in his own high chair and eat from his own dinner plate at mealtimes. From family letters one gains the sense that it was safe to love and laugh at the antics of the pet puss in a way that was denied to the children. Years later Marie remembered bitterly that one Sunday when the joint of beef was carved, her mother said: 'That's too rare for Fluff, give it to Marie!'[11]

Henry adored his daughters, but he was often away from home and when he was present he was frequently preoccupied by his books and his boxes of stones. Although he did not interfere with the little girls' religious training, his puritan background made him draw the line at dancing lessons. For once, it was Charlotte who insisted that Marie should share dancing lessons with three other local children. She herself missed the outlet and one day when she was teaching Marie a few little steps admitted that it was 'a pity your Papa does not like dancing as well as I do'. 'Never mind, Mama, perhaps some other young gentleman may fall in love with you who likes dancing better,' Marie replied. Charlotte pointed out hastily that after marriage people could not change their minds.[12]

That summer, July 1886, the evidence of an incompatible marriage was beginning to pile up. On the 30th, Henry wrote an impassioned letter to his wife who was at the seaside with the girls, pleading for a closer union. After seven years together he felt the coldness between them:

Dearest, will you not put from you the teachings of your splendid brain and look only into the depths of your heart and see if you can but find there the love that every woman should hold for the father of her babies? . . . We would put from us the seven blank years that ended and commence the truer honeymoon.[13]

Charlotte did not respond. Sex had proved distasteful to her and she later confessed herself pained by the 'sensual look' on Henry's face when he was a young man. For her the seven years of marriage had turned out to be a period of intellectual deprivation in which she 'could not read, let alone write a book'. As the years passed, Charlotte began to develop interests outside the home and to spend time researching into the Women's Cause in Record Offices and Museums, while Henry's letters became respectful but distant. He signed himself: 'Yours dutifully'.

The same day that Henry had written that plea to Charlotte, he also answered Marie's little note, which was full of warm affection: 'My dear Papa, I love you and I want to write a letter to you. I am glad you are happy and good.' Henry replied:

Think, is it not you are happy because you are good? Be kind to the cockatoo and to Winnie too. Play with the sand and the tiny little waves. The mightiest force on earth loves to play in the sunlight with little girls. Listen to the murmur of the ripples and hear what they say to you.[14]

In September, from the British Association, he wrote to her on a more practical note: 'I hope you have not bitten your nails, if not, tell Annie to give you a penny.'[15]

As if to console each other, Henry and his elder daughter drew close together. Increasingly it was her father who provided the guidance and tenderness. When she was five, the future sex reformer asked her mother where her new sister had come from. 'When I went to bed Winnie wasn't there and the next morning she was,' she was told. Not that Henry would have given her a more explicit answer. Sex was never discussed in the family and although both Charlotte and Henry were progressive and broadminded in accepting intellectual ideas, Marie and Winnie were brought up in the clamp of Victorian prudery.

In her own way, Charlotte did love her children and she was determined to give them a good educational grounding. With her scrubbed-clean appearance, neat features, lips pressed together, firm jaw and hair scraped back, she looked every inch a schoolmarm. Naturally, as a former governess, she held decided views on the upbringing of children. She gave her little girls few toys to play with, preferring them to learn to amuse themselves. Henry and the aunts were warned sternly never to repeat the children's sayings to discourage them from being self-conscious. They were not to be spoilt. Admirable and well-thought out as Charlotte's regime was, it was also arid. She was quick to find fault but neglected to hug the children, to praise them and to show her pride, and all her life Marie felt a compelling need to prove herself.

Marie's first experience of education was as Charlotte's pupil, since her mother did not consider that any of the schools in the district were suitable. Every morning, when the housemaid turned the nursery out, five-year-old Marie tottered into Charlotte's room carrying a pile of books balanced on a large atlas. While Charlotte read to her from the *Tales of Greece and Rome* or *The History of Scotland and England*, Marie carefully followed the stories on the map in the big atlas. The front cover, she always remembered, showed a picture of the earth surrounded by clouds, rolling round the sun and she had to repeat 'The earth is round and rolls in space'. The ambitious syllabus also included the roots of English language, Grammar, Composition and the theory and practice of music. Charlotte attempted to teach Marie Latin and

Greek but even she could not manage to instil a knowledge of the classics into a five-year-old.

By the time Marie was six, both of her parents would go away on visits independently. With such an emancipated mother, Marie came early and easily to take for granted women's equality in every sphere. In 1887, when Marie was not yet seven, Charlotte travelled up to a meeting of the British Association in Manchester. From the train she wrote to Marie: 'I have left Winnie greatly in your care and I expect that you will be extra kind and careful of her while I am away as you must be little mother and big sister at the same time. Manchester is a smoky, dirty place,' she added, 'no fun for little girls, otherwise I may have brought you.'[16]

Fun was notably missing in the Stopes's home, where every activity, even dancing, had to be taken seriously. When Marie was sewing her doll's clothes, it gave her mother an excuse for a homily: 'Careless sewing is neither good for dolly – or for you.' Marie was always being warned by Charlotte to work hard, to be virtuous and kind, yet no matter how she tried never seemed able to win her mother's approval and the burden of rectitude lay heavily on her shoulders.

By the time Marie was eight, her mother expected her to take on household cares. Again, Charlotte was away at a meeting of the British Association, this time in Bath. 'Papa has gone to London,' she wrote, 'and it is quite possible he may go to [Norwood] tonight. Annie had better get ¼lb of nice salt beef and a kipper and if he does not come, you can eat it up. You will remember his breakfast medicine, of course'.[17]

Charlotte was a prominent member of the Rational Dress Society, in rebellion against the corsets and stays, flannel petticoats and flounced and frilled skirts worn by Victorian ladies. In 1889, at the Annual Meeting of the British Association in Newcastle-upon-Tyne, she presented a paper on the subject, informing her audience that, according to two leading London couturiers, the fashion for tight lacing was going out.

Early photographs of Charlotte show her wearing tightly-waisted crinolines but, in middle-age, she wore loosely flowing garments – without corsets. Persuaded by his wife Constance, who edited *The Rational Dress Gazette*, Oscar Wilde decided to take up the subject in his illustrated magazine *Women's World*, and asked Charlotte to write him a 'bright, piquant article'. She was, of course, delighted but the consequences of Charlotte's commitment to rational dress were less happy for Marie and Winnie. Victorian children wore long stockings and body stays, stockingette knickers, a profusion of petticoats, flannel in cold weather and, as they grew up, fitted corsets. All these layers were topped by a tight-fitting miniature version of their mothers' dresses. Charlotte's girls, by contrast, were put into loose-fitting, knitted garments that allowed them much greater freedom of movement. But like all children who look different, Marie and Winnie felt awkward and miserable in sensible clothes and were teased by their Scottish cousins when they met.

Charlotte's food fads, too, singled out the girls in a way which was outwardly trivial but deeply hurtful to a sensitive child like Marie. At the time rock cakes studded with raisins were all the rage at children's parties. Charlotte distrusted dried fruit; at her home she offered the children plain and iced cakes but *no* rock cakes. Marie felt this as a humiliation and came to dread giving tea parties. Since they did not go to school, the Stopes sisters were isolated in childhood and no 'best friends' were made. The three-and-a-half years difference between the sisters meant that Marie was always looking after Winnie, a docile, rather delicate little girl; the two were thrown together but were never real companions.

By the late 1890s Charlotte's diverse literary, political and scholarly activities were taking up more of her time. She had joined the Women's University Club, was a reader at the British Museum and was gaining in confidence and experience as a speaker and writer for the Women's Movement, interested in the participation of women in local government as well as in women's suffrage. When Charlotte was otherwise occupied, a governess was sporadically engaged to teach the girls but Charlotte had begun to realize that they needed regular schooling. She felt little confidence in the English education system.

In Edinburgh, where Charlotte kept up her contacts in the Suffrage movement, her women friends had spoken well of a girls' school founded by suffragists to give pupils a sound educational grounding. Charlotte accordingly arranged for the girls to stay with a suitable family in the neighbourhood.

In the summer of 1892, before term started, Charlotte had taken Marie and Winnie to a spa at Matlock to recuperate from coughs and colds, while Henry remained in town. In a letter to her father, Marie asked for news of Fluff, the cat. 'I do miss him so much', she said and added tellingly, 'I do hope you will come to see us in Edinburgh when we go there.'[18] She sent sixty huge rows of kisses for father and thirty-three for Fluff. Henry, too, was missing the family. 'I am glad you wrote to me as I wish so much to know how you all are. You do not say why Mama cannot write . . .'[19]

In the past Henry had designed breweries successfully in both London and Colchester but now his architectural practice had begun to lose money. He had neglected it badly, taking months off for his archaeological expeditions and spending a great deal of time writing learned papers on the art of brewing and on pre-history. In September 1892, just before the girls went to school, H. Stopes & Co. moved to smaller premises, No. 31 Torrington Square, London.

Marie started her first term at St George's in Edinburgh in October just before her twelfth birthday. She found herself backward in some subjects due to Charlotte's idiosyncratic teaching methods and she was put into a form with girls much younger than she was. Marie was a proud child and she felt the humiliation intensely. 'Went to bed very cross,' she noted in her school diary, dated 4 October 1892.[20] But a week later she was put up from the Lower Third to the Upper Third and began to work hard, eager to please her teachers. Charlotte tried to console her, in her fashion: 'It was not your fault that you were left behind in some things,' she wrote reasonably, 'the only things I blame you for are carelessness and inexactitude. Do set yourself in earnestness to cure yourself of these faults. Remember, you are learning not for a day or a week or a year but for life.'[21]

At home, marital and financial affairs were in difficulty and Charlotte wrote to Marie as if she were an adult, giving her a full account of her activities as a member of the Rational Dress Society and of the Aristotelian Society, of her work at the British Museum or darning father's socks. Often her letters were shot through with self-pity. She was lonely, missing the girls, business was bad and father involved in a lawsuit; he had not worked for months and had no money to buy stones. 'At times I feel that if it were not for my children I would lie down and die.'[22]

Decades ahead of her time, Charlotte was struggling to be an independent woman, work outside the home and take care of her family. The effort kept her in a permanent state of muddle. She sent the girls to Edinburgh with dirty nightgowns she meant to have mended, and forgot to send clean vests. Since sewing took up hours and hours of her time, she decided that Marie and Winnie must devote half-an-hour each evening after school, homework and piano practice, to mending their own clothes.

Charlotte needed the freedom to pursue her own interests, but was unwilling to delegate authority, so she gave the girls endless instructions.

They were to rub their chests with olive oil every night, and not to go out in cold weather. Marie had to supervise visits to the dentist for Winnie, whose teeth were bad. Their round was austere. Charlotte asked anxiously how many times they visited church on Sunday and Marie was reminded to read the Bible. She collected shells and stamps and occasionally had an opportunity to practise her chess. In almost every letter, Charlotte reminded her to visit this old friend or that elderly aunt, or to collect signatures for a suffragist register. Even the treats Charlotte organized for the girls in Edinburgh, through her friends, were something of an ordeal. A Miss Menzies, interested in Iceland, read the sagas to the girls; on Saturday afternoon her cook taught them to make ginger-bread and scones, which was better. But Miss Mair's parties were truly terrifying. After a gorgeous tea, each child was asked to entertain the company with a clever remark!

Most of the letters to both girls were addressed to Marie, who was used as a go-between by both parents. 'Papa never remembers my birth-day,' her mother complained. As the elder sister, Marie bore the responsi-bility for Winnie's health. At eight Winnie often suffered from chills, headaches and inexplicable rashes. Marie gloried in her sturdier consti-tution: 'Don't you think Winnie is greedy?' she wrote to her father on 12 March 1893, 'she has not given me the least bit of measles but kept it all to herself.'[23]

Marie's own weakness was her horror of criticism and teasing. Both girls drew well (Charlotte's father had been an artist and she took pains to teach them) but Marie had boasted of her own skill and the girls at school teased her arrogance. She suffered horribly. From a distance, Charlotte tried to help and encouraged Marie to confide in her: 'There ought to be perfect confidence between mother and child,' she wrote. Since her mother was always so critical, Marie was never open with her. As always it was her father who monopolized her affections. Despite business worries and a lawsuit, in 1892 Henry rented Swanscombe Manor in the hamlet of Swanscombe in Kent, rightly convinced that the vast gravel pits close by would yield relics of prehistory. He soon dis-covered prehistoric hand-axes and wrote to Marie with enthusiasm of his find of seventy beautiful work flints and a 'dear little baby elephant tooth'.

As a small girl Marie had enjoyed accompanying her father on his digs, watching him gently prise the stones out of the rock with his hammer. Later, she helped him to wash, catalogue and label hundreds of stones. In her letters she 'sent her love to the flints and the flints sent their love back'. It was an enchanted world they secretly inhabited. The flints are, Henry confided 'full of a rich, long story of brave, true struggles in the past of right against might'.[24]

After the Christmas holidays of 1893, Henry sent Marie back to school with a collection of flint implements to be donated to the Society of Antiquaries in Scotland. Proud to be entrusted with the package, Marie gave such precise and detailed information about the nature of the flints and the best way of labelling them when she handed them over, that the curator, Dr Anderson, amused and impressed, persuaded the headmistress of her school to allow Marie to lecture to the girls on the fossils: 'My first lecture, oh, dear, it was dreadfull!' she wrote to her father, 'then I had to do it again for the students, those are the ones who are going to be teachers.'[25] But she felt the first glow of recognition: 'I have the honour to inform you that your acceptable donation will be announced and exhibited at one of the ensuing meetings of the Society of the Antiquaries of Scotland,' Dr Anderson wrote to her.[26]

That was the first time that Marie had distinguished herself at school. Her spelling, as Charlotte was quick to point out was 'dreadfull' and, by now, her mother was dissatisfied with the progress her girls had made. Miss Buss's school, the North London Collegiate, like Miss Beale's Cheltenham Ladies' College was highly thought of in progressive circles. Miss Buss herself was a prominent supporter of the Women's Cause and the school's reputation was such that staid middle-class parents, used to establishments which offered more genteel accomplishments for young ladies 'put up with the mathematics' in order to give their girls a sound education. With her experience of marriage, perhaps Charlotte appreciated the contemporary rhyme about the two headmistresses:

> Miss Buss and Miss Beale
> Cupid's darts do not feel:
> How different from us,
> Miss Beale and Miss Buss!

Despite the fees, which Charlotte warned Marie in a letter were very high, Henry made a formal application for Marie's admission at the end of July. Winnie was to attend the school's preparatory section for two terms before joining the Senior School. That summer the family moved from Norwood to Denning Road, near Hampstead Heath. When the moving van appeared with stacks and stacks of boxes of fossils, a neighbouring Professor of Geology was horrified: 'Good God,' he spluttered, 'we've got a grocer moving in next door'.

The move to north London was of immense importance to Marie, who was almost fourteen. At the pioneering school girls received a thorough and comprehensive grounding in all subjects in an atmosphere of emancipation. Four years before Marie joined the school, an annual sports day was held in defiance of convention. The pupils wore special sports uniform of light-coloured knee-length skirts, white blouses loosely belted at the waist and striped caps. When they walked about in their ordinary garb of long skirts and high-necked blouses, North London Collegiate girls swung their arms vigorously to show passers-by that they were 'freed from the trammels of tradition'. Many of the old girls were pursuing careers in the new professions of medicine, school teaching and journalism, opening up to women in the 1890s. In the school magazine there were reports of women travelling the world, climbing in the Alps, bicycling and golfing. To widen their horizons, at the end of each term experts in a variety of subjects, from the music of Mendelssohn to the influence of photography on modern art, lectured to the girls. Through her friendship with the headmistress, Charlotte took the opportunity to give a talk on sixteenth-century women students in Shakespeare's time, which must have embarrassed her elder daughter.

After Marie's first term, the ageing, white-haired Miss Buss was succeeded by Dr Sophie Bryant as headmistress. Dr Bryant, a strong feminist and a graduate of London University, was the first woman to take a degree in science. Chemistry was her subject and fortunately Marie showed some promise in science and was given encouragement. Otherwise, she seemed to the staff to be rather a dull student in her first year at North London. In spite of, or perhaps because of, Charlotte's efforts to tutor her at the age of five in Latin and Greek, she found those subjects extremely difficult. The children were in any case at a disadvantage, since they were not allowed to go to school in the afternoons, presumably to save money.

Nevertheless Winnie won prizes, for holiday work in Scripture and Science. Marie, as fascinated as her father with fossils, spent part of her holidays and weekends at Swanscombe helping him.

Charlotte was extremely busy, lecturing and writing. In Stratford-on-Avon in April 1896 she heard the American Ambassador give a commemorative speech on the Bard's birthday. '. . . he made some slips,' she wrote to Marie. Charlotte seized eagerly on the errors and corrected them in a letter to the press. After her letter was published, 'the Ambassador and Lord Ronald Gower asked to be introduced and things were pleasant', she crowed.[27]

It was typical of Charlotte that, although she wrote Marie a sermoniz-ing letter on her sixteenth birthday, exhorting her to 'purity and good-ness', she had not bought a present. 'I have been so busy that I have never been out since I saw you,' she wrote, 'so I think the present must be decided when I see you.'[28]

Aware of how little mothering Marie had enjoyed, her father wrote to assure her that she was 'never forgotten if seemingly overlooked'.[29] In almost every letter he wrote praising his wife's outstanding qualities to Marie, telling her how privileged she was to have such a mother:

'With so great a mother life is (and must be) different in some of its aspects to [sic] other children's. It is now time to tell you that with such advantages as you possess you have to do ... for yourself and others what your mother did with so few advantages ... I want you to feel that you have the warm, loving arms of a father round you. With fondest love your affectionate father'.[30]

Marie hardly needed reminding that she had to measure up to her mother, but fortunately that year she had begun to come into her own. A week after her sixteenth birthday she was elected to the Committee of the Science Club and gave what the School Magazine described as a 'most interesting paper on Prehistoric man, illustrated by a beautiful collection of flint tools'. For the second time in her school career her work with her father, digging up fossils, had brought her recognition. As she grew into womanhood, she met many of her father's scientific friends, Norman McColl the Editor of the *Athenaeum*, Professor Sayle the physiologist, and a man whose views were to influence her in later life, Sir Francis Galton, who argued for the existence of a natural élite in mankind and coined the word Eugenics.

The Vice-President of the Science Club, Clothilde Von Wyss, a former pupil and now a young teacher, inspired passionate devotion among the older girls. Marie was one of the select group who accompanied Miss Von Wyss on expeditions to Pinner to gather wild flowers or to Epping Forest where the party went pond-dipping with nets and jam-jars to fish out water-snails and sticklebacks. Marie's was an ordinary schoolgirl crush on Miss Von Wyss but, because of her temperament, more painful and intense than most. She jostled fiercely with the others to sit beside her idol and hold her hand on trips to the country and bring flowers for her to school.

Marie was at that painful time of life when she was seeking spiritual as well as emotional fulfilment. Unfortunately she associated religion with her mother's reproving attitude:

> 'The love of God was formalized for me
> By Church and State and rigid home decree;
> I listened while the printed prayers were said,
> And meekly heard th'appointed service read,
> Feeling it sterile, weary, dry and dead.'

she wrote in a long narrative poem, 'The Brother', published almost twenty years later.[31] In adolescence, it was only when she and her father went to Friends' Meeting together, where they sat in silent communion, that Marie was transported.

Six months after her sixteenth birthday, while staying in the country, she decided to visit a Quaker Meeting House alone, looking for inspiration. She was deeply disillusioned. Hoping for acceptance, she felt the worshippers were cold and excluding, their dress too fashionable, their mode of service too formal. Instead of the spontaneous outpourings she had imagined, speakers read from notes and the congregation sang from hymn books. Worst of all, when a clumsy workman blundered in, Marie felt that he was looked down upon; she shared her hymn-book with the newcomer. Suddenly, in the silence, the workman rose to his feet and confessed to the congregation that he had killed his brother and asked them to pray for him. To Marie's disappointment, she sensed a chill of disapproval run through the Meeting House. Later three of the Quakers followed the sinner out of the Meeting to ensure that he gave himself up to the police. Marie spoke to no one of the incident but remembered it for years, convinced that her poetic account was 'absolutely true and unvarnished' although it was extremely rare for hymn books to be used in Quaker Meetings at the time. The incident led her to dissociate herself increasingly from formal religion, yet she never doubted that she possessed a personal means of communication with God.

At last, in the second half of her teens, Marie also began to develop her intellectual potential. She read widely, obviously influenced by her parents, the whole of Darwin, Swedenborg, Kant and Confucius, but emotionally she remained a child. In the spring term of 1898 she managed to matriculate at the age of seventeen, delighted with even a second-class pass. 'You didn't deserve to get through, how did you manage it?' her Latin mistress remarked dourly. 'I concentrated on the things I knew and ignored the things I didn't know,' Marie answered shrewdly. As she pointed out to her father, nearly half the girls failed and even the four they thought would shine didn't win prizes. Highly competitive, Marie always liked to point out the failings of others to enhance her own position. She was developing well at school, especially in chemistry, where she was encouraged by Miss Aitken, the chemistry mistress. She made friends; Olga Kapteyn, a girl of Dutch origin, became a friend for life. Marie was also made a prefect that term. Yet, like many gifted adolescents, Marie showed a marked imbalance between her intellectual and emotional development. 'Dearest father', she wrote on 20 July 1898 in one breathless sentence: 'I am so sorry you are ill but I am so happy I have passed matric after all . . .'[32]

Apart from her father, Marie lived both at home and at school in an almost exclusively female society. Her father over-protected her, perhaps to make up for her mother's neglect, perhaps for more complex reasons. The girls were not allowed to hold dances at home and only on Charlotte's insistence were they reluctantly given permission to attend dances held at their friends' homes. At school in North London she dissected frogs and discussed their reproductive organs, but human sex was taboo. The only instruction she had at home was from her father and that was entirely negative. To kiss a boy before marriage was impure and no girl from a decent home could consider marriage before the age of twenty-five. Henry Stopes was both possessive and unconsciously prurient in his attitude to his beloved daughter. In a letter of 9 April 1899, he cautioned Marie not to read too many novels and to avoid going to the beach before breakfast. 'It is so very probable that some gravely unpleasant flotsam may be washed up and it is better to avoid it . . .'[33]

In the meantime Marie had been seeing a good deal of Clothilde Von Wyss. With three other girls she sent Clothilde a present of a brooch:

'not so much as a token of our love but as the outward and visible sign of a deep inner tie to friendship: a bond of unity which has, under your influence, drawn us all together and made us kin . . . May we . . . according to our individual light, seek to gain a more perfect knowledge of mysteries yet unsolved . . . thus with the aid of love, the eternal light, may we endeavour to illuminate in some degree, however small, the dark, unfathomable enigma of life.'[34]

Perhaps it is not fanciful to see the hand of the author of *Married Love* in that effusion. Clothilde herself displayed an unprofessional preference for her pupil, inviting Marie to come and see her beetles and frogs ('you and Winnie, of course') in May. By August she was writing Marie mystical letters, rich with hints of delight. 'Maybe we shall never in this life complete that glorious song of truth, insight and adoration for which our soul craves! . . .'[35]

During the year the two exchanged gifts. Marie sent Clothilde a tablecloth she had embroidered with pink roses, while Clothilde sent Marie a volume of Thoreau's essays with a throbbing message: 'Whenever I think of you a strange gladness creeps over me and I feel rich in the thought of your love and less lonely.' For her birthday, Marie sent Clothilde a picture, with her love as always. 'Is it the same each time? I think not, grown a little wider, deeper, wiser, it loves you more and feels still more the impossibility of true expression . . .' It seems unlikely that the 'true expression' that Marie referred to was a full sexual relationship between the two, for she was still more or less unconscious of her own body and its desires, a clean young woman, sporting and studious. As for Clothilde, she was so overcome by Marie's missive that she went for a walk through a 'ripe cornfield ablaze with dream-flowers and gave myself up to passionate thoughts'.[36]

At the time Marie was much taken up with thoughts of her future career. She had at last won the approval of one or two of her teachers. Her chemistry mistress, Miss Aitken, impressed by Marie's remarkable application and memory, gave her special tuition. On one occasion, when Miss Aitken was absent for several weeks with scarlet fever, Marie Stopes went to Dr Bryant and said with remarkable self-confidence that she felt she could take over the teaching of the subject for the school if she were given the chance. She left school in December 1899 with a £5 leaving scholarship in science and a new-found belief in herself, boosted no doubt by the devotion of Clothilde Von Wyss and schoolfriends who had begun to perceive the strength and ardour that lay beneath Marie Stopes's outwardly demure behaviour.

North London Collegiate helped her in her selection of a university. Two years before she left school, her headmistress, Sophie Bryant, argued powerfully against the case for a separate women's university at a public debate.[37] 'There was', she argued, 'no demand in the schools for a separate University for women . . . Indeed I have never met with a woman who for herself wanted a Women's University . . .'[38]

And, as a second-generation emancipated woman, Marie was eager to compete with the men. She applied to study in the Science Faculty of University College, London, where she would find the best teachers. Through staying on at school, Marie found she had covered most of the Chemistry degree syllabus and the Zoology. With her newfound confidence, she asked permission to omit the intermediate examination in Chemistry and to work for an honours degree at once. Her unusual application was turned down. But the Professor of Botany, F. W. Oliver, noticed an earnestness and eagerness in the young woman. He encouraged her to make Botany her chief subject, with Chemistry second, and took her on.

2

Scholarly Pursuits

At university, for the first time, Marie began to show signs of a strong will. As a child she had felt helpless, dominated by Charlotte's wishes and tastes and even at the progressive North London Collegiate School she was constrained by innumerable rules and regulations. But at University College she enjoyed the new freedom to organize her work and enrolled secretly for evening classes in zoology at Birkbeck College, determined to prove that she could better the men. In Queen Victoria's England young ladies did not meet young gentlemen without a chaperone; the students at mixed colleges in London were the privileged exception. At that stage of her life Marie worked alongside male students in the laboratory and in the lecture hall quite unselfconsciously, unaware of her own femininity or of male attractions. She regarded the men students as competitors, not possible suitors. But they noticed her. Stocky and full-breasted, with a brilliant brain and those penetrating, deep eyes that betrayed her, Marie was not conventionally pretty; her jaw was too strong and her nose too prominent, but she gave out an air of vivid intensity which she sometimes tried to disguise in posed portraits.

Socially she mixed almost exclusively with women, in the hockey team and at the Women's Debating Society. She was an eloquent speaker and when in her second year she became President of the Debating Society, she introduced joint debates with the men, to the consternation of the University authorities, taking the chair in the first debate herself.

The University suited her, she contributed to the College *Gazette* and, in the vacations, accompanied her tutors and other (male) students on field trips, digging for specimens in the pouring rain and relishing the adventure of camping out. Professor Oliver who had initiated the field work, encouraged her, and Marie did not let him down. She walked ten to fifteen miles a day, never allowing herself to flag in front of the men.

When in London, she went with women friends to the theatre, savouring the new independence of her life.

During the Easter vacation of 1901, Clothilde, who was taking a course in further education in Cambridge, invited Marie to stay for a few days. Marie arrived, bringing a white lily for her hostess, but was horrified, on unpacking, to find she had no nightdress in her case. 'Don't tell father, it's too disgraceful.' she wrote privately to Winnie.[1]

The two friends gardened together and spent evenings discussing the mysteries of theosophy, and Clothilde exacted from Marie a promise of chastity and devotion. The intensity and frustration of the friendship with Clothilde haunted Marie for years. A quarter of a century later, in an educational book, *Sex and the Young*, she described the disillusion of it in an obviously autobiographical account:

> A teacher in a large girls' school was most popular with both mistresses and pupils ... there was always a long train of girls wanting to walk home with her ... and to bring her flowers picked in their own gardens or purchased on the way to school ...

About a dozen girls, selected as special favourites, were made to swear vows of eternal chastity and dedication.

> Each separately deluded girl felt herself pledged to remain all her life in a highfalutin kind of secret Order based on a mixture of mysticism, pseudo-theosophical fantasies of purity and crude personal expression of personal love and sex feeling. The teacher accepted presents from the girls far beyond their means, which involved deprivations and saving up of pocket money ...[2]

The hurt of competing with the other eleven girls, as much as the unhealthiness she implies attached to the friendship, emerges from Marie's revealing account. At the time she was unaware of homosexual love and her intense revulsion later suggests how deeply the attachment affected her.

Both Clothilde and her father had wrested promises of purity from Marie without her understanding the sexual implications of her pledge. She felt honour bound to refuse an offer of marriage from Guy Pilgrim, a fellow student, who fell hopelessly in love with her. Guy tried to persuade her: 'I am afraid you don't realize what a hopeless blank the future looks to me without you,' he wrote, ... 'I am very miserable.' With more perception than tact, Guy suggested that Marie did not appreciate the intensity of his love. 'You probably speak from experience of a schoolgirl attachment which made you feel unhappy for a bit!' he wrote.[3] Guy, who lived near by in Hampstead, put his letter personally through Marie's letter-box. When she opened it she was indignant at the suggestion of a schoolgirl crush and drew a pencil line through that sentence. 'How dare you,' she wrote, 'Not I!'

Marie had an exalted view of love and romance gleaned from literature – she had never seen her parents exhibit much affection, let alone love towards each other. She liked the idea of a young man at her feet – at a distance. In her reply, she urged her suitor either to find 'one of the sweet women in the world', or else, if his devotion was strong enough:

> . . . you can make it a lifelong blessing, for you can carve your life so that it is like some strong beautiful solitary mountain . . . For there is nothing in the world I so reverence as beauty, whether of the world of character or in a soul . . . if you are a true knight, you will strive to the uttermost to build what I could admire, whether I see it or not . . . forget me please, but remember that it is of infinitely more value to be a grand, than a sensually happy man.[4]

Marie had unwisely written to Clothilde of Guy's infatuation and offer of marriage and something of Clothilde's influence and language pervades Marie's reply to her suitor. Clothilde's own urgent letter, fearing her hold on Marie slipping away, was intended to subvert any possibility of romance:

> Dear Little one, I am sometimes filled with a vague dread that you are drifting beyond my reach . . . You have outgrown me little one and our life streams make different windings . . . The bed we will make deep, you and I and the banks fertile – so that our work will be the same in intention and in value. I am proud of all the things you have done . . .[5]

Clothilde referred directly and reprovingly to Guy's proposal to Marie:

> This thing ought not to have happened Marie, I do not blame you for it, but it ought not to have happened. It is like a stain on your garment of purity . . . I know that you in no way led the man to honour you with the offer, but I can't help thinking that, if you retired into an inner coil of your shell – you would be safer from the touch . . .

Clothilde's language makes clear that, consciously or unconsciously, she wanted Marie for herself. Love, passion, sex were all veiled by embroidered visions and flimsy dreams and Clothilde's advice only helped to trouble Marie's already confused attitude.

Work, as usual, was taking up most of her energy. At the end of her first year she heard the news that she had won a gold medal in Botany and had come second in her class in Zoology. University regulations laid down that as an internal student of University College, Marie had to spend two more years studying for an Honours degree. She was beginning to sense her own ability and secretly determined to find a way of at least trying to take the papers for an Honours degree at the end of her second year. She discovered that if she registered as an *external* student at Birkbeck College, she could obtain an Honours degree (in two subjects instead of three) if she could pass with honours in one subject and get a first-class pass in the second.

When she sent in her name, the Registrar of the University, Sir Frank Heath, tried to discourage her. He warned her that the whole idea of taking Honours in two years was ridiculous. Opposition always brought out Marie's courage and obstinacy. She kept her own counsel, did not tell her mother, but chose Botany and Geology as her subjects. Further work in geology was necessary for her botanical studies and Marie enjoyed the field trips. She worked furiously to succeed. Even if she failed it would be good practice, but Marie did not mean to fail. She enjoyed showing the men that she could beat them. Her own experience at home, where both her mother and her father worked, accorded women a natural superiority that filled her with confidence, so that she was surprised but not unduly disconcerted by the patronizing attitudes of some of the men she met at college. She thrived on competition and was extremely ambitious. In a copy of the University College *Gazette* for March 1902, Marie heavily underscored a skit on Gilbert and Sullivan's 'Patience':

> If you're anxious to appear as a sort of pioneer in
> the march of learning's van
> You must advertise the bent of your beneficent intent
> in every way you can.
> With announcements clear and shrill, set your light
> upon the hill where the world can see it shine,
> For they fancy education is a mild hallucination if
> they see no outward sign.[6]

Whether Marie was the anonymous author of that verse or not, she grasped the need for self-advertisement early on and it was to prove invaluable to her in her career. She loved work and college life and was happier than she had been for years.

Since she had become a student, the affection and understanding between Marie and her father had deepened; in the late summer of 1901 they attended the Annual Meeting of the British Association at Glasgow together. Henry now spent most of his time at Swanscombe or at nearby Greenhithe, where a rich philanthropist had offered him an acreage of land rich in archaeological potential. Charlotte too was often away from home, lecturing and writing on behalf of the Suffrage Movement or researching scholarly contributions to the detailed knowledge of Shakespeare's origins and environment. Charlotte found it hard to organize either her work or her home life and remained underrated, particularly at home. Henry now wrote to his elder daughter as an equal and they chuckled in their letters about Charlotte's muddle and indecisiveness. 'Mother got off to Aldeburgh today at last,' Henry wrote, 'It began to remind me of the launch of the Great Eastern!!'[7] And Marie confided her dislike of Jane Austen, a favourite of Charlotte's, in a letter to Henry. The novels were, she opined: 'A dull record of dull sayings and duller doings of dull people.'[8]

Marie cherished the close contact with her father but unfortunately it was not to last. In 1902 Henry Stopes, who was fifty, was suffering from cancer of the intestines. In April Marie heard the news that he was feeling unwell but did not realize the seriousness of his illness. By August the gravity of his situation could not be concealed. She had already enrolled for an energetic geological survey and was not told the true nature of Henry's complaint. It became plain, however, that he would not be able to work for a long time. Charlotte impressed on both girls, particularly Marie, the precarious state of the family's financial situation. In spite of Charlotte's labours, the rewards for her scholarly work were pitifully small and she had no head for business. With that streak of practical sense that was to develop, Marie borrowed twenty-five pounds from a family friend to enable her to continue her studies. She flung herself into the work on the Yorkshire moors at Malham, near Leeds, enjoying the simple meals (two eggs, five pieces of bread and butter and two cups of coffee) and the 'stupendous' geology. She told her father, who could share her enthusiasm, that she had found the tail of a trilobite (a fossil crustacean). She told Winnie of more indecorous feats, such as shinning down river banks and crawling up waterfalls. Winnie could never compete with the energies of her sister; she was not such a strong swimmer, she could not walk so far and was frequently ill. A gentle, thoughtful girl, she was overshadowed by the towering personalities of her mother and sister. Their father, she told Marie in a letter, was not much better. His 'homerage' (presumably haemorrhage) had stopped and 'he was eating well – for him'.[9] In September, Marie went down to stay with her father, helping with the chickens and ducks and enjoying the cream served with every meal.

A few days before Marie sat for her Honours degree, in October 1902 Charlotte wrote from Swanscombe to tell her that her father was dying. He did manage to write to her for her twenty-second birthday, telling her how much her letters meant:

> . . . It is a pleasant world to those who have a superfluity of its goods . . . but to the needy it can be intensely hard. I know all this and have known it for long and yet I can only offer you good wishes. These, dear, I send you and may you be able to build upon the wide foundations I have done my best to spread for you . . . I have equal trust that my sweet girl will live up to her possibilities. I hope your life will be bright, useful and filled with gladness. Ever your affectionate father.[10]

Marie wrote back two days later, the kind of cheerful, chatty letter that she knew her father liked to receive. She adored him, so it must have cost her an effort: 'My own dear father, The umbrella is exactly the thing I needed and is a very nice one.' She told him that her College paper had asked her to write a paragraph on the geological expedition on the Yorkshire moors, that she was expecting a pine seedling to be sent to him and, in a later letter, that she was getting 'very grand indeed' at College, working in the usual laboratory *and* in a research room. In November, Henry wrote a little note to Marie and Winnie to thank them for their letters. He was in considerable agony. Marie's reaction to the tragedy was to work even harder. Professor Oliver was sympathetic, even fatherly, and agreed to let her have her exam results before official publication in the hope that her father could see them. On 28 November 1902, she received a postcard with an outstanding result: she had won her degree with double honours, a First in Botany and a Third in Geology. She sent the news immediately to her father. To her mother, who was with him in his last days, she wrote a studied, rather patronizing letter:

> My dear mother,
> . . . I have now something to tell you that will take some very careful

understanding – you know that I am to take my degree next year and that I have worked for one year and the courses are arranged for two. Well, I thought this year that I had better keep my work up and that it would be good for me to practise by taking the papers. The most unlooked for news is that *this* year I have got my degree, I am now B.Sc. Not only have I got it, I have done very well, I have got First Class Honours in Botany with the marks qualifying for a scholarship . . . I also have got Honours in Geology, Third Class and am the only candidate with Honours, the others (men only) all failed . . . As it is supposed to be impossible to take one Honours in a year, to get two is very nice . . .[11]

Marie added that she had missed several of the botany lectures in order to swot up for her exams and would have to attend them next term instead. She was pleased to be able to tell her mother that she need not worry about the fees. Her exam results had entitled her to a scholarship and had saved a year of her life. All that, she pointed out, she had done in spite of objections from the Registrar, the Dean, Professors and students (except for a few). Her father died on the day Marie wrote that letter (5 December 1903) and in the Christmas holidays, condolences and congratulations arrived at the same time.

Marie was now launched on what promised to be an outstanding academic career, but Winnie's future was more uncertain. She had artistic talent and was taking a course in bookbinding at Shoreditch. But in order to set up as a bookbinder, she would need a little capital for leather, goldleaf and other materials as well as premises and, just as important, the drive and personality to attract clientele. Winnie had neither the energy nor the push of her mother and sister and Charlotte was now seriously worried about the future. Both of the family houses at Swanscombe and Hampstead were rented and Charlotte was left with an income of only £80 a year to keep Winnie and herself. Henry had left them a legacy of hundreds of boxes of fossils. But it was not until eight years later that Marie managed to sell them to a museum. Charlotte could not conceive of living without servants, as she wanted to pursue her own ill-paid research and studies.

Even when Marie was a child, Charlotte had looked to her to take on some of the burdens of the home and now she turned to her elder daughter for support. But Marie was keen to escape from Charlotte's nagging and to work where she was appreciated. Professor Oliver, who was immensely fond of her, appointed her as his assistant at University

College. Paleobotany, the study of fossil plants, was then in an exciting phase of development associated with coalballs, chalky nodules of rock embedded in coal seams, containing the petrified leaves, twigs, fruits, stem and seeds of primitive plants, hundreds of million years old. Marie immersed herself in the work and published two erudite papers on ancient plants, 'The Leaf-Structure of Cordaites' and 'The Epidermoidal Layer of Calamite Roots', in botanical journals. She was also elected in 1903 as a member of the British Association for the Advancement of Science. As her mother said: 'Marie is in luck all round'.

The scholarship she had been awarded was sufficient to support Marie in a year's post-graduate study at a university abroad. At first she explored the possibility of working in Zurich, where her old schoolfriend Olga Kapteyn lived, but on the advice of Professor Oliver decided that Munich would be the best place. The head of the Botanical Institute there, Professor Goebel, had a distinguished international reputation and possessed the largest collection in existence of cycads (the most primitive form of fern-like seed-bearing plants) both fossilized and living.

Despite Charlotte's grumbles at her staying away from home, Marie spent a few days' holiday in Appleby in Cumberland, away from the family, before boarding the boat-train for Munich. She had plenty of time and the fact that she chose to travel just two days before her twenty-third birthday reveals just how little she regretted leaving home. 'A birthday is not half a birthday without you,' she had written to her father when he was absent on her seventeenth anniversary. From babyhood onwards, one or both of her parents had spent part of the year travelling, so that she had never known a settled home in childhood. Although she was fond of Winnie, the 'kid' as she called her, they were very different in temperament and ability. Now that her father was gone there was nothing to hold her, and Marie left England without regret. Her success in College and the independent academic line she had taken had combined to make Marie into an outwardly self-contained and self-confident young woman with a splendid academic record, vigorous health and an appetite for both work and pleasure.

Most women students of the day were anxious to appear serious; they wore deliberately dowdy or strictly tailored clothes. Marie favoured frilly lace collars and trimming, flowing gowns and elegant buttons and gloves. There were mutterings from academic colleagues of frivolity and vanity but Marie was impatient of learned women 'sterilized by study'. 'There is hardly anything in the world so gloriously beautiful as a woman's body', she wrote in an unpublished autobiographical novel.

'And while I am one, and a young one, I think it would be wickedness not to enjoy the loveliness of it.'[12]

In Munich, at last she began to sense her femininity and realize the impression she made on men. She bought herself a little black fur cap to top her soft, chestnut-coloured hair. When she wore her new fur hat in the street with 'a long cloak, a very short skirt and nailed boots, a strange Herr held open the letter box for me and took off his hat with a sweep,' she told Winnie.[13] From her upbringing Marie had learnt to shun corsets (although she did wear long combinations against the freezing German weather) so that her physical attractions were apparent and she was beginning to be aware of them. If Marie was original among intellectual women in glorying in her body she did not exploit her attractions. She was still bound by the conventions of the time and her father's code which turned a kiss into a sacred vow and made marriage before the age of twenty-five unthinkable.

In Munich she began to be aware of how unworldly her upbringing had been. She saw the beautiful dresses that fashionable women wore and understood how little she or Winnie knew of the 'usages of good society and the way to carry on and lead an intelligent and interesting conversation with either sex . . . We have had next to no social intercourse with anyone – and none with well-educated young gentlemen – the people of all others to polish and refine women'.[14] A shop girl or a typist knew more about the 'feminine arts' than the highly educated Miss Stopes. Yet, though she was still unaware of it, she was passionate by nature and strongly sexed.

This dangerous young woman was welcomed by Professor Goebel and his students with grave formality and a good deal of curiosity. The Botanical Institute was attached to the University and, although other women from the University attended the Botanical lectures, in her first term she was the only woman among 500 men at the Institute. Marie worked in the laboratory where some of her colleagues were postgraduate students like herself. Conscious of her status, elevated above the average student, she tended to seek out the lecturers and professors in her spare time. The élite Student Corps, the beer-swilling youths who swaggered through the streets in gaudy silk caps and sashes, their faces scarred from the ritual duels they fought, did not impress her in the least. 'What a crew!' she remarked and was disappointed to discover that there was little social or intellectual life in the University, no Debating Society and certainly no joint debates with women. One night she discussed socialism, women's education and politics in her heavily accented German with a group of students. 'The Germans are not out of the Middle Ages, although they have a few faint glimmerings about women', she wrote pityingly to her mother. And she told Winnie that German students thought women were 'not intended to come to Universities – though they are very polite, I think they think Englishwomen are half masculine.'[15]

Marie was always at her best with older men, looking up to them in a filial yet easy manner. She admired Professor Goebel who spoke very good English, and described him to her mother as a fine man, hugely tall, well-proportioned and clever! The English girl interested Goebel by her earnestness and her avid reading of the literature about cycads in French, German, English and Swedish in the Institute's library. At first she was afraid that she would not be able to take her PhD at Munich. 'I think they demand three years and let you off with two if you have a foreign degree,' she wrote to her mother at the end of October.[16] Marie's intense commitment and hard work had, however, made an impression and Professor Goebel had 'quite taken up' Marie's cycad work, suggesting that she should collect all the past work on the ovules (the unfertilized seeds) of the cycads from all over the world, add her own contribution and submit a thesis that would become a standard work. If she succeeded she would become the first woman permitted to take a Munich degree from the Institute of Botany. There was, she assured her mother, no time for sightseeing.

To the lay person, the reproductive habits of ancient plants may not at once stir the imagination, but Marie was immensely enthusiastic about her subject and unsparing of herself. She boasted to a colleague that she would be famous one day, and was ambitious and competitive. By 8.30 in the morning she was already working in the lab, never missed a lecture and spent hours working in the library or at home in her lodgings, a tiny room on the Hesse Strasse, near the University. Sometimes, at the week-end when she was immersed in a research problem, Marie would sit up the whole night in her icy, drab little room, brewing beef tea on the spirit lamp to keep her going. The Munich winter was cold and she sat wrapped in two heavy dressing-gowns over her outdoor clothes, ironing her bed before she dared to get in. Her life was nothing but work and sleep she told Charlotte and Winnie, who were struggling and quarrelling in Hampstead on a reduced income. To her mother in particular, she stressed the rigours of her life.

She stayed in Munich to work over Christmas, when she found the attraction of the city irresistible. '... the streets were crowded with students, every young girl had a portfolio or a music roll under her arm. Every bookshop was a veritable treasury of rare books and old prints and fascinating new editions.'[17] Marie disliked the smoky atmosphere of the beer halls but developed a taste for opera, delighted with the elaborate stagings of *The Magic Flute*, enjoying Beethoven's *Fidelio* but discovering that it was Wagner who suited her temperament best. When the Ring Cycle was performed she visited the Opera two or three times a week, though never allowing her work to suffer. She adored dancing and, during Carnival Week in February of 1904, she joined in the masked and fancy dress balls that took place every night, but to Charlotte was still priding herself on her virgin frigidity:

> ... It is the boast of Munich that every woman who goes to Café Luitpold or any café Fasching Tuesday night, gets kissed. I can boast that I went and did not get kissed – I was with two men and looked all the time like a block of ice and had my quietest clothes and a big cloak on – but usually that is not enough. Still, it would be a strange man that wanted to kiss a block of ice![18]

In Munich, the nightly performances of Isadora Duncan were driving the student population to frenzy: 'Night after night they [the students] harnessed the horses from my carriage and drew me through the streets, singing their student songs and leaping with lighted torches on either side of my victoria . . .'[19] Isadora herself wrote. Even Marie fell prey to the mania. Just before the dancer was due to leave the city, Marie was persuaded to go to see Isadora and, despite herself, was carried away. Isadora was dancing to the music of Beethoven in a packed Munich hall. She performed on a large platform covered with soft, dull green baize which matched her Greek tunic. Accompanied by piano and orchestra, Isadora dazzled her audience with her interpretations of 'The Moonlight' and 'the Pathétique' sonatas and the Seventh Symphony. 'She was truly wonderful in the Allegretto and Presto Agitato, her light, skipping movement miracles of rhythmic motion.'[20] The audience cheered, clapped, waved handkerchiefs in wild excitement and Marie was swept up with the crowd that followed Isadora to the station, where railway officials had to shovel students off the steps of her departing train.

How could such a simple and beautiful way of dancing have become a lost art? Marie mused, and how was it that it took a twentieth-century American girl to rediscover it? Back in her cold little room she danced in front of her mirror in flimsy garments, imagining herself in Isadora's place, entranced by the glamour and success of the evening. Hard-working and frugal as her student life in Germany was, she was glorying in the freedom and impatient of the news she heard from home where her mother was (in Marie's view) making too much of running the house at Hampstead at the expense of intellectual interests. 'Of course go to the Gray's Inn Hall Dinner,' she wrote to Charlotte, 'it would be absurd not to – can't you turn the key in the door and leave the house to Daisy and the beetles . . . ?'[21]

She wrote to Winnie secretly when she could, sympathizing. '. . . I know just what must be going on, poor kid, poor old wretched family that we are, altogether absurd . . . I need to give you cooking lessons. I cooked beefsteak, eggs and veg for five on my spirit lamp – it didn't prevent me from acting hostess gracefully.'[22] Two other girls shared her lodgings and Marie occasionally entertained them and other students. She enjoyed improvizing and produced homemade jam and apple cake in her little room.

In the spring Professor Goebel took senior students into the country to collect specimens on excursions which began at 4.30 in the morning. Marie was in her element and envied the men who went on hiking tours in the mountains, eating simply and enjoying the intoxicating air and the views of the Dolomites. One man told Marie of a ten-day tour that had cost him seven shillings. She longed for such adventures but recognized reluctantly that it was impossible to go along with a man and 'the women are all so silly'.

The name of one companion, a co-worker in her lab, began to appear regularly in her letters home. Kenjiro Fujii was fourteen years older than Marie, thirty-seven to her twenty-three, an assistant Professor from the Imperial University at Tokyo, on leave to study at Munich. Also, he was married, with a daughter. Professor Fujii was an expert on the structure and reproduction of the rare Ginkgo or maidenhair tree, considered holy by the Buddhists. He worked in the same lab as Marie, studying cycads with Professor Goebel. She described him to her mother as 'very nice, very interesting and wonderfully Western and observant'. Fujii mixed English and German in his speech. Their work was in the same field and Fujii encouraged Marie and helped her. He was tiny, even his hands were smaller than hers, so that she did not feel either threatened or compromised by this gentle Japanese, in fact she rather patronized him. 'I am sorry for him with his wife in Japan while the [Russo-Japanese] war is on,' she told Charlotte. 'He is a splendid botanist too, I have learnt heaps from him.'[23]

Fujii was subtle in his compliments, telling Marie that he thought German women dressed very badly and that the English must be a better and prettier dressed race. Charlotte did not even consider that this tiny, married Japanese professor could be an entanglement. Presumably, even she would have been alarmed by the letter that Marie wrote to Winnie, knowing that their mother was away (for Charlotte had an uncomfortable habit of prying into the sisters' letters). Marie described a thrilling expedition in the wilds when she and Fujii had visited a remote lakeside to collect ovules for their research. They spent hours searching for specimens until it was too late to go home and at last had to put up for the night in a little inn. Marie made it clear, indeed it was implicit, that there was no impropriety involved. But she did revel in the details of breakfasting with Fujii at 6.30 in the morning, on the veranda, overlooking the lake, with the reflection of snowcapped mountains glittering in the rising sun. The pair hiked twenty-four miles to catch the 1.50 p.m. train back to Munich just in time to attend a sacred opera the same evening. 'The sun got hotter and hotter till little Fujii nearly collapsed, all that saved him was a great patch of snow on top of his little bald head . . . I shall never look on little Fujii as a solemn and learned Professor again – after that snow on his head . . .'[24]

In the lab everyone said that the adventure was 'just like Miss Stopes', but there was no suggestion of scandal. Marie was so fresh, so enthusiastic and such a novelty in the University that more than one young man was in love with her. According to her own account she was almost swept into marriage by an ardent young German without even realizing it. On a botanical expedition in the Alps, the German youth courted her in a stream of flowery language that bored her so much that she just said 'ja, ja,' to everything he said. When it emerged that she had promised to marry the boy, Professor Goebel had to intervene to soothe the hurt pride of the student's family, since Marie showed herself to be utterly indifferent and mystified by all the fuss.

Despite the distractions, within the academic year, Marie Stopes had written her thesis in German on the fructification of the ovules and egg cells of the cycads, the most primitive of the seed-bearing plants. A Swiss student helped her with the German phrasing and she read and defended it in public: 'Of all the gruesome, beastly enough to make you cry sort of things, the exam, lasting two wretched hours in German is the worst,' she confided to Winnie.[25]

After the gruelling ordeal Marie won her doctorate with distinction and was the heroine of the hour, presented with armfuls of roses and shaking hands until she ached. She wrote to her mother immediately with the news of her great achievement. 'No question, Marie's a genius,' Winnie's friend remarked! She was the first woman in Munich University (and a Briton at that) to take her Ph.D. in Botany with Honours. The course usually took at least two years and it seems clear that Professor Goebel, and Fujii too, had helped her considerably, but no one could deny her brilliance.

The academic honours added to her aura in Munich. Another suitor, Alvara Humphrey, a South African, who had eyed her for some time, wrote to her inviting her to accompany him on a three-to-four-hour walk. Perhaps, he suggested, deliberately provocative, the exercise would be too much for her. That did it. Marie replied witheringly that in her case the phrase 'too much' was totally uncalled for. She would be ready to start at any time after 6 a.m. The two talked long and earnestly as they walked through the woods and a few days later at the end of June, Alvara Humphrey went to the station to see her off, only to find, to his annoyance, that she was deeply engrossed with Professor Fujii.

She was reluctant to leave Munich, where for the first time in her life she had been completely free, and was anxious about her future. Before she left, hearing that a junior lectureship in Botany had fallen vacant in Manchester, she sent off a carefully phrased letter of application.

After the triumph of Munich, Marie felt hemmed in when she came home to squabbles over money, housework and the servants. Charlotte took it for granted that Marie must assume her share of domestic responsibility – 'woman's work that is never done,' she grumbled to Alvara Humphrey – so she fitted in her scientific research, 'man's work', when she could. During August, she decided to stay in the empty house in Hampstead, in charge of the cat and the maid, and get on quietly with her work while Charlotte and Winnie went to the seaside. She was waiting anxiously for a letter from Manchester University.

From Munich Alvara Humphrey continued to correspond. A perceptive young man, he considered himself something of a student of human nature and was intrigued by Marie's unusual qualities. Would she like him to send her a frank character sketch, he offered? Marie responded enthusiastically, asking him for his honest opinion. His analysis was unflattering: 'I think that in the interests of science you could let your spirit of investigation conquer your human nature and that you could be capable, if not of cruelty, at least of hardness and a forgetfulness of true perspective,' he wrote.[26] Her reply was that he had not understood her at all.

In another attempt at advice at Christmas, Alvara suggested that Marie would do better as the headmistress of a finishing school for girls rather than as a university professor. 'The personal factor weighs so enormously and your personality is so eminently attracting and inspiring.'[27] And indeed there *was* something of a Miss Jean Brodie in Marie's vivid intelligence and crusading ardour. She did not see it at all. She was not, she insisted, the sort of woman with a mission, 'so convinced of my superiority that I set about trying to influence others for good . . . I am not unconscious of a certain power but I consider it unhealthy'. She crossed out the last sentence in her draft but left a telling remark: 'I deliberately tried to give you a false impression of my aims in a desire to make you dislike me . . .'[28] Marie may have been deceiving herself with that comment.

'Dr Marie Stopes, a daughter of Mrs Carmichael Stopes, who took the degree of Doctor of Philosophy, magna-cum-laude at Munich last June has been appointed assistant lecturer in botany in Owen's College Manchester, being the first woman appointed', the *Daily Mail* reported on 22 October 1904. (The *Mail* was a little out-of-date; Owen's College had recently become an independent university.) Marie was furious at the publicity, convinced that it was her mother's work, although Charlotte denied it strenuously. Dr Stopes had been warned by the head of the Scientific Department at Manchester, Professor Weiss, that the university authorities would be watching her progress carefully. He knew her work and had supported her application but the university council had expressed grave misgivings and it was only after a lengthy debate that the appointment of a woman demonstrator was ratified. Weiss also pointed out that the chances for other women scientists to gain a foothold in the university depended largely on Marie's performance.

Just before she took up her first post Professor Fujii arrived in London. Marie had encouraged him to come to England and she invited him to her home and introduced him to her mother and Winnie. The whole family undertook his English education. Charlotte advised him to see a production of *The Tempest* and Winnie lent him a volume of Tennyson's poems. Fujii was to work at University College, London with Marie's former professor, Professor Oliver. They saw each other only briefly before she left for Manchester but during the term Fujii did take the trouble to attend one of Charlotte's lectures on Shakespeare and Winnie noted that he 'didn't look too bored'. Marie also discovered that Fujii's wife had fallen in love with another man and wanted a divorce, a rare occurrence in Japan. Gradually and delicately an entirely unsuitable love affair between the quiet, Japanese professor and the intense English-woman, fourteen years his junior, developed. Letters flowed between London and Manchester (Fujii at a considerable disadvantage because of his halting English). They explored oriental poetry, Western religion, and other highflown themes across a cultural chasm. Fujii tried to initiate Marie into the mysteries of the higher Buddhism, the philosophy of living in the present, struggling to express himself in English:

> Care not for death. What is death? Live as you live: die as you die. All is nature. Why do you think about the future life? Why long for the continuance of life: live not for reward but live for life. Immortality? do you understand what life really is? The ideal is the only reality. Reality is the only ideal . . .[29]

To which Marie replied that she could not go with him to the limits of his philosophy:

> Forgive me, but it seems to me too small. I may not have understood it rightly but you seem to me to be beautifully idealistic – yet so materialistic. Can you conceive of a worm seeing in the sky at sunset all we see in it? Can you not conceive of us as beings whose powers are as limited in relation to other forms as a worm is to us? But, as I think a worm would waste his time trying to understand sunsets, so I think we are absolutely incapable of understanding those above us and the fate of us all.[30]

She was sorry, she added, that he had missed her lectures on cycadofilices, the best she had ever given.[31] The language of botany was the one they could best share. For the rest it was better to talk 'eyes to eyes' as Fujii put it. There were so many opportunities for misunderstanding in what was, at that stage, a purely intellectual love affair.

Marie was busy enough in the 'real' world establishing herself at the university. She had wanted to take lessons in voice production before she left London but time was short and, with her usual good sense, she attended lectures in other departments, picking up points from different lecturers. She managed to present a confident front, sailing about in her gown, which she found a great moral support. 'I feared possible ructions from the men but they are perfectly good and don't mind my lecturing to them and ragging them about their work. I don't think they are awake to the fact that a little revolution is going on quietly . . .', she told Alvara

Humphrey.[32] Although she was in love with Fujii, she could never bear to let go of those who were fond of her.

For the students the presence of an attractive, modern young woman, well versed in her subject, was a distinct asset. At twenty-four she was of an age with most of them, one man at least was older than she was and had published more. Marie took her handful of botanical students out for walks, invited them back for tea, and organized a dance, very bold behaviour since all students' social events were required to be chaperoned. Outside college she liked to look as feminine as possible and in that first term made herself a white silk blouse with a pink rose embroidered on it that she was 'perfectly in love with'. The faculty and their wives viewed both her appearance and her disregard for convention with some disquiet. '. . . my husband says and I feel so strongly too that it would be very inadvisable to invite individual students either to your rooms or to go with them to concerts, theatres, etc.', wrote Mrs Weiss, wife of her professor.[33] Marie accepted the letter of the advice but not perhaps the spirit of it. She continued to organize fancy dress balls and social events to enliven the Science Department.

One extra-curricular activity that no one could fault was her lectures to Manchester working men of the university Ancoats Settlement at Ancoats Hall on the 'family tree' of the plant world. The audience was enthusiastic and respectful, so keen to learn that Marie enjoyed lecturing to them and discovered that she had a gift for popularizing a highly technical subject. 'I could understand every word she said,' muttered one old man, a shoemaker, in disgust. She was depressed by the city of Manchester, the mean streets, the smoke and everlasting rain. By November thick fog hung over the city, making everything filthy. To neutralize the acid of the fog, Marie placed dusters soaked in ammonia across the open windows in her lab and escaped, whenever she could, to find glorious country outside the city. Manchester was not Munich, nor was Professor Weiss Professor Goebel, but nevertheless her first term as a lecturer was a success and she came home for Christmas justifiably pleased with herself.

While Marie was in Manchester, Fujii had called on Charlotte and established himself as a friend of the family. Her biographers have until now accepted Marie's account of the affair as authentic, if superficially disguised. Her novel, *Love-Letters of a Japanese*, written in 1910 under the pseudonym of G. N. Mortlake, reveals through correspondence the course of a love affair between a young Englishwoman of Marie's age and an older Japanese man. (Privately Marie implied that the book gave a factual account of her love story with Fujii.) She changed the names and occupations of the protagonists, Marie Stopes became Mertyl Meredith and Kenjiro Fujii, Kenrio Watanabe; the two meet as artists, not scientists. While one or two of Marie's letters in the novel are very similar to her drafts in the British Library Manuscript Collection, the fact that so very few of Fujii's 'real' letters remain in the archive is disturbing. His only love letter to her, elusively poetical, appears both in the Manuscript Collection and in the novel.[34]

Early on Marie displayed a tendency to veil the real events of her life with layer upon layer of flimsy fiction and never more so than in this intense and idealized love affair. The language in her novel gives expression to an effusiveness and sensuality not yet revealed in her personality. She described every nerve in her body tingling with longing, every pulse 'throbbing with desire'. 'Dearest of all . . . When you are away . . . it seems too strange, too sweet, too absurd, too like a strange novel too impossible that I could have found so early in my life, the man who can be perfectly my own, whom I can love . . .'[35]

The contrast between this and Marie's ordinary language, the concision with which she described her scientific work and her outwardly brisk, sporty personality is marked. In Fujii she had found, she believed the bridge between her matter-of-fact world and her yearning for love, the answer to the deep schism in her nature.

Over Christmas Marie saw Fujii at home. They visited the Botanical Gardens at Kew, picnicked on Hampstead Heath on Boxing Day, went to concerts and talked and talked. In his halting English Fujii tried to explain Chinese and Japanese poetry to her and they even considered his wife's wish for a divorce and the possibility of a life together. Fujii obtained permission from his university in Tokyo to extend his stay in Europe and followed her to Manchester, where they planned future work together.

For Marie, the first kiss in the spring of 1905 was a momentous event: 'He had won from her lips the first kiss she had ever given to a man, a kiss that she considered as binding as a marriage service,' Marie wrote in her *Love Letters of a Japanese*. She was almost twenty-five, sexually and emotionally immature, and quite unprepared for such a heady and unconventional love affair.

Since Fujii, as a Japanese, was not practised in the art of kissing (there was no Japanese word for the act, it took place only between mother and child), and Marie had never kissed a man before, the result, as she wrote later, was 'quite horrid'. Nevertheless it marked a new stage in their love affair. Fujii sent Marie a box of red and white flowers with a poetic inscription: 'Dear – a bunch of flowers followed you, they could not help starting after you. White of the lily as pure as my love and red of the rose as deep as my love. It will be as it is. Good night, dear, good night.'[36] That is the only 'real' love letter from Fujii in the archive. Marie pencilled on the back: 'received 5'oc 26.IV.05'.

For Fujii, as for Marie, this love affair with a Western woman was exotic, uncharted, light years away from his everyday life in Japan where marriages were arranged, courtship virtually nonexistent and love and passion no basis for marriage. To find an attractive and gifted young Englishwoman so infatuated must have been immensely tempting. Both of them dreamed, yearned, quite unrealistically for a perfect marriage.

Love, however, did not deflect Marie from her work; it seemed to give her more energy. In the spring term as well as demonstrating and lecturing to her students, she played hockey, rowed and worked for her Science Doctorate (a pure research degree and a higher academic award than her German Ph.D. Then there were the troublesome letters from home. Sensing that her elder daughter was growing away from her, Charlotte wrote once or twice a week, anxious, complaining letters, trying to involve Marie in household decisions and responsibilities. Marie looked careworn, Charlotte wrote, she was working too hard. She urged her to rest more, but Marie told Winnie that she was far more careworn when she was twelve! Both proud and resentful of a daughter who was fulfilling her own life's ambition, Charlotte was envious of Marie's free and scholarly life. To gain attention she dramatized her difficulties and demanded Marie's help: 'I want you to write at once with advice on how to act in an emergency,'[37] Charlotte wrote imperiously in January 1905 when Marie had just returned to Manchester. She had been offered a house in Downshire Hill, Hampstead, she described as a bargain. Ought she to take it or not?

Since Marie had not seen the house she could hardly give advice but Charlotte was disgruntled. 'I am sorry you do not spend the amount of intelligence and understanding on my letters, my position and my difficulties that you spend on your own work . . . I made up my mind that I would rather starve than not have a pied-a-terre for my daughters . . .'[38]

Marie wrote back reasonably, pointing out that as she was not on the spot, she felt that she must leave it entirely to her mother's discretion and try not to grumble if she was not happy with the result. 'Do what you think best, then at any rate you cannot reproach me for giving you bad advice . . .'[39]

At that time Marie and Winnie were close, Marie offering advice on subjects ranging from cookery to dressmaking and trying to drum up business for her sister's bookbinding efforts, and Winnie admiring and supportive of her older sister. They grumbled together about their impossible mother and clubbed together to buy her presents at birthdays and Christmas. Marie offered to take financial responsibility for Winnie. But Charlotte was reluctant to give up her grudges and resentful of the sisters' relationship. 'I am sorry that you are so indifferent to your mother's difficulties, not even to read and answer my letters. The message you sent through Winnie was a very improper one'.[40]

Mother and daughter vied to impress one another. Charlotte mentioned her involvement with the Suffrage Demonstrations and the Shakespeare Society. 'At High Table I was the only woman in her own right, the others were all wives and daughters of the men.' But by now Charlotte could no longer compete with her daughter. Marie's life and interests were expanding all the time.

In February 1905 Captain Scott the explorer came to the University fresh from his Arctic expedition. Marie was invited to a lunch given for him and later to a dance, when she waltzed with him and tried to persuade him to take her on his next expedition. Marie explained that fossil plants might be found in the Antarctic which would help her to make valuable palaeontological discoveries on the origin of coal. They might also discover usable coal in the region. Scott would not promise but he was interested enough to visit Marie in her laboratory so that he could see the fossil plants likely to occur in Antarctica. She longed to uncover new worlds. 'I must have some exploration and coal mines are the only things here to take the place of mountains or tropical forests,' she wrote to Professor Goebel.[41]

Living close to the Lancashire and the Yorkshire coalmines, Marie had become interested in the formation of coal seams and the beautiful coalballs she had first come across as Professor Oliver's assistant at University College. Unlike other botanists who sent down requests for the specimens, Marie preferred to go down to the coalface herself, enjoying the adventure. Coal-owners were flattered by her interest and her searches and the shrewder of them realized that her findings might help them discover rich new deposits. One pit owner gave her his own fossil collection and in it she discovered a rare species of fossil fern and named it *Tubicaulis sutcliffi*, in honour of Mr Sutcliffe, the mine owner.

Her work was attracting international attention, and in May 1905

Marie wrote to tell her mother that the Royal Society had granted a sum of money to enable her to pursue her work in the mines. She was careful to point out that she could only spend those funds for scientific purposes, since she had to submit accounts to the Royal Society. This was presumably to forestall Charlotte, who was always complaining of outstanding gas or grocery bills.

She also received her doctorate in Science that year and became the youngest Doctor of Science in the country. Recognition came quickly. The British Museum's Geological Department invited her to prepare a catalogue of the Cretaceous Flora in their Natural History collection, which took her years to accomplish. In June 1905 she was invited to lecture to a Scientific Congress in Vienna. The occasion gave Marie and Fujii an opportunity to meet in Munich afterwards. To allay any suspicion Charlotte might have Winnie agreed to spend some time in Munich. Charlotte obviously had no idea of their involvement because when Professor Fujii visited her to say goodbye she wrote to Marie saying that she was almost sorry that Professor Fujii was to be in Munich for he would keep her at work. Fujii looked smaller than ever, she commented.[42] To keep them closely in touch the two botanists planned to produce a paper on the research they had been working on in England on the nutritive relations of the surrounding tissues to the Archegonia in Gymnosperms.[43] Fujii returned to Japan in July but Marie was so busy that she scarcely had time to miss him.

For the rest of the vacation Marie went to Caen University to consult a Professor Ligner, a leading French paleobotanist about her research with Fujii. Then she visited Munich and was allowed to work in Professor Goebel's laboratory in the Austrian Tyrol. High up in the mountains she made a study of the process by which the male sperm fertilizes the ovum and feeds it with food granules. Her work on the reproductive system of plants was to prove of immense importance when her life changed.

The only accounts of Fujii's feelings towards Marie during the lovers' separation are fictional, but Marie's draft letters to him make it clear that she considered herself totally committed. Back in Manchester, in November 1905, she gave a lecture to 300 members of the Openshaw Working Men's Brotherhood and was invited to tea afterwards with the secretary and his wife, both spiritualists. For a scientist Marie had an unusually gullible streak. She was delighted when the wife foretold her future and wrote to tell Fujii:

Sweet Heart . . . He and his wife are quite simple people, but so real . . . She told me that everything I do in my life will succeed (so far that has been true) and it is a pleasant thought. She also said that the man who is everything my heart desires is not yet born as I set my aims *so* high – but that I shall marry wisely and well and that my marriage will be out of the common in its perfection – she said I had not yet thought of a definite man to marry which was silly of her! But I told her that for fun. It amuses me so much to hear people's views about my possible marriage! and I dare not hint at the truth, that thou and I are one – dear heart it is known only to us, how sweet! . . . She also told me people had seen me and told her I was beautiful! I was awfully glad for noone here has told me and I feared I must be ugly in their eyes – and for your sake I wish that people find me a little beautiful. Dearest, I wish so much that your wife is beautiful, good, distinguished – all that is splendid so that men and women may think . . . [the letter breaks off here.][44]

In her letter, Marie reveals her insecurity and naïvety, yet professionally she was doing well. In 1906 she wrote her first book, *The Study of Plant Life for Young People*, a textbook 'written with a breadth of knowledge not before met with in an English elementary book' the *New Phytologist* commented.[45]

In the summer of 1906, Marie set out on a challenging journey to the Arctic circle with Frau Resvoll, a botanist friend from Norway whom she had met while studying in Munich. The two women trekked through mountain passes, rucksacks on their backs, sleeping in little huts. Marie gloried in the northern snowscape, the white-capped mountains and the rich pine and birch in the valleys. They saw many reindeer and Marie was disappointed not to see a bear, although the guide was relieved!

Frau Resvoll, the only woman professor in Norway, was prominent in the women's cause. But at the time, unlike her mother, Marie was not active in the Suffrage Movement. She said openly that although she sympathized with their aims she did not want to jeopardize her professional position, and was contemptuous of the militant, breakaway wing of the Suffragists, the Women's Social and Political Union. Mrs Pankhurst, in Marie's view, had done a lot of damage and was now 'a vulgar byword in the streets and in pantomime'.[46] In a letter, she warned Charlotte not to join them: 'You know that you don't dare take the risk of hurtling and getting put into jail. Your special work writing and lecturing on the Movement is quite a different line'.[47] In her disapproval of militant Suffragettes, Marie was echoing the University's attitude. In October 1905, Christabel Pankhurst, a student at Manchester, had barracked a Liberal Party meeting in the city, unfurling a VOTES FOR WOMEN banner. She was charged with obstruction, imprisoned and threatened with expulsion from the University.

Marie dreaded Charlotte interfering in her own professional world and rather cruelly dashed cold water on her mother's proposal to lecture to students on Women's Suffrage. Charlotte's name was unknown to those members of the University interested in the women's cause, she asserted, and besides, as her daughter, she did not want to introduce her mother. Of Marie's secret life, Charlotte knew nothing. From Japan Fujii had written to tell her that his divorce had come through in January 1906 and she was longing to see him. She found the solution in the unlikely field of angiosperms.

Like many botanists at the time, Marie was puzzled by the sudden rise in the dominance of the angiosperms, or flowering plants, propagated by seeds protected by an ovary, over the fern-like more primitive form of plants, the gymnosperms. She wanted to discover why the flowering plants had flourished and spread so fast. It was common knowledge among paleobotanists that angiosperm impressions had been discovered much earlier in Japan and elsewhere. But Marie was eager to find a petrified specimen of angiosperm which would reveal the whole structure of the ancestor of modern flowering plants and, perhaps, the secret of its evolutionary prevalence. She was convinced that petrified specimens might be found in the Island of Hokkaido, off the north coast of Japan. She wrote urgently to Fujii, hardly daring to hope, but asking him to send her the most likely rock specimens from Hokkaido that he could obtain. The parcel with the specimen rocks arrived shortly after her twenty-sixth birthday in October 1906 and Marie took the rocks immediately to be cut into sections. The first thin section cut revealed an angiosperm. Marie was tremendously excited and lent the evidence to Professor Weiss in Manchester and Professor Oliver in London. In a carefully worded letter to the Royal Society she reasoned that it was possible to predict where petrified specimens of angiosperms could be found and asked that learned body to give her a financial grant to travel to Japan to find those descendants of ancient plants that she was sure could be found there.

The undertaking was bold and original, particularly for a woman. Even in the British Isles her geological field trips, 'bareheaded and behammered', caused interest and astonishment. In March 1907, while waiting to hear news from the Royal Society, she spent a fortnight in the Scottish village of Brora, on the north-east coast, where she was delighted to find two tree stumps well preserved and a splendid belemnite (a cigar-shaped fossil). The reply from the Royal Society took months. Professor Oliver of University College in London backed her project while from Japan Professor Fujii wrote 'inestimably valuable letters' proposing that Dr Stopes should work in the Imperial University in Tokyo. Tact was not Marie's greatest strength and she wrote to her lover patronizingly, pointing out that he was a botanist, not a paleo-botanist, no expert in fossil plants as she was.

> It is true, dear, that you do not know enough about these things to be the only person in Japan who works at them. I have done so much now, in coal mines and in nature that I think I and Mr Watson [her colleague at Manchester] know more about them than anyone else at all . . .[48]

That year Marie had just learned to ride and she enjoyed a gallop in the open country outside Manchester; she also swam in the summer, skated in the winter and kept herself in first-class health, which was important for her strenuous life and made the waiting easier.

Not until May 1907 did Marie finally get the confirmation of support from the Royal Society. 'I am apparently going off in grand style,' she told her mother. Sir Edward Grey of the Foreign Office wrote to the British Chargé d'affaires in Tokyo asking him to render to Miss Marie Stopes 'such assistance as he properly can'. On 3 July 1907 she boarded the *Prinz Regent Luitpold* bound for Yokohama, wearing thick knickers and vest knitted for her by Winnie, with her favourite China doll 'Frenchie' mended and carefully packed for the journey. She told Winnie that she would make dresses for Frenchie on the journey and lend her to Professor Fujii's little daughter, but *only* if she turned out to be a very nice little girl would she part with Frenchie.

Marie was nearly twenty-seven and longing for love. 'To be kissed, I sometimes long so much that I take a girdle and bind it tightly, so tightly that I can hardly breathe, round my waist and then close my eyes and dream that it is your arms around me. You know', Marie went on in less exalted mood, 'I have never worn corsets. I have always been scornful of women who did. But do you know dear, this teaches me that this is why so many women like to have them very tight.'[49] There spoke the future sexologist.

On her sixteenth birthday her father had written, 'I want you to feel that you have the loving arms of a father round you'.[50] Although she protested in a fictionalized love letter that 'every nerve in my body is tingling with longing for you, every pulse in my body throbbing with desire,' it seems probable that Marie was yearning not only for a lover but also for the warmth and the protection of a father. Highly gifted intellectual she might be, but she was, as she wrote of herself later, still a child in a woman's body.

3

Japan

For five weeks on board ship, freed from her books and her lab work, Marie enjoyed the first restful holiday she had had for years. She was still the most lively and energetic of passengers and made the most of her journey. While the rest of the passengers dawdled over coffee, she explored Port Said, alone and on foot. Daily she wrote her journal which was sent home to be circulated to friends and colleagues. In the evenings she enjoyed a waltz with the ship's doctor or a game of chess and during the day she basked in the steamy weather. She adored the sun and felt 'all the blackness of Manchester drawn forth' as she sat in her deck chair. But she always put up her parasol to make sure her skin remained becomingly pink and delicate. When she arrived at Yokohama to meet her lover she felt ten years younger and was up at five that morning to see the sun's rays gleaming through the mist as they docked.

The reunion of the two lovers, who had reached such an elevated plane in two years' correspondence, remains significantly undocumented. Whether it lived up to expectations or was a wretched failure, for once she left no record. Her visit was official and she was greeted with ceremony and courtesy. Leading scientists and government officials came to her hotel, the Imperial, Tokyo, to work out a plan for her fossil-hunting trip to Hokkaido, the remote island in the north of the country, inhabited partly by aboriginal Ainos.

To her mother, who still had no idea of her emotional entanglement, she wrote that Professor Fujii had met her and smoothed her way through the Customs. In her journal she recorded that by the second day in Tokyo, 11 August, she had given up travelling by rickshaw ('where one is simply a parcel of goods to be delivered') to find her own way by the new trams. She got hopelessly lost, 'then my guardian angel (in the shape of Professor Fujii) turned up and rescued me though, as I had planned this expedition without his knowledge and spoken of it to no one, it was nothing short of a miracle.'[1]

In their letters and conversations, Marie and Fujii had discussed philosophy and Japanese poetry, touched on the infinities of religion and talked at length about the minutiae of fossils; they had, however, neglected more mundane matters, with the result that Marie had no clear idea of daily life and customs in Tokyo in 1907. For over fifty years Japan had been opened up to trade with the West and Japanese women were gradually beginning to staff the offices and new brick-built factories. The majority of the typists and telephonists travelled to work in overcrowded trams but the bolder spirits had begun to ride bicycles.

In high society and at official gatherings the Empress decreed that European dress was compulsory and 'Japanese ladies were therefore got up in garments which they do not thoroughly understand and therefore cannot wear with grace,' Marie remarked discerningly. But, despite the outward signs of emancipation and progress represented by women working outside the home, in offices and factories, and the new University for women where the authorities concentrated on teaching child care, the underlying attitude to women remained feudal. Japanese men demanded total obedience from the Japanese woman: obedience to her father when unmarried: obedience to her son when widowed. When a married couple went out, the wife was required to ride behind in a separate rickshaw and at home women played a submissive role, called upon to behave graciously and gratefully, to serve at tea but not to enter into conversation. 'Most Japanese men make no secret of their disdain for the female sex,' observed a travel writer in 1904, three years before Marie's visit.[2]

In her first two months in Japan Marie Stopes completely reversed that role. She battled through the northern jungle of Japan, leading a party of thirty men in her quest to find fossils. At the planning stage, she enjoyed teasing the hidebound Japanese by dressing to underline her femininity in a white muslin frock with a pink silk sash, while assuring them that she was quite happy to walk 'several miles up a river bed' and that she didn't mind 'sleeping on stones'. The journey to Hokkaido, the northern island, took two days. When she set off on her expedition she changed into more practical clothes: short, blue Japanese trousers and jacket, cloth leggings and stiff socks to be worn with straw sandals.

Her party included a Japanese professor (not Professor Fujii) who acted as an interpreter, a surveyor, an official from the Ministry of Agriculture, a policeman (presumably to defend her honour but he proved his usefulness by catching fresh trout for breakfast and carving chopsticks out of bamboo) and numerous coolies.

A lone, young, white woman traveller was a figure of great curiosity at that time and Marie became used to local officials calling to see her and crowds of people gathering at stops on her travels. When she went to bathe, women and children marvelled at her white skin and wondered why she put on a 'dress' to go into the water. At Yubari on 21 August, en route for the wilds, the party was put up in the Club House of the local coal mine. The room allotted to Marie Stopes served also as the party's dining and living room. 'The last gentleman came after I had prepared for bed,' she noted, 'and I conversed with him in my nightgown which, mercifully, was long and rather like a tea-gown but he never turned a hair – coming in on me before I could put on a dressing-gown.'[3]

On another occasion on the train from Tokyo, a Japanese businessman sitting opposite her slipped out of his suit, stripped to his shirt and then donned a kimono because of the heat, and on the boat to Hokkaido, Marie had to share a three-berth stateroom with two men. She remained cool and amused and approved the attitude of the Japanese who would not peep or pry but would stare frankly through open doors if occasion arose.

If the Japanese men felt sceptical of the small, confident lady in charge of the fossil-gathering expedition, they soon came to respect her as she led them through prickly forests of tall sasa (a plant of the bamboo species) and up river courses, carrying only a fan and a hammer. The coolies followed with the tents, food and equipment for the party. Marie scrambled along steep banks of friable shale, chipping out the rocks, indefatigable in her quest for the nodules which contained the fossils she needed. The work was laborious and exhausting but glimpses of blue hydrangeas and passion-flowers overhanging the water, and of snowy peaks seen through forests, lifted her spirits. At night, Marie decided where they would pitch camp and would sit alone huddled by a roaring wood fire in torrential rain as the coolies cooked the evening meal. They tried hard to please her and carried a chicken for her to eat but since they would 'only cook it for ten minutes or so it was as hard as the stones we are hunting for'.[4]

By the beginning of September, heavy rains had made the rocks treacherous and, without the clinging grasp of straw sandals, Marie would have been unable to gain a foothold. A coolie carried her on his back to cross the swollen rivers:

Without a couple of my escorts to put their feet to make steps or to give a hand round corners, I could not have got along at all . . . In crossing a river we all keep hands . . . how the loaded coolies could manage I cannot imagine. It was only the feeling that as I was the leader I daren't show fright, that kept me going. However, we were rewarded, for the fossils I got that afternoon were the best obtained so far and after several hours of brilliant sunshine the water perceptibly lessened.[5]

The expedition brought out the best in Marie, her courage and disregard for convention, her capacity for leadership and devotion to work. Three days later, on 4 September, she was back in Sapporo, the capital of Hokkaido. Her exploits had made her a heroine and when she gave a lecture on her expedition at Government House, the building was filled with women as well as men.

Two weeks later she returned to Tokyo where Professor Fujii had found her rooms in the house of the widow of a Japanese officer, close to the Botanical Institute. Safely home she wrote to Charlotte to reassure her that the only harm that had come to her on her expedition was a little black mark on her thumb where she had hit it with a hammer!

In her new home Marie adopted the Japanese style of life as far as she could. She admired the taste and simplicity of the local houses, the small rooms 'exquisite as seashells' furnished with only a few handsome paper screens. As a seasoned camper, it was no hardship for her to sleep on the floor on velvet futons and she even enjoyed the predictability of the Japanese diet, mainly rice, raw fish and eggs. It saved her the bother of designing different menus for her maid to cook every day.

A physical challenge, the spice of danger, seemed to satisfy a need to escape from the mundane for her. She wrote on 22 September, with enormous gusto, of a real 'Japanese experience':

I was wakened at five o'clock by a tremendous sensation in my walls and floors, as though they were trying to part company and I started to rush downstairs, my room being the only one on the second floor. Then I rushed back, thinking of all the tales of robbers I had heard . . . A figure approached, I accosted it angrily and demanded it to give an account of itself and be off! It was some time before I recognised myself in the glass! All the time the floor was swaying violently . . . when it suddenly stopped I lay down feeling very seasick. Then and then only did I remember that I was in a land of earthquakes.[6]

At first, Marie enjoyed her excursions into Tokyo society. As a 'specialist' lady she was a novelty, invited both to the Western Hallowe'en party and then to the Imperial Chrysanthemum party at Akasaka Palace. 'It is frightfully select and I am awfully pleased to go,' she wrote home. Marie had inherited her mother's snobbish tendencies and was thrilled by the 'numerous Princes and Princesses, Ambassadors and the élite of Tokyo Society,' although less impressed by the food. '... the Imperial allowance was about one plate each and on this the guests put ham, tongue and chicken, jelly, rolls and ice-cream, sweets and cakes ...'

In a letter to Charlotte she remarked that she had met some very charming people: 'I am quite in "High Life": Barons, Counts, Ambassadors, Military attachés, etc. .... Isn't it a change from the days of my early youth when fossils were the staple article? I am rather a lioness here, as there is no single real scientist in this place among the foreigners ...'[7]

Marie would not, of course, admit to her mother that her professional and social life was anything but a success. At first the sheer novelty of her experience absorbed her. She made further journeys, searching for fossils, none of them quite as spectacular as her journey to Hokkaido. Within a month of her arrival she had learnt enough of the language to be able to travel by herself. She visited the No, the highly stylized dance drama of Japan dating from the fourteenth and fifteenth centuries, sitting on the floor from 9.30 in the morning until 4.30 in the afternoon, and was so intrigued and discerning about this form of theatre that she later wrote a book about it with a Japanese collaborator.[8] Marie had given 'Frenchie', her china doll, to Fujii's daughter but she soon discovered that in Japan dolls were not mere children's playthings but 'wonderfully dressed figures of ancient Kings and their attendants, Court ladies and ministers with houses and exquisite lacquered furniture,' accorded a feast and a ceremony once a year.[9]

Fujii escorted her to the famous popular chrysanthemum show where millions of colourful blooms represented life-sized models of famous actors and actresses. On 1 January she drank saki out of lacquer cups with Japanese friends.

Nevertheless, in letters to her sister, for whom she bought thoughtful presents of comfortable sandals and decorative buttons, there were hints that not all was well in her private life: 'I am glad you made a pretty nightgown,' she wrote to Winnie, 'a girl ought to have pretty clothes and ought to have someone to encourage her to get them by admiring her in them but that, alas, fate often withholds ...'[10]

In Hampstead, meanwhile, Charlotte was complaining to Winnie that Marie ought to think of her family, come home and settle down, find a husband and take a house where they could all live. She wrote to Marie in this vein and Marie replied fiercely:

What steps have you ever taken to assist either of us to get married? What dances have you ever chaperoned us to? What young men have you introduced us to?

When I mix, as I do here, among ordinary people and see the kindly helpfulness (not to be confused with husband-hunting) of mothers for their girls in the way of social things, I sigh indeed for my abnormal youth and for Winnie even more. I, of course, could have been married often, it is my own high standards as regards certain things that debars me . . .[11]

And she reminded Charlotte, who had fought all her life for women's emancipation, that she, Marie, was carrying out work that 'is at any rate, rather unique for a woman . . . The honour of being sent by the Royal Society is great, perhaps you don't realize just how great . . .' Marie guessed rightly that lack of money lay at the root of Charlotte's complaints but insisted that, mixing as she was with the 'upper ten' and travelling expensively because transporting her fossils cost a lot of money, she had nothing to spare.

Despite the interest of her surroundings and the genuine absorption in her work, her journals and letters indicate that her private life was not the ecstatic union that Marie had longed for. She spent her twenty-seventh birthday down a mine in Japan, enjoying the adventure but conscious that the years were passing and she was getting dangerously near the status of permanent spinsterhood. No letters from Fujii to Marie survive from this time, no record of betrothal on his part exists. On the basis of cold fact, it appears that Marie had, in her own mind, transformed a gossamer foreign romance into a cast-iron commitment. The name of her beloved Fujii appeared less frequently in her journal (where the use had to be discreet) or in her private letters. Curiously enough, she did not once mention Professor Fujii's daughter by name. Nor does the little girl's name appear anywhere in her novel, *Love Letters of a Japanese*, which certainly reflects Marie's attitudes. In her book, Mertyl (Marie) suggests that the girl should be brought up by aunts: 'The child . . . must not be allowed to spoil the sweetness of our marriage . . . At present I cannot love it, for it is a pain to me always that you were married to the bad woman and the child reminds me of it every time . . .' Also, in her journal, Marie told a story of a Japanese professor who arrived two hours late for the lecture he was due to give because, he explained, his child had been naughty and it had taken care and thought to admonish her appropriately. Marie cited that as a justification for her view that the Japanese were 'capable of very much less mental activity in a day than a corresponding Englishman or woman'.[12] These passages seem to suggest that the child had come between them. Perhaps Professor Fujii, faced with a fiancée who was demanding on every level and spectacularly different from any Japanese woman, retreated.

Early in 1908 it was clear from her Journal and her letters that Marie felt disillusioned and lonely in Tokyo, at home neither among the polite and ritualized world of the upper-class Japanese nor at the tea and tennis parties of the diplomats and businessmen of the British colony. She soon found 'the social round petty and inconsequential', and disliked the conventional calls where the talk was of clothes, engagements and marriages. Travelling in Tokyo was slow, addresses hard to find, the roads muddy and largely unsurfaced and it all took time from her work. 'It really is sad how the material hampers the intellectual.'

By the spring of 1908 she was longing for a day's shopping at the sales and for some stimulating conversation: 'Only when I can get a respectable middle-aged man, can I get such decent intellectual conversation as I have been accustomed to have nearly every day in England,' Marie grumbled in a letter to Winnie.[13] Despite herself Marie was drawn to Western circles for company. She was 'bullied' into playing hockey and that is not easy to imagine. She bought herself a bicycle and went everywhere on it, even to diplomatic parties, causing the footmen who had to lift the machine up the British Embassy steps to raise their eyebrows. When she turned up by bicycle, dishevelled and be-spattered, for an evening-dress party, the French Ambassador remarked sardonically 'très moderne'.

Like her mother, faced with the narrowness of life in a London suburb, Marie in Tokyo, tried to create her own intellectual climate. She organized a society of London University men in Japan (with at least one woman on the committee). She also founded the first Woman's Debating Society in Tokyo, in May 1908, recruiting missionaries and diplomatic wives as members. Not surprisingly, the motion at the first debate, 'that chaperones should be abolished', was overwhelmingly defeated. In another debate in the autumn on the motion: 'that the unmarried life is happier', Marie made it clear where her sympathies lay: 'I did not need to speak against the ranting type who rave against men and marriage and prove themselves deformed . . . The ranting type seems mercifully to be confined to big communities; I suppose it is an inevitable result of city life where some must sterilize.'[14] She had read in the London newspapers of the Suffrage movement where women were on the march, speaking at street corners. Marie was thankful to be out of it. '. . . though I don't have much sympathy with the rowdy ones, I should probably have got drawn into it and should have seriously damaged my career as a scientist . . .'[15]

The pain of her situation, with her hopes of love, marriage, the mental and physical union she yearned for as elusive as Fujii himself, was excruciating. Intensely guarded, she had kept her affair private, so she did not have to suffer public humiliation. Yet her loneliness was almost tangible and a hint of her misery appears in a letter she wrote to Charlie Hewitt, a colleague from Manchester, who had himself broken off his engagement to a Miss McNichol because his doctors had suspected tuberculosis – then incurable. Marie deplored his behaviour and offered to be his confidante: 'To a woman who deeply loves a man a broken betrothal is as death itself . . . an endless agony of pain . . . that turns every simple daily duty and pleasure into torture . . .'[16]

Fortunately she had her work. To her satisfaction, Fujii had managed to install fossil-cutting machinery in the Botanical Institute during her stay and Marie worked there from ten in the morning until four in the afternoon quietly busy over her fossils and excited to find the structure of the plants under her microscope with the leaves, stem and roots all with their cells well preserved. That she did know more than Professor Fujii about this form of fossil was incontrovertible and Marie was incapable of pretending to modesty. That, of course, made their relationship more difficult and Professor Fujii seemed more and more aloof. He didn't like to dance, usually arranged to meet her in the company of others and refused to work in the lab with her in the evenings because of the scandal it might cause. 'I often go for days with only half a dozen words of business to Professor Fujii', she told Winnie.[17]

By the spring, emotional deprivation accomplished what no amount of physical hardship could; Marie fell ill with influenza. On 10 March 1908 she spent the day in bed feeling 'so seedy I did not get up at all'. Not since a bout of measles as a child had she ever succumbed to illness. She began to find certain features of life in Tokyo insupportable. At the end of April, Marie sat next to a leper in a tram and, transfixed with horror, noticed that 'some of his finger tips were eaten away and one eye was blinded . . .' Though the Japanese assured her that they did not believe leprosy to be contagious, Marie was so fearful that she never boarded a tram in Tokyo again. At night, with the increase of robbers in the city, she went to sleep with a sword in her hand.

Most distressing of all, Professor Fujii was ill, so ill that once when she called he could not see her. 'Do get engaged while I am here and can buy and send home some underthings for your trousseau,' she advised Winnie. 'Professor Fujii is ill, awfully ill and it is distinctly a trouble to me from many points of view and also I am a worry for him. It is his eyes again, he has overworked so very much . . .'[18]

Fujii's illness which lasted for months was never satisfactorily diagnosed or explained. His sight was badly affected and he had to spend some time at home, away from the Institute. To Professor Oliver, her co-sponsor from London University, Marie wrote explaining her difficulties in completing the work, the life in Tokyo was so slow and time seemed to be of no importance to the Japanese: 'also, Professor Fujii, my nominal colleague is busy – and now is ill, really very seriously ill, in danger of losing his sight.'[19]

A month later, Marie was feeling desperate about the situation. She had smothered her secret; no one knew of what she considered to be her 'betrothal' to Fujii and there was no one in whom she could confide. In desperation, she sent off a wild and passionate letter to her kindly professor in Manchester – not so wild, however, that she did not keep a draft copy.[20]

Before she poured out her troubles to Professor Weiss, Marie swore her recipient to secrecy. 'There is no good beating about the bush,' she wrote, 'so I must plunge in. I am in love, thinking about marrying . . . Now please don't be vexed and throw the letter down and say, "of course, another woman lost to science" . . . I will be no worse scientist because I am married. Are you?' At the time prejudice against married women working in the professions was so strong that they were often dismissed. After confessing that Professor Fujii was the man she loved, Marie explained that Professor Fujii's eyes were bad, he had been off work for a month and although he was gradually recovering he would never be fit again. 'I can't bear it, it is so painful to think of his life's work spoiled.' The work had fallen behind and Professor Fujii refused to spend the evening hours with her working, as he would not expose either of them to gossip. If they were married, she argued, she could read to him, discuss her work with him all night if necessary and they could produce their work jointly. 'He is ballast and I am the sails in our work generally, but without ballast I am likely to tip over.' Marie reminded Professor Weiss that she had mentioned these matters only to show him how science entered into the argument. If the two scientists were married they could work all night without reproach!

But what was to be done? In order to complete her work for the Royal Society, Marie had to return to England. She could not finish her paper based only on the fossils in Japan. So she proposed to return to England for a year or two, lecture in Manchester, settle her work for the Royal Society and then possibly return to Japan or 'perhaps, if Professor Fujii is well, bring him to England . . .' But would the University appoint her if she were married, she asked Professor Weiss? 'Professor Fujii fears sometimes that we should not marry, he sees the disadvantages for me, particularly in his health,' she said naïvely. But she wanted badly to marry soon, 'if I do not get a little happiness now I may never get it at all, his health is so very bad'.

If a reply came from Professor Weiss to that extraordinary letter it no longer exists. What is not at all clear is how far Professor Fujii, the 'ballast' in the partnership, had been consulted about her plan. Marie had been so self-sufficient all her life, accustomed to taking her own decisions and keeping her own counsel that she may not have told him. A week after she wrote to Professor Weiss, Marie told Charlotte that if she had one hundred pounds to spare she would come home for the summer, the weather in Tokyo was far too hot. And a letter from a close friend, Olga Kapteyn, makes the most important comment on the Japanese episode. 'It struck me as rather remarkable that you should have come to exactly the same conclusion as I have, namely that *sex* is the key to everything.'[21]

Hoped for, imagined, romanticized, Marie's and Fujii's love had not come to fruition. The situation was intolerable for both of them, thrown together publicly in their work, their private life in tatters. Marie put in long solitary days at the laboratory. By the middle of August, she was bitter and disappointed. 'Are the gods never going to have mercy and stop their cruel play of battering Professor F. and, through him, me and our fossil work', she wrote in her journal.[22]

> . . . he came very late with the horrible news that he had just heard that the people who lived in this house before him (he moved last year) had a leper in the family! Consequently, he and his household have stood in grave danger of getting this ghastly disease and may actually have it now, the latent period is so uncertain . . . I am not

really afraid for Professor F. and through him, for myself but I fear the removal will still further hinder the progress of our fossil work.

In September, the strain of the situation again broke Marie's health. She took to her bed with a temperature of 104° for the second time in Tokyo and called a doctor, despite her deep distrust of the profession. The real source of Marie's illness and the sixty-six warts that appeared mysteriously, and Professor Fujii's weakness, has never been traced. In *Love Letters of a Japanese* earlier Marie (in the guise of Mertyl Meredith) writes after a lover's misunderstanding:

> I hated you fiercely for not only had you cruelly broken my dream of beauty and happiness but you seemed not worthy of my love . . . my pride was wounded and cried out for revenge. I planned how I could kill you and, had you been in my power, I believe I should have done it . . .[23]

The failure of her dream, the rejection by Fujii, profoundly affected Marie Stopes. Never again did she let her defences down so completely, and her acute sense of her own dignity, from that time on, often led her into ridiculous situations. In November 1908 an eminent Swedish biologist, Sven Hedin, visited Tokyo and lectured in the University. Marie met him at tea beforehand and he visited her laboratory. The following day the British Ambassador, Sir Claude McDonald, held a large reception for him. Marie knew about the reception, had heard others talk of it, but had received no invitation herself. She took the unprecedented liberty of writing to Sir Claude, asking him if her invitation had gone astray: 'tomorrow representatives of the university [of Tokyo] are coming to you to meet Sven Hedin – and if they find that I – the only British scientist in Japan and one, moreover, for whom they have put themselves so much about – am not invited to meet Dr H. at my own Embassy – what will they conclude?'[24]

Sir Claude McDonald was clearly annoyed by Marie's presumption. He replied that he *had* sent her an invitation and added that he found her remark that she would not have written to ask him 'were it merely for the trifling pleasure of a social function' discourteous. '. . . you are perhaps unaware that there is no obligation whatever on my part to entertain anybody in this Embassy outside the strictly official and diplomatic circles.'[25]

Marie had been precipitate and over-sensitive but, throughout her professional career, she was constantly slighted by the system and sometimes by male colleagues who resented her unrepentant knowledge of her worth. Although her work was regarded as original and valuable by the Royal Society, as a woman she could never become a Fellow and enjoy the privileges of membership, or even lecture on her own work there.

For the rest of the year Marie worked hard to complete, as far as possible, her research for the Royal Society which barred her presence. Professor Fujii worked with her in December but, by then, the love affair, the future together, was no longer discussed. She sailed for home on 24 January 1909 and Kenjiro Fujii was among the small group of friends who came to see her off. She had spent eighteen months in Japan but it took her many years to get over the love affair and perhaps contributed to her subsequent disenchantment with science. Professor Fujii's side of the story has never been told but he did write a letter to Professor Oliver, praising Marie's work in Japan. The very qualities that had attracted Marie to him, his gentleness and discretion, would have made it impossible for Professor Fujii to brazen out such a wildly unconventional marriage in his own society.

That they both suffered during that extraordinary eighteen months is indisputable. Fujii did not succumb later to leprosy, blindness or, indeed, any serious illness. He lived until he was eighty-six and had two common-law wives after Marie left, finally marrying the second in his old age. When he visited her at Christmas years later, when their lives had gone their separate ways, Fujii wrote no ordinary 'thank you' letter: 'For myself December 25, 1925 was the most happy day I ever had for twenty years . . .'[26]

Back in England, for years Marie felt betrayed and hurt and she wrote both published and unpublished works about her loss. Undoubtedly, it contributed to the chauvinistic outlook she developed and to her deep distrust of mixed marriages, expressed in an unpublished comedy in verse about a treacherous Japanese nobleman who persuades a pure English girl to initiate him into the art of kissing:

> Oh British maids: to British men
> Betroth yourselves, if love you must.
> All other love will turn to dust.[27]

4

Independence

Pain and disappointment made Marie prolific. She found solace in her work and with her ingrained self-discipline schooled herself to spend even longer hours at her desk. Back in England at the end of February 1909, she stayed at home for two months finishing up her work for the Royal Society and sending off her 'Journal from Japan' to Blackie (the firm who had published her book *Ancient Plants*, the first popular account of the subject). Professionally she received encouragement on every side. The British Museum invited her to prepare a monograph on cretaceous plants and the Linnaean Society, founded in the late eighteenth century to promote the study of flora and fauna, elected her a member and a Fellow. Although she had not discovered coalballs in her cluster of rocks, Marie had found Japanese fossils of value and interest, including one of the earliest examples of the ovary of a petrified flowering plant. Her scientific papers on the fossils of Japan, published in 1909–10, were to enhance her reputation. She was frequently invited to lecture on her Japanese journey by schools and universities. As a speaker, Marie's great strength was her ability to gauge the mood and receptiveness of her audience and to vary her delivery accordingly. Although inwardly uncertain she came into her own with an audience. She joined the Poetry Society, founded shortly before she arrived back in England, and in March read her poems aloud to a small gathering.

At Manchester University Professor Weiss created a new post for her as Lecturer in Fossil Botany. Marie went back there in May 1909. During the summer vacation she found rooms for Winnie and herself, away from her mother, in a tall, red-brick, semi-detached house, a few strides away from Hampstead Heath.

She was now well established in the scientific world and beginning to be known in literary circles, she belonged to several clubs and frequently dined out – a fully independent woman.

Yet her private life remained chaotic. Deeply frustrated by her stay in Japan, Marie had plunged into a hopeless entanglement. Leaving the ship at Vancouver, she travelled by train across Canada where she had arranged to look at fossil plants and to lecture to women's groups on her Japanese experiences. As a speaker, she was immensely popular among Canadian women. The contrast between her feminine, fur-wrapped appearance and her self-confident assertive manner as she related her adventures quickly made her into a heroine. She became the symbol of the new woman, telling the Canadians, who were longing for emancipation, that they were wasting their lives washing dishes and must find satisfying careers for themselves. Hearing her speak in Toronto, Helen McMurchy an unmarried woman doctor in her fifties, in the field of public health, became one of Marie's most enthusiastic admirers. To this sympathetic stranger Marie poured out all the hurt and disillusion of her love affair with Professor Fujii, and Helen was only too happy to console her.

Marie, bisexual by nature (although she later denied it fiercely) was attracted to women, as two naïve passages in *A Journal from Japan* reveal. With surprising sensuality, she wrote of a beautiful American she had met at a diplomatic party: 'On her soft neck were the loveliest little blue veins, I never saw anything so suggestive of living marble. She was like white marble with an under-flash of rose and violet. Why do I always fall in love with women?'[1] Women's necks and shoulders in particular fascinated her and in an earlier *Journal* entry, written in November 1907, Marie had remarked on a girl of mixed race, half-Japanese, half-English: 'She had such lovely shoulders that I longed to be a man and marry her . . .'[2] That Marie wrote so publicly of her feelings suggests that she was completely unaware of their significance. At the time, even in intellectual circles, the subject was quite literally unmentionable.

However, after Tokyo Marie was yearning for sexual experience and by the time she left Canada, Helen McMurchy was completely enthralled and Marie herself had demonstrated that she wanted to be loved. From Toronto Helen wrote:

My darling, That is what I have been wanting to call you ever since the express took you away from me to Montreal. At that moment I knew I loved you when I found it in my heart to take you into my arms and kiss you. It hurt my heart all day, every day that I knew I had to let you go . . . Will you really have me dear, I am so glad. I am old enough to be your adopted mother ... You have 'got me' dear and what a sweet thing that you knew that you had got me and were a little glad about it.[3]

And then Helen McMurchy, as much would-be mother as would-be lover, added generously:

There will be true lovers for you darling, instead of that cruel and false one, other men will love and admire you ... I claim you for mine, dear – forever – as you said. I shall always have a share in you and in what you do – You dear genius ... It must be goodbye – and was I the only person who kissed you in Canada! You darling – what am I to call you? Ever yours affectionately, Helen McMurchy.

The time was too short for the friendship to deepen beyond an over-whelming infatuation, and Marie visited McGill University and Yale in America before sailing for home, aboard the SS *Lusitania*.

Marie usually kept drafts of her own letters but none exists of her correspondence with Helen McMurchy. From Helen, however, the let-ters came constantly, reassuring Marie that she was indispensable. Poor Helen was overwhelmed and could hardly believe that Marie cared for her. Yet, when one of her letters seemed less devoted, Marie chided her. Once back in England at the end of February, the love affair depended on letters from abroad and Marie desperately wanted an admirer nearer at hand.

In the scientific community, she found young men to go about with. In June 1909 she went for day cycling trips with Henry Bassett, a chemist friend from Liverpool University who had admired Marie, first, at Munich, when they were fellow students and, later, when she came to Manchester. Over the years Marie had treated Henry rather off-hand-edly. She had, it is true, sent him her photograph to admire, asked him to hear her lectures and invited him to an occasional dance at the University. Henry was a mild-mannered, tame young man who lived a secluded life with his parents. Of course, he adored her, called her his 'dear little sunbeam', and assured her that she was the only person who understood him. But though steadfast, Henry could not be described as exciting. Marie told Winnie he was 'of no account'. At the same time, Marie was collaborating with Charles Gordon Hewitt, an entomologist in the Department of Zoology of her University and an infinitely more attractive prospect.

They had corresponded when Marie was in Tokyo and she had

pleaded with Hewitt then not to break off his engagement to Miss McNichol because of his suspected tuberculosis. Now he was engaged again this time to Edith Garner. Marie had brought back some fossilized insects from Japan and they co-operated enthusiastically on their esoteric work, a paper on 'The Tent-Building Habits of the Ant, Lasius Niger Linn, in Japan'.[4] That collaboration led to an intense friendship trembling on the edge of mutual infatuation. On holiday in Filey in Yorkshire, Charlie Hewitt was missing her. And Marie wrote urging Charlie to 'pluck the flower of life in youth . . .' He wavered, uncertain: '. . . is there not such a thing as plucking a flower and regretting it afterwards? Is not youth synonymous with inexperience? It is because I feel . . . the awful risk of snatching a few moments' happiness – of a very transient nature – that I hesitate.'[5] He did, however, send her a snapshot of himself camping with his dog, captioned 'Human Friend with Dog!' and from Well Walk, Hampstead, where she and Winnie were now installed, Marie wrote him one of her high-toned letters:

'Best beloved of friends – all last night I slept little but there was a feeling in my hands . . . that I held in them something, rare, beautiful and sacred. Even if we never were to meet again I would thank you for that vow on bended knee. Difficult – you said – sweet knight I know, but not too difficult for your beautiful strength.'[6]

What the vow was is not clear but according to Marie the two had never kissed. She might have asked him to swear eternal love, or total abstinence. Entangled and obligated both to his fiancée and to Marie, Charlie Hewitt decided that it might be the right moment to take up an academic appointment in Ottawa. However, he found Marie's intellect, her command of language and, above all, her sweeping ideals of love and marriage almost mesmerizing, even across the Atlantic.

And Marie seemed to court entanglements. Under her influence, Charlie wrote to Edith Garner breaking off his engagement. Edith, a trusting and direct young woman, was devastated by his letter and, knowing of Marie's friendship with her fiancé, she wrote to Marie from Warwick: 'Do you love Charlie Hewitt and do you wish to marry him and does he return your love? . . . if he wants you I shall pass out of his life and never trouble you again.'[7]

Marie replied that she was extremely busy but she would try to unravel the tangle. She coolly invited Miss Garner to spend the night with her. 'I could put you up, if you didn't mind partly sharing a big bedroom.' She asked Edith to bring any recent letters from Charlie with

her. Not surprisingly, Edith Garner declined the invitation at first and
Marie wrote again on 15 March 1910, stressing that Charlie had been
entirely loyal to his fiancée and only in the last few letters had there
been anything more than friendship. 'I needn't tell you, he has never
kissed me (Ah! how I envy you) . . . He wrote to me that if we were
married he would feel a brute to you – also that he felt he ought not to
marry for years as a penance. (Oh, if you really loved him, you could
not wish that for him.)'[8]

In the meantime Marie reported her correspondence with Edith to
Charlie, asking him not to tell Edith that he knew of it. She hated, she
claimed, to see her rival clinging to the false hope that Charlie still loved
her and begged him to make that clear to Edith. 'I think from what I
have observed that if she was once definitely convinced that you would
never see her again she could find happiness later on with someone else.'
Marie was manipulating the correspondence and the relationships and,
two days later, she urged Edith to write to Charlie and tell him she no
longer loved him: 'it would be so good for him . . . (you know what
false ideas he has about his value in women's eyes) . . . You are worth
more stable love than he gave.'[9]

Charlie tried to disentangle the incestuous correspondence in a long
letter to Edith, pointing out the reality as he saw it. He had been in love
with her (Edith) until Marie came back from Japan; 'unintentionally she
gradually seemed to change things . . . It was on account of my feelings
towards her [Marie] that I recognized the unenduring character of my
love for you.'[10] Nevertheless, Charlie insisted that it was Marie's ideals,
not the woman herself he had loved. Charlie revealed to Edith that when
he had broken off his engagement, Marie had written asking him to
marry her, since she knew, she said, that Charlie would not dare to
propose to her himself.

Thus cornered, Charlie asked for three months to think it over. But
Marie would not have it, Charlie explained. She wrote dictating her
terms. If they were to be married the marriage must take first place in
his life; Marie would want to come to England every year for two
months and she was only prepared to wait six weeks for his answer. 'I
feel she is more in love with Love than with me. I can see that to her
the man is only the personification of her great ideal love – that I cannot
be,' he wrote perceptively.

Marie had insisted that Edith should send Charlie's letters on to her
and she reaped a bitter benefit. When she saw Charlie's letter, turning
her down, she sent it back to Edith immediately (carefully copied out

for her own record). And she first wrote and then cabled to Charlie, telling him to send all her letters back because she wanted to read them through carefully to see how the 'unimaginable situation' had arisen.

To Edith Garner she denied Charlie's version of the affair but without her usual vehemence. Above all she wanted to be in control of the disaster. Almost thirty and still unmarried, Marie felt if she could only understand the tangle she might at last find happiness. She had grown up in an atmosphere of emotional sterility, and consequently as an adult she tried to resolve all her problems intellectually. When she was a child, she said, she had recited the Lord's Prayer daily. Now she asked not for daily bread but for understanding. It was a heartfelt plea since Marie's emotional blindness, both towards her own feelings and to other people's, caused havoc. In May she had applied for a post in Paleobotany at the University of Toronto. A letter in June 1910 regretting that the Botanical Department was 'not yet educated up to the subject' dashed that hope.

Soon after she had written to Charlie in Canada, asking for her letters back, Marie wrote to her old faithful, Henry Bassett, rousing a hope in him that he might win her love. He had waited, hoping against hope that she would come round, and abased himself. 'Luckless wretch that I am, that I cannot urge my cause more fitly but can only lay my simple honest love, quite unadorned at your feet . . .'[11]

Marie told Henry cruelly that she felt on consideration he was not of the right temperament or calibre. Although he liked camping and the outdoor life, he lacked appreciation of music, books and painting and did not seem to notice beauty. The poor man gained some good marks but the overall report was unfavourable. 'Your steady faithfulness is much in your favour but I am a very complex person and could not have too many of my sides left lonely always.'[12]

Even Henry cannot have been surprised that the love affair did not flourish. Marie yearned for a knight who was exotic, as intellectually and aesthetically gifted as she was and, of course, abjectly in love. The disadvantages of possessing brains and ability, yet being a woman, were only too apparent to Marie. In her early years at Manchester, although tacitly and implicitly a feminist, she had opposed the militant tactics of the Women's Social and Political Union, the breakaway faction of the Suffrage Movement, afraid, as her letters make clear, that open involvement might hinder her scientific career. Now she was established in her professional life, but disillusioned with men. The General Election of January 1910 resounded with talk of Women's Suffrage.[13] On 16

December 1909, she wrote to *The Times* urging the case for women's suffrage, giving her address as Manchester University:[14]

Dear Sir

... It is important that the nation should realize how wasteful and short-sighted is the policy of the men who refuse women the vote. (The vote, by the way, which they have exercised in the past and which the law allows them.) There are in the country thousands of women who not only 'want' the vote but who are absolutely determined to get it. And they will get it. Behind them is working an invincible power stronger than any opposition – the force of evolution.

Why does the nation waste its energy and money in the petty sex wrangles over the question? It is an unnatural and ridiculous thing that men and women, who were made to love and help each other, should fight as they are forced to do at present, and the cost of the fight is a terrible drain on national resources ... There is another indirect but vital loss to the country. Men are undermining the national reputation of Englishmen for chivalry – even for honesty and justice, which is an invaluable national asset – the Norwegians can despise us. [As early as 1901, Norwegian women over a certain income were allowed to vote in municipal elections. By 1909 they were campaigning for the full franchise which was granted in 1913.]

It is clear that as the vote for women has to come, the sooner a stop can be put to the degrading struggle to get it the better. Then the reckless waste of money, energy and honour which is now going on may cease. The country should be made to understand that those in power who protract the struggle are the nation's enemies.

Yours etc
MARIE STOPES

Ever since her return from Tokyo, Marie had felt restless, sexually stirred, and unable to settle. To a friend she wrote that she planned to go round the world in two years' time. Reports she had read of Shackleton's account of coal deposits found in Antarctica intrigued her and when she heard that Captain Scott was planning a second expedition to the Antarctic, she offered him her services in a careful letter. Just before Christmas Marie received a disappointing reply from the Expedition's Offices in Victoria Street, London:[15]

Dear Dr Stopes
I should have acknowledged your letter of the 16th and enclosures

before. I am very much obliged for the trouble you have taken in giving me information concerning your particular work as far as it can be conveyed by written explanation. I appreciate fully how far this must fall short of the possibilities which might result from your personal examination of the coal seams which may be found, but difficulties which would result should a lady be included in the staff of the Expedition appear to me practically insurmountable and even if these were overcome, there would remain the strong probability that you would be unable to reach the interesting localities which you had especially come to see.

I must ask you to be satisfied with this expression of my sincere gratitude for the results which I hope will be of great benefit to our geologists.

Yours sincerely
R. SCOTT

Marie's rage and disappointment at that reply can only be imagined. Captain Scott was only too willing to accept her scientific work but not her presence. Arguably she would have stood up to the ordeal of that last expedition as well as any of the men.

In private, in her rooms at Manchester and at home in Hampstead, Marie began to turn more and more to self-expression, to write her way out of her difficulties. As early as 1906 she had confided to close friends that she was writing a novel, and of course she produced scientific papers from the time she graduated. But in her thirtieth year she wrote poetry or, rather, she believed that poetry ought to write itself with facility and some technical skill, each poem a 'flashing message'. Unfortunately, she also published it.

Her poem, 'The Idealist's Love', was written in 1908 when she was in Tokyo:[16]

> My lover hurt me, but I would not moan:
> For love was mine, and I was his alone.
> What though my lover as a mortal man
> Did break his truth – no mortal ever can
> Do all he would. I had no wish to blame
> And kissed his lying lips next day the same.
> Thus to my lover I was true, because
> Truth in great love is one of love's great laws.

In London in 1909, a poem entitled 'Wine that turned to Vinegar' outlined her disappointment even more explicitly:[17]

> To have loved, to have kissed
> And – oh, God! – to have missed
> The completion of Love!
> To have turned to one
> As the only sun
> In one's sky above
> And to find that his beams
> Had merely in dreams
> Their radiant light.
> What so deep as the woe
> Of those who did know
> The joy of the height.
> A more pitiful thing
> Than the broken wing
> Of a bird that soared,
> Is one driven by fate
> To return with hate
> Where she once adored.

Despite some technical skill, Marie's talent was not perhaps best suited to tragic love poems. That year she offered a volume of poetry to the publisher Chapman Hall but was rejected. Her sheer energy and output were daunting. As well as making a sensitive and imaginative translation of the No plays with a Japanese, J. Sakurai, she wrote *Love Letters of a Japanese*, an account of her love affair with Professor Fujii, based on their correspondence, five reports of new discoveries for learned journals, and founded and edited *The Sportophyte*, The Botanical *Punch*, the first humorous magazine of the botanical world. In the magazine, which she wrote almost entirely herself, she took the opportunity to review her own book *Ancient Plants*: 'Blackie must have been a Brownie to have dragged this book to the light of day. It is not a bad book, however, because it deals with plants which can no longer wriggle about to convolute our own theories'; and included some spoof definitions: 'Polygamos – a plant that drops its seeds everywhere'.[18] This skit on their work was much enjoyed by the international botanical world.

An unpublished novel, 'A Man and his Mate', obviously describing a young English girl's life in a German university, was discovered in 1990,[19] dedicated to:

those who understand that in the world are but three things worthy of our Passion:

Beauty, which is goodness
Truth, which is sometimes called Science
And Love, which is life itself.

Marie drew a border of oak leaves and plants round the frontispiece and marked the story ready for the printer. On the last page she wrote: 'The work and property of Dr Marie Stopes, 14 Well Walk, Hampstead Heath, N. W. But this fact is to be kept strictly secret and it is to appear under an assumed name'. The name she adopted (among other pseudonyms) was G. N. Mortlake. But neither 'A Man and his Mate', nor her playlet in verse, *The Two Japans*, was ever published.

Marie used her novel to provide a happy ending for her disastrous romance in Japan. The heroine of 'A Man and his Mate', Marjorie, a charming and brilliant twenty-three-year-old English post-graduate student studying at a German university, has all the professors at her feet. Significantly, it is an Englishman, Kenneth Lawrence, a married paleontologist with a wife languishing in a lunatic asylum, who captivates her heart. After a passionate, if pure friendship between the two, the Professor's mad wife dies and the couple are free to marry. Interleaved in the torrid romance: 'When their lips met it was the meeting of two mountain torrents . . . dashing over the bare rocks and sending white spray high into the sunlight . . .', feminist sentiments impinge. Marjorie, the heroine, sees herself as on the borderland here, the first woman to take a place in this little community of scientists. 'Might not it symbolize the real work which she had to do in the world and of which she had hitherto no vision . . . ?'

In addition to all her literary and scientific work (and by now she had a typewriter and a dictaphone) Marie organized fortnightly 'Cinderella' dances at the Women's Union which she herself and many of her colleagues enjoyed. She had not given up hope of finding Prince Charming. In demand to lecture to botanical and geological societies in the universities, she also received invitations to lecture and attend scientific conferences in America and Canada.

In May 1910 Marie was elected as a fellow to University College, London, able to use their laboratories and resources. At what stage she took the decision to leave Manchester is not clear. She suffered from headaches and neuralgia and persuaded her physician that the fogs of Manchester exacerbated her condition. Conveniently, her Hampstead doctor gave her a certificate in July 1910 stating that in his opinion it was 'advisable, on account of health, that Miss Marie Stopes should *not* live in Manchester'.

Professor Weiss and Marie's colleagues there were genuinely sorry to see such a bright scholar leave (particularly as they were forced to soldier on through the fogs and rain of their city). But Marie was now free to concentrate on her writing and lecturing and was spared the tiring railway journey. Her salary, £150 a year, had been small and she was confident of her ability to earn money from other sources. In August Marie and Winnie went on an inexpensive camping holiday to Studland on the Dorset coast, then Marie travelled to Berlin, to stay with her old school-friend, Olga Kapteyn, now married.

In the autumn the Canadian Government invited her to make a study of the carboniferous flora of New Brunswick. She still had her contacts in Canada, Helen McMurchy and Charlie Hewitt, and Marie had hopes of broadening her scientific knowledge and perhaps finding a suitable husband at last. She was in the New World for Christmas.

According to her diary, Marie arrived in Minneapolis on Boxing Day and on the 29th at a Botanical Dinner at St Louis, at a meeting of the American Association of Science, she sat next to Reginald Ruggles Gates. A pallid-faced man of medium height, with pince-nez, a fine broad forehead and a sweeping moustache, Gates was a bachelor from a religious background in Canada. Sensitive and highly-strung, he was two years younger than Marie. He was already distinguished in the new field of genetics and very conscious of status in the academic world. To Marie, whose parents had met at the British Association, the coincidence was striking. They met next day at tea, attended a scientific meeting together and went on to the theatre in the evening. On New Year's Eve, after skating and a dinner at Gates's cousins, Ruggles proposed and within a week was accepted. Marie had always wanted to marry a botanist, to be fulfilled as a wife and mother as well as a scientist; she was overjoyed. She had to leave her fiancé for almost two months to pursue her scientific engagements, but she was in top form, working hard, dancing till three and meeting 'heaps of jolly people'.

On 4 February she wrote enthusiastically to Winnie from Baltimore:

Dear Kidlet

I had a really and truly heavenly time in Washington. The Ambassador was asked to dinner and I put next to him. He is the third most popular man in America and some say the greatest Englishman alive . . . He wrote a letter to Mr J. to say he was 'much impressed by my intelligence and knowledge!'[20]

She hugged her secret to her for a week and then wrote again to Winnie:

My dear kid
Tho' I can't be sure till I am actually married, I want that room for a man! A man who will be my husband before I sail I expect, if he stays as nice as he seems . . . Except that he has a stupid little nose, he seems absolutely perfect. I couldn't have made him better myself. He is a Canadian and a darling. Don't tell a soul. It is a dead secret. You see I am a sudden person and in the middle of the ceremony I may say no![21]

Secret notes to Winnie instructed her to have the rooms in Well Walk painted and repaired. Her bedroom, in particular, Marie explained should be a 'pretty, restful sweet-memoried place'. Gates had no private income, as Marie had thought at first, but was comfortable enough to be able to live without a post for twelve months, if necessary. Marie was confident that Winnie and Ruggles would like each other but dreaded the meeting with Charlotte, afraid that her mother would cross-question and overpower the gentle husband, so Charlotte was kept in ignorance. Ten days before her marriage, Marie was staying at Government House in Ottawa with the Governor General, Earl Grey and his wife. She wrote a bantering letter to her mother, boasting of her temporary grandeur without a word about her engagement. 'At breakfast a glorious A.D.C., in his gold tasselled uniform rose from his own honourable meal to fetch me mine'.[22]

Her work was going well and she found Ottawa delightful although she and Ruggles were temporarily separated. They had a rapturous reunion and were married at the Windsor Hotel, Montreal by a Methodist minister on 18 March 1911. The loyal Helen McMurchy was one of the witnesses and Charlie Hewitt was among the guests. 'Married' Marie cabled to Winnie, who was left to break the news to Charlotte and arrange a party for their homecoming. The couple arrived aboard *The Empress of Britain* on 1 April.

Ruggles Gates was delighted with his new wife, with her charm, her scientific ability, her Englishness. He realized when he married her that Marie would make an unusual wife but he had not quite grasped the reality of it until he came to live in her Hampstead home. Housework she despised, just as her mother had done. Scrubbing floors and cleaning windows, she once said, played havoc with highly-strung women; as for washing dishes after meals, that, in her view, was the hardest task in the house. They had one maid-of-all-work but Marie made it clear that Ruggles had to do his share of the housework. He also had to accustom himself to her habits. She insisted on sleeping with the bedroom doors and windows open and putting up her sister in the house. Then, Ruggles had not realized the extent of her literary ambition. When she came home from Canada she found a parcel containing a returned manuscript which completely absorbed her. Before she had left she had sent Maurice Hewlett, a well-known romantic novelist of the day, her account of love and marriage, already turned down by a publisher, and begged him for his advice. Maurice Hewlett replied carefully. He recognized the enthusiasm of the work, he wrote, but added:

> It is a kind of first sketch of a thing which, when complete, might be romantic, poetical, philosophical . . . it is much too short and has no conclusion: the verses are not really part of the book. It looks to me as though the narrative . . . has been made to connect the verses. That is quite legitimate, of course, but it should be done with more art. As for the verses themselves . . . I think you trust too much to the first impulse or inspiration . . . One or two of them, though, put into the mouth of the heroine seem to be addressed to a woman . . . I recognized, as I began by saying, your enthusiasm at first blush . . . the question you must decide is whether there is enough of it left in you to urge you to begin again and make a book of it.[23]

No copy of that early version of her life's work exists. Marie said later that she had intended to write a series of a dozen novels, each with a single idea featured, describing love and marriage in her time.

Marie hero-worshipped Hewlett, adored his novels and took his advice literally. She burnt most of the book and eventually encapsulated the themes in it into *Married Love*, the best-selling work which was to make her famous and sell over a million copies.

Another, less welcome, reminder of his wife's accomplishments came one morning in Hampstead when Marie handed her husband a copy of a small, handsomely bound volume: *Love Letters of a Japanese* by one G. N. Mortlake. 'They purported to be the letters which passed between her and K. Fujii,' he recalled years later. 'My reaction was one of mild shock but I accepted it as one of the minor disabilities of being married to a literary woman!'[24]

If Ruggles needed further confirmation that he had married an extra-ordinary woman, he received it when she showed him a copy of a circular letter in July 1911, three months after their marriage, informing all her friends and acquaintances, including her own mother, that she intended to keep her own name:

Dear –

As there is a considerable diversity of opinion among my friends as to what they should call me, and as I find there is a very widespread misconception as to the law regarding married women's names, I think it may be useful to make a definite statement regarding both these subjects.

In the first place, notwithstanding my marriage, my legal name is Marie C. Stopes. As I have been for some time, and still am entitled to the courtesy title of 'Doctor' the situation is relieved of any difficulty regarding the application of either 'Mrs' or 'Miss' to that name. Privately, for the few friends who cannot escape the bonds of custom, I add the name of my husband by hyphen – Stopes-Gates. This name we also use when he and I wish to stand coupled on any occasion.

The letter went on to explain the general law about names and con-tinued:

When a woman marries, it is commonly the custom for her to take her husband's name . . . in the eyes of the law she makes this change of name voluntarily . . . I have taken the necessary steps to retain my own name as my legal one . . . and it is also the name I use in all my scientific work. It is, in short, my real name.[25]

Marie's friends accepted her decision, with kindly teasing, in the case of the elderly academics and with enthusiasm in the case of young women who realized that Dr Stopes was furthering the cause of women's inde-pendence. Ruggles Gates was not too enthusiastic, nor did he care much for his wife's championing of the Married Women's Tax Reform League. 'He [Gates] will come round to the view of Votes for Women as I did,' wrote Helen McMurchy from Canada.[26]

Years later, Ruggles was to say that if he had realized the extent of Marie's sympathy for the movement he never would have married her. Marie had dreaded Ruggles meeting her mother but strangely enough the two got on well and Ruggles took to calling round for tea to Charlotte's house in Kemplay Road, Hampstead every Sunday after-noon, whether Marie was free or not. Her son-in-law had pleased her because he was aware of her reputation as a Shakespearian scholar before he met Marie and his religious upbringing was in his favour. Besides, both of them were perhaps secretly a little jealous of Marie's success in academic circles.

For her husband, Marie's prominence and position in the closed circles of the London botanical world was the bitterest pill. In June 1911 she went to Stockholm to work at the Natural History Museum there, while Ruggles returned to America, to the Missouri Botanical Gardens in St Louis, disappointed that he could not find a suitable post in England. Ruggles returned to England in the autumn of 1911. A distinguished graduate of McGill and Chicago Universities, he had had hopes of eventually gaining a Chair in Botany at University College but Professor Oliver, Marie's fatherly mentor, gave *her* a lectureship in Paleobotany in the spring of 1912.

Marie's presence lent sparkle to academic occasions. At her inaugural lecture on Paleobotany a *Daily Chronicle* reporter remarked on her 'dainty pink costume and youthful and unprofessional appearance'. Learned Societies, The Royal Society, The British Museum, the Geologists' Association, all craved a lecture from Dr Stopes. Dr Gates, on the other hand, was reduced to accepting a post well beneath his abilities as a lecturer in Biology to medical students at St Thomas's Hospital. Nevertheless, for over a year the marriage appeared from the outside to be a success.

In the spring of 1912 Marie was sparring with the Royal Society for not giving her her proper title in advertising a course of lectures when all the other learned doctors were duly advertised as such. 'May I ask whether this omission is by accident or design?', she wrote icily.[27]

If she was prickly about her own status, she was also anxious about Ruggles's lack of recognition and devised a devious, if generous, plan to enhance his reputation. Acting through her solicitors, Stibbard, Gibson & Co., Marie offered £20 to Imperial College for a special course of lectures on the breeding of plants for the scientific study of heredity and mutation, the precise field in which Ruggles had specialized for years. After the anonymous donor had turned down one or two unsuitable candidates, her solicitors wrote on 4 June 1912: 'Dear Dr Stopes, I enclose a letter received by my firm from R. R. Gates of 14 Well Walk, Hampstead. The plot thickens.'[28] Gates, of course, was the successful candidate.

'I am so glad you are so happily married,' wrote Isabel P. Evans, a colleague from the National Museum of Washington, that November.[29]

'May the kisses never grow less . . .' Unwittingly, Isabel Evans had touched a raw nerve. Despite the kisses and embraces and the great hopes and excitement of both of them when they first married, the sex life of Dr Stopes and Dr Gates was a complete flop. Ruggles could not satisfy Marie as a lover but, in public, he embarrassed her by fondling and caressing her, even putting his hand in her dress. Possibly he found out about Marie's 'plot' to further his career. That June the tensions and dissatisfactions within the marriage exploded in a violent quarrel. Marie threatened to kill her husband and herself and left Ruggles briefly.

As a Canadian academic, Ruggles Gates felt ill-at-ease socially, particularly among Marie's growing circle of literary and suffragist friends, unsure of himself where Marie shone. He resented her for not being content to be a working botanist and a wife, and tried to assert himself. First he presumed to choose her friends and her books and that was dangerous: he even 'banned' her from buying *The Times*, saying that one newspaper was enough for them both, although he took it out of the house with him. When she described the possessive type in *Married Love* later, she surely had her husband in mind: 'This man posed to himself . . . not only as a romantic man but as a model husband and he reproached his wife for jeopardizing their perfect unity whenever she accepted an invitation in which he was not included . . .'[30]

By December, after fifteen months of marriage, Marie was feeling dissatisfied and bored with her husband. At a Hampstead dinner party on 12 December she met an older man who intrigued her. Aylmer Maude was fifty-four, twenty-two years her senior, married, and with four sons. He looked distinguished and fiery, with thinning white hair, a beard and a moustache. In literary London Aylmer Maude held a considerable reputation; he had grown up in Russia where he met Tolstoy in 1888 and became his biographer and official translator. The two talked together throughout the dinner; Marie was impressed by his knowledge of a world that attracted her and a spark of sexual attraction flashed. After the party, Aylmer Maude wrote asking Marie to dine and continue the conversation; although she declined, she sent him a teasing note: 'Do you dance? I think you looked jolly enough to be a dancer . . .'[31] Two days later she went further: 'Don't you find life desperately in ruts and lacking in sparkle: Why shouldn't we do absurd things?' The Christmas holidays were already arranged and Marie and Ruggles took a walking tour in Cornwall, but by January Aylmer Maude had agreed, 'with fear and trembling', to come to a dance, since he was a novice, so long as Marie would keep as many dances for him as she could. She had already sent him her publishers' announcements about *A Journal from Japan*, *Ancient Plants* and *Love Letters of a Japanese* and he had talked to V. H. Collins of the Oxford University Press, suggesting that Marie should call on them with ideas for educational science books. They met at dances and dinners at vegetarian restaurants to cater to Maude's taste. Aylmer Maude also escorted her to a Belloc-Shaw debate and tried, unsuccessfully at first, to introduce her to Shaw and his wife, whom he knew well.

Maude was lonely in London, on distant but not unfriendly terms with his wife, who preferred a platonic marriage and lived in the country in Essex. At a time when Marie's marriage was strained, she began to dine with Aylmer Maude fortnightly and the friendship ripened rapidly. Winnie's health was causing concern again, and her efforts to make a living bookbinding continued to be unrewarding, so that Marie often had to support her sister as well as herself. She was delighted to find a friend who was so generous with his contacts in the literary world. Immensely flattered, Maude was delighted with his new friend and told Marie that he 'never knew anybody like her'.

At the end of February, Ruggles had 'flu, and money, as always, was short. Even with Marie's growing scientific reputation and published books, her financial rewards were small and Ruggles's post as lecturer at St Thomas's Hospital was poorly paid. Aylmer Maude needed lodgings in London and Marie had room at Well Walk, so it seemed natural to offer to put him up. Surprisingly, Ruggles agreed, tempted perhaps, by the extra income. Late in February Aylmer Maude moved in, paying £25 a month for bed and breakfast. His new landlady wrote from a cycling holiday in Surrey:

> Oh! Maudie dear, I am so very sorry you are being so miserably neglected in my house . . . I did want to make you comfie and happy – and there you are like a martyred saint while I am revelling in blue sky, white billowing clouds and pine trees and moors of golden gorse – and heartache. My husband is beside himself with rage against the women [the Suffragettes] and his wife too for not condemning them.[32]

To Maude, an experienced older man, Marie could pour out her frustration and disappointment. Ruggles was growing jealous, inclined to read her letters, petulant and critical of everything she did. More and more, Marie turned to Maude as confidant and friend. In August, when she was away with her husband and Winnie on holiday, she sent him a plaintive letter describing the scenes and reconciliations she had had with her husband and her fears that she would never achieve success as a writer. When Maude replied with a love letter, Marie professed herself surprised. At that stage, she wanted Aylmer Maude's devotion and sympathy more than a commitment. For Maude she had a 'bigger, impersonal love, admiration and tenderness,' she wrote. She did not feel justified in leaving Gates, 'If he was angry or unjust just *once* I should leave him quietly and once and for all . . . He is only a spoilt and undeveloped child, he isn't bad at all, and very sensitive and extremely affectionate, loving and lovable. But the strong always have to suffer for the weak.'[33]

She mentioned casually that Ruggles had told her he intended to shoot Aylmer Maude as soon as possible. 'I don't think his aim is very good and I am not sure if he has a gun but dear one, don't laugh!' And, in a passage surely calculated to inflame her elderly lover, Marie added:

> If I give him a few kisses and play a little as my buoyant physical nature finds it easy enough to do – all is well. At present we have had twenty-four hours of light and happy calm and kisses. Real kisses would still matter to me immensely – his I put in a different category. They don't really matter. But you don't want kisses like that! If ever I kiss you it must be with a piece of my soul . . .'[34]

Marie sent Maude poems and in every letter confided her ambitions. At thirty-two, she was still haunted by the feeling that she had an important mission to accomplish, a feeling reflected in her unpublished novel, something she could lose herself in and die for if necessary. In one letter to Maude she wrote that she was feeling happy because she had, at last, come to grips with an idea that had clung to her for years. Now, she confided, she knew that she must gain preliminary information and work slowly and thoroughly to make her idea effective. Marie was surely describing the themes in the manuscript she had sent to Maurice Hewlett in 1910, the themes that were to become *Married Love*.

In the autumn it was largely due to Aylmer Maude's intervention that she still had a post at the University. Her subject was little known in English universities and funds were hard to find. In the spring of 1913, through influential friends in the city, Aylmer Maude had arranged for donations towards 'a grant to University College for Dr Stopes to give a series of lectures on Paleobotany for three years from 1913–1916'.[35]

Marie and Ruggles attended the Annual Meeting of the British Association where she was delighted to see Madame Curie honoured. She sent Maude a postcard with one line: 'The thought of you brings deep and sustaining joy.' But the sterility of her marriage nagged her and she confided her worries in a letter to Olga Kapteyn.

Intensely interested in Marie's affairs, Olga, now living in Berlin, had talked at length to a Russian nerve doctor. 'He says that people very seldom have the same sexual temperament or tempo and, in many cases, it is the husband's fault for not developing his wife's sexual instincts in the right way . . .'[36] Olga asked Marie if she had ever managed to get hold of the English translation of the *Karma Sutra*.

The basic trouble, Marie was to tell her lawyers later, was that Gates indulged in foreplay for hours but could not get a real erection, leaving Marie feeling drained and unsatisfied. By September 1913 she had already visited her solicitors to find out about the possibilities of obtaining a divorce in Canada. A letter sent on 13 September from a Canadian legal firm, Brown, Montgomery & McMichael of Montreal, brought the depressing news that divorce in Canada was only granted by Act of Parliament and would be expensive. But Marie was a fighter, determined to gain her freedom. Through her London solicitors she asked the Canadians what she had to do to obtain a divorce. Was the use of abusive language by the husband sufficient grounds? Was one act of adultery by the wife, provided she did not return to her husband, enough? Or, if not, how long must the errant wife stay with another man? And how much would it all cost? Again, the replies were disappointing. A divorce would cost her between $1200 and $1500 and the only grounds on which she could gain a divorce was by her husband's adultery.

Marie's insistence that she was ignorant about sex during her marriage, and her sensational preface to *Married Love* (see page 78), led her biographers to believe that she was innocent and unaware that her marriage was unconsummated. She wrote a play, *Vectia*, re-creating her real life situation in drama, with Vectia (Marie) a 'delightful English girl' married to William (Gates) 'thin and ascetic-looking with pale, dun-coloured hair and face'. Vectia longs for a baby but not until Heron (Aylmer Maude), her next-door neighbour, 'a well-groomed, virile, attractive man', obligingly shows her a diagram of the sex organs of human physiology does Vectia realize that her husband is impotent. *Vectia* was not ready for production until 1926, but was in fact never staged, since the Lord Chamberlain refuse to grant it a licence. A note to the producer insisted that Vectia and Heron (Marie and Aylmer) must make it plain that their relation is a 'pure and straightforward one and that there is not the smallest hint of flirtation or love-making on either side . . .'[37]

Marie claimed that this play told the literal truth about her situation, that it was only in the late autumn of 1913, after reading voraciously almost every learned treatise and medical account of sexual theory and practice in English, French and German (in the restricted access section of the British Museum known as 'the cupboard') that she understood married love. After poring over innumerable legal tomes, she realized that the non-consummation of her marriage, very rarely invoked in those days, would give her grounds for divorce.

No one can know for certain what took place in the bedroom of Gates *v.* Gates. But new evidence suggests that Marie was neither as innocent nor as ignorant as she made out. An unpublished letter from the British Library collection reveals that less than six months after her marriage to Gates, Marie offered advice on birth control to F. H. Brewin, a clergyman whom she met on board ship. (She travelled to Stockholm alone that summer.) She obviously wrote to him, although no draft survives. He replied on 26 October 1911:[38]

Dear Dr Stopes

I came back from a Diocesan Conference to find your letter waiting for me . . . I talked to another parson at the Diocesan Conference and we both regretted that bachelor bishops should tackle this subject. At the same time, I think you will agree that where deliberate limitation springs from selfish motives, it is to be condemned; you will also agree, I suppose, that the decrease of the birthrate is and will be a source of danger to the Empire.

We have four children and our assured income is £500 with a position to keep up; also we have no Vicarage. We have come to the conclusion that it would not be right or fair to anyone to increase our family until our income increases. *On board you volunteered, I mean of course in answer to my request, certain information* [author's italics].

It was not very definite – you recommended a solution of quinine, but you said nothing about quantity, etc., or whether it was to be administered with a douche or how long beforehand. You would be laying us under a great obligation and be doing us a great kindness if you could give us definite instruction . . .

Yours sincerely
F. H. Brewin

The writer of that letter must have assumed that Marie Stopes was familiar with the sexual act. It is hard to imagine (though not impossible in the climate of the day) that a scientist with an inquiring mind, who had studied zoology and the reproductive habits of fossil plants, would not have discovered how the reproductive organs in men and women functioned and the nature of the sexual act. And, although she might have been ignorant of the technicalities of orgasm, she would surely have known that her husband's penis should have been erect and not 'so limp as he struggled to enter that he pushed it in with his fingers', as she graphically described it in her statement and claim for Nullity of Marriage.

'In my first marriage I paid such a terrible price for sex-ignorance that I feel that knowledge gained at such a cost should be placed at the service of humanity . . . I hope [this book] will save some others years of heartache and blind questioning in the dark,' Marie wrote in her preface to *Married Love*. Hundreds of thousands of couples were to benefit from her advice in that book and the publicity obtained from the claim that she was a 'virgin' wife undoubtedly helped to popularize it but her claims to ignorance remain in question. In 1919, when there was a suggestion (completely disproved) that Marie had contracted venereal disease, her personal physician, Dr Armand Routh wrote to reassure her: 'I never thought of such a thing in you . . . I merely thought to myself that if you had been infected it was *in some way* [he added the words above the line] by your first husband.' Perhaps the most puzzling and equivocal document is the certificate of her status by her family doctor: 'I have today examined Dr Marie Stopes: in my opinion there is evidence from the condition of the hymen that there has not been penetration by a normal male organ', signed Dr E. Taylor.[40] Marie told her lawyers that during her travels in the tropics she had been advised to use a wide-nozzled douche.

Ruggles Gates was a virgin when they married and his version of their sex-life has never before been told. He maintained that Marie was 'super-sexed to a degree which was almost pathological'.[41] According to Gates's statement, Marie insisted that her fiancé should visit a doctor before their marriage and learn about methods of contraception. (This seems at least possible in the light of the Brewin letter.) Gates was a prim and timid man and found the experience unpalatable:

The doctor only agreed to give me the information when I said that I would cease using such methods as soon as I got a post in London. I ceased using any condom contraceptive method soon after I was appointed lecturer in Biology at St Thomas's Hospital in January 1912 but she insisted on continuing to use pessaries. This was the beginning of the rift.

At our first sexual congress she had twitted me with having had no sexual experience. This was true. Although I had been greatly tempted many times, I had managed to lead a celibate life as a result of my strict religious upbringing combined with hard scientific work. I was probably clumsy at first, through lack of experience, but we were soon having intercourse frequently enough to satisfy a normal woman. If she had ceased the use of pessaries even in 1913 she could have had a normal child . . . She no longer desired to have a child by me because her desires and aims were already set in a different direction. The use of contraceptives, however, detracted from the joy of these experiences for me and doubtless acted as an impeding factor in my own sexual activity.'[42]

Ruggles did not contest the case, but soon after the annulment in 1916 claimed that he was examined by Sir Alfred Fripp, a well-known phys- ician, and given a certificate of 'perfect normality'. Whether or not Gates was impotent initially or throughout the marriage can never be known now. But Marie's great expectations and great disappointment may have sapped his confidence sexually. What seems certain is that the pair were incompatible, both sexually and in temperament, Marie vigorous, self- confident and highly-sexed, Ruggles, timid, gentle and under-sexed.[43] Ruggles admits that he was clumsy on the wedding night (Marie described him 'hurting her horribly but chiefly by digging his elbows into my breasts . . . in the long struggle to enter'). Just as her triumphs and professional standing almost certainly contributed to his lack of faith in himself (something she understood when she secretly arranged lectures for him), so he felt undermined sexually. He remarried but had no children and died in 1962. The year he died, Ruggles Gates's widow deposited his testimony about the affair in the British Library.

In late 1913 they were both desperately unhappy, hurting themselves and each other. By the Christmas holidays, Ruggles knew that Marie had written to Canadian lawyers and the atmosphere at Well Walk was bitter. They boarded the train for Switzerland together for appearances' sake but separated en route, Ruggles bound for Interlaken and Marie for Villars.

The sun and snow always refreshed her, physically and mentally. Dressed in a short, swinging, green skirt to the knees, with a green cap to match, when she looked at herself in the mirror she thought she looked about fifteen; the years had dropped off. 'Dear Heart', she wrote to Aylmer Maude on New Year's Eve, 'A Happy, Happy and Prosperous New Year to you! I have just seen the little new moon over the mountains and I thought of you. It seems such a little time since I left – oh!, I don't want to get caught again by the iron bands of all that gloom and misery! God bless the New Year and you.'[44]

Back home, she persisted with her writing and Aylmer Maude was a great source of encouragement. She had given him a one-act playlet, which he pronounced a work of 'genius' and he offered to show it to Granville Barker, actor, playwright, producer and eminent man of the theatre, when it was ready. But by 8 February 1914 Gates finally found the courage to tell his lodger to leave Well Walk. For Marie, it was a wretched time. Her sister, Winnie, always a source of worry because of her delicate health and lack of funds, was now suffering from heart trouble and rheumatism, and was pronounced seriously ill by the doctor. Marie tried to persuade herself that the doctor was 'over-anxious – we do recover so wonderfully in our family'. Unfortunately Winnie had none of the resilience of either her sister or her mother. Marie, as often before, bore the financial burden for Winnie. She was also tired of the endless scenes with her husband and the effort involved to put up an appearance of normality at the University.

Even her precious friendship with Aylmer Maude began to suffer. Marie's suffragette activities were a source of dissension since they took up much of her time. She had been critical of the militant branch of the Suffrage Movement in the early years in Manchester, but had joined their ranks in 1912 and now carried banners in the street, and expected, even hoped, to go to prison for her activities. In the intervening years, the cause of Women's Suffrage had become increasingly prominent, with the processions, protests and imprisonment of the militant Suffragettes constantly in the headlines and the organized meetings of the societies set up to press for constitutional reform growing in frequency and numbers.

After a snatched meal together in February 1914, shortly after Aylmer Maude had been forced to give up his lodgings in Well Walk, Maude had criticized Marie for advocating Tax Resistance, and their pleasant evening was ruined. She could not bear any criticism and replied with a trenchant letter complaining that he had never been to one of their meetings. 'We strike no blows,' she said, and told him graphically of having street garbage flung at her head and the soft flesh of her neck stung with horse dung. 'Where do you think the crowds of good Pharasaical suffragettes would be today who belong to "law-abiding societies and condemn those who take any real burden on themselves?".'[45] Only militancy would move the authorities. (Nine months earlier, Emily Wilding-Davidson had sacrificed her life by throwing herself in front of the King's horse on Derby Day.)

'You urge me to resist Ruggles' private impositions and wrongs,' she wrote, '. . . Why can you not see it in the case of bigger and impersonal issues?' Tension between the would-be lovers grew, with her husband suspicious and wary of all her movements, and the opportunities to meet limited. In mid-March, Marie suggested that Aylmer Maude should come to Well Walk at lunchtime when Winnie would be in the next room and the servants were about. 'Ruggles will probably never know and if he does, be hanged to him!' Maude grew increasingly edgy, beset by his own business worries, with a jealous husband at his heels and a mistress who remained elusive. The pair quarrelled over politics. Maude was a Socialist while Marie, innately Conservative, became a revolutionary only when her own interests were involved. By April, Maude was hoping to fade out of her life. Marie, on the other hand, was preparing the way to make her situation public. In a letter to *The Times* dated 6 April 1914 she ostensibly protested against the ban the London County Council had introduced, preventing married women from practising medicine. She argued cogently that the disqualification would stop some women doctors from marrying at all; discourage others from qualifying at all, while 'women of more perfect balance who demand the right to be both normal women as well as intelligences would either have to conceal their marriage from their employers or live in union with a man without the legal tie of marriage' – a perfectly good argument so far; it is the next paragraph that was unexpected.

> My own experience of three years of marriage, in which I have discovered the innumerable coercions, restrictions, legal injustices and encroachments on her liberty imposed on a married woman . . . has brought me to the point of being ready to condone in any of my educated women friends a life lived (if in serious and binding union) with a man to whom she is not legally married. Three years ago such a course would have filled me with horror.[46]

In that letter Marie not only drew attention to the difficulties of married women who wanted to pursue a career but also tried to make 'living in sin' respectable provided the woman was of a certain class, paving the way for her to live openly with Aylmer Maude in the future and, incidentally, humiliating her husband. She used her own life as the raw material to wreak change in social attitudes with startling courage and with equally startling indifference to other people's feelings. Aylmer Maude, infatuated with her despite his irritation and chivalrous by nature, did not desert her. When she made the final, painful break with Ruggles, he was waiting.

On 6 May she saw Dr Taylor, who gave her a certificate of qualified virginity; broke the news to Charlotte, who remained friendly with Ruggles after the separation; had a difficult talk with her old friend Professor Oliver, who knew her husband as a colleague; and prepared for a lecture which she had to give the following day. Back at Well Walk, she supervised the removal of her furniture in readiness to leave. In the confusion, the men packed two boxes of Ruggles's papers. Marie had to go to the warehouse and get them sent back. At Well Walk, Ruggles was blustering about the lease, in their joint names, and the keys to the house. Fortunately Aylmer Maude had had a copy of the lease typed out and sent to Marie. Ruggles insisted that she give up the keys and 'all rights' in the house on leaving it. But Marie stood her ground, said that she would only give up her door key if the lease was transferred 'legally and bindingly' to a single person, either Ruggles or a tenant but not held jointly in her name.

Five days later Marie moved to stay with friends at the end of the road, Heathside, Hampstead, taking Buster (her cat) who needed comforting, to sleep with her. 'Winnie was there at the last,' she wrote to Aylmer Maude, 'so there was no scene'. Feeling tired and shaky after the stress of the past months, Marie went to stay with a friend, a Mrs Russell in Hindhead, in the Surrey hills, where she always felt reinvigorated. To Aylmer Maude she wrote almost a love letter:

> . . . when I think of all you have done for me, your tender consideration when I was so nearly submerged . . . I feel that I owe you all myself, but at other times I know I was put in such a position in order that you might have the joy of saving me and that I should afterwards be the medium of a divine message to people who could never have opened their hearts to me otherwise . . . The last moment that I saw you yesterday will live in my memory . . . you stood looking up, your face half-turned towards me smiling . . . and the light flushed you rosy so that all the lines went out of your face and your flesh was warm and full of calm, your white hair looked so beautiful you symbolised ageless manhood.[47]

5

Breaking Out

Between 1914 and 1918, the period of the First World War, Marie Stopes was to find, at last, the mission she had been seeking and to emerge from comparative obscurity into a blaze of publicity. Just before war broke out, however, her prospects had rarely looked so grim. She had left her husband, surrendered all rights to her home in Hampstead and placed herself in an awkward and embarrassing social and financial position. Although she had an international reputation in the obscure field of Paleobotany, the financial rewards for her scholarship were meagre.

In July 1914, unable to find suitable inexpensive lodgings, she pitched her tent on a ridge of sand dunes on the bleak Northumberland coast near Longhoughton. She needed a period of peace after the break with Ruggles, to escape from curious eyes and work out her future. Lord Grey, who as former Governor-General of Canada had been her host, had offered her refuge on his estate. Marie loved sleeping out, it gave her a sense of tranquillity and freedom and she had sewn the two sides of a large eiderdown together to make a sleeping-bag. But neither the weather nor the world situation was in her favour. The rain pelted down unceasingly and the sea was too wintry even for her to bathe in. By 17 July 1914 she had no methylated spirits left to cook with and her food store consisted of fresh farm eggs, butter and lard, apples (from Aylmer Maude) and pockets full of bulls-eyes. The nearest village shop was at least two miles walk up the coast.

In her frequent letters to Aylmer Maude, Marie made light of her trials but a note of rising hysteria belied her words. She gave her address as 'The Dog Kennel', 'The Rabbit Hutch', and 'The Arck' when 'a savage thunderstorm makes me into a small waif'. And, though she had found a local woman to give her dinner daily, she ran out of methylated spirits and went without tea, supper and breakfast. Too proud to bother her landowning neighbours, it was a relief when the Howicks (Sir Edward Grey's nephew and his wife) invited her to dine on 2 August. Even in that far-off corner of England, it was typical of Marie that she should have access to the latest news. Sir Edward Grey, now Foreign Secretary, had apparently told his nephew that 'Everything possible would be done to keep England out of the war'. Two days later, on 4 August, war was declared.

Marie wrote to Aylmer Maude urgently that day, acutely aware of how exposed and vulnerable her position was: 'Dear Love, This isolation and anxiety is intolerable! Come to me.'[1] She desperately needed advice and human contact and bombarded Aylmer Maude with questions. Would it be best for her to enlist in the local Red Cross? Lady Howick had suggested it. Would it be possible for her to live in London at all? Would the museums and universities remain open? Marie had been at school during the Boer War but that was remote and had not affected daily life at all. In this war bombs on London, even invasion, were feared.

The next day Marie wrote again from her little tent, calmer now that she knew war had broken out. 'I have plenty of money for the next two months, if not, well than I shall gaily laugh – I can live here on twelve shillings a week – and stay here indefinitely.'[2] By then, she added, one or the other of them might be rich. She had followed Lady Howick's suggestion and enlisted in the local Red Cross but, since the Howicks did not know that she had left her husband, they would think it natural if she had to go home at a day's notice. 'I shall come to you at once, dear, if you get too worried and depressed or if London is in danger,' wrote Marie, yearning for a heroic role. At present, it seemed wisest to stay put; also it was the cheapest course. Aylmer Maude's investments were dwindling and business was becoming more and more difficult. He had, as well as Marie, a wife who co-operated with him in translating Tolstoy from the Russian and a home to maintain in Essex.

Meanwhile, on the Northumberland shore where Marie was camping, three warships hovered in the bay and aeroplanes flew overhead. One night, three soldiers with fixed bayonets, patrolling the beach, shouted 'Halt!' outside the tent where she lay in bed. 'Don't be silly,' she called, 'how can I halt when I'm lying down anyway?' 'I'm beginning to wonder myself whether it is bravery or foolhardiness or a joyous callousness which keeps me here solitary nights,' she wrote in an uncharacteristically self-critical mood.[3]

Whatever the motives, her original intention to stay in Northumberland where she could rest, write poetry and redirect her life was now thwarted. By September Marie was back in Hampstead, anxious to return to her home in Well Walk. Ruggles did not contest the nullity and he sailed for Canada that summer after some unpleasant wrangling between the couple over payment of rent and rates and the division of the furniture. By October, she had cleaned up her house and invited Aylmer Maude as well, of course, as Winnie to lodge with her again.

She had also filed her nullity petition in the Probate, Divorce and Admiralty Division of the High Court of Justice. Clause 3 pleaded: 'That the said Reginald Gates was, at the time of the said marriage, and has ever since been incapable of consummating the said marriage and *that such incapacity is incurable*'[4] [author's italics].

A more conventional woman than Marie Stopes might not have stood the strain of breaking up a marriage on such unusual grounds. But, although she kept her separation as discreet as she could, Marie had always accepted that her role would be exceptional both in her public and in her private life. Her scientific training helped her to achieve a detachment in dealing with her own tangled emotions. As well as reading up learned volumes about sexual relationships, she had begun to analyse her own sexual reactions, clinically, as a scientist. In her notes for *Married Love* which date from February 1914, the very month Aylmer Maude left the house at Well Walk, she had begun to record her own feelings and sense of frustration. Her *Tabulation of Symptoms of Sexual Excitement in Solitude* analyses her own sensations at different times of the month with devastating precision:

a) Through constantly reverting in the midst of other business, to feelings of tenderness in kissing.
b) Through the sensitiveness of breasts, so that one is conscious of their shape.
c) Through a desire to be held closely round the waist, till corsets become tempting though normally they are abhorrent.[5]

She was still, of course, giving lectures illustrated by lantern slides, and specimens, on the various modes of preservation of fossil plants for students and teachers taking Geology for their Bachelor of Science examination and also writing learned articles in botanical and geological journals. But nearer home was the cycle of desire she charted for other women as well as herself. In wartime many women were deprived of their men and, through emancipated friends in the Suffrage Movement, Marie gained their co-operation. One woman doctor reported that when her husband was away from home during the Boer War, she was ready to 'jump out of the window at any man who passes'.[6]

A medical man to whom she showed a draft of her findings agreed broadly with her ideas of peak periods of desire during the monthly cycle but suggested that she should augment her knowledge by taking a medical training. 'You would then get . . . a legitimate platform from which to speak.' (The grand old man of sexology, Havelock Ellis, had acquired a medical degree although he never practised medicine; his interest, unlike Marie's, was in the abnormal.) Marie had little respect for medical practitioners and did not accept that sound advice.

As a scientist, she did not flinch from recording her own sexual feelings in charts and notes. As a woman, though seemingly candid, she was inconsistent, sometimes secretive. She hoarded most of her letters and kept drafts of many she had written herself, yet no single letter from Ruggles Gates to her exists and all the letters from Aylmer Maude from the time he left her home in Well Walk in 1914, until May 1918, a period when she was, in his words 'the chief feature of my life', have been destroyed. She wrote to him often during that time, sometimes twice or three times a week.

Their strange friendship proved the most influential in Marie's existence. They talked about everything and Marie tried out her ideas for fiction and fact on Aylmer Maude. His influence can be seen in her books; in *Married Love* she cites Tolstoy as an example of a married ascetic who withdrew from sex-life in old age; in a later book *Enduring Passion*,[7] Marie cited Tolstoy again and specifically acknowledged Maude's help.

Marie dedicated *Married Love* to 'young husbands and all those who are betrothed in love'. In the book she makes three references to a form of love-making known as 'Karezza'.[8] She described it as a type of male continence which demands:

a control by the man of his ejaculation: the idea being that after mutual passion has been roused and union effected, instead of encouraging the excitement by movement . . . an attempt to reach complete calm, both mental and physical should be made. This is achieved by the cessation of all physical movement and the centring of thought on the spiritual aspect of the beloved. In my opinion, an average, strong and unimaginative Englishman is not likely to achieve success in this type of union.

That Marie should have included a description of the technique of

Karezza at all in a book written for 'those who enter marriage normally and healthily', seems curious, particularly as a colleague of hers, Dr Ernest Starling, advised her to 'omit the Karezza part . . . it is only possible with the (inward) control or diminished ardour which comes with diminished years'.[9]

In her handbooks on sex, Marie often wrote autobiographically. She frequently asserted, for example, that the more intellectual and spiritual type of woman did not develop full sexual feelings until she was in her thirties. Therefore, it seems probable that Marie's interest in a form of love-making in which an under-sexed man could conserve his 'vital energy from the loss of which he suffers' while 'giving the woman the sense of union and nerve-soothing she requires' sprang from personal experience. Aylmer Maude was neither average, nor strong, nor unimaginative.

Throughout the war, Marie was writing – articles, novels, plays – and Aylmer Maude encouraged and criticized her work, introducing her to useful contacts whenever he could. As Honorary Treasurer to the Society of Authors and a member of the Executive of the Fabian Society, he was able to put her in touch with writers and publishers. His admiration of Marie's intellectual power was genuine and he remained devoted and undemanding through her most creative years. Marie maintained – insisted in her play *Vectia* – that her relationship with her next-door neighbour (i.e. Aylmer Maude) was a 'pure and straight-forward one, with no hint of flirtation or love-making on either side'.[10] Her letters tell another story. She was constantly provoking him, describing herself in the country, dancing round the flower beds: 'I had nothing on but my thinnest nightie and pranced round like a mad thing with joy at the feel of the grass between my bare toes.'[11] Or, writing from near Land's End, when Maude had just returned to London, she described her day in a little sheltered cove, 'so quiet that I was garmentless all day . . . I am now writing to you all as God made me . . .'[12] A year earlier she had addressed Maude as a 'precious Pattern of Patience'. Since they now lived at Well Walk without Ruggles's inhibiting presence, he would have been remarkably patient if Marie remained, as she claimed, a virgin. Winnie lived in the house but was often ailing and far too retiring a person to intrude.

'Don't wrinkle your face up and get drawn and narrowed and old so that your look pierces my heart like a sword and inhibits bodily love,' Marie wrote to him soon after she left her husband.[13] Ironically, the twenty-two years between them had begun to tell now that Marie was free physically, if not legally, of Ruggles. In her mid-thirties she looked ten years younger, charged with health, vigour and confidence while, at fifty-seven, Aylmer Maude tired more easily and suffered from indigestion and chills. She was increasingly patronizing about his age and lesser physical stamina. 'You will be relieved to hear that there is a letter-box and a decent hotel half-an-hour's walk away from where I have pitched camp,' she told him in a letter dated 1 August 1915. 'You aren't a camper yet!'

'I wish I could be nicer to you, for you are a dear,' she wrote in the spring of 1916, 'Do get rid of all your colds . . . it is these perpetual colds that make you feel so slack.'[14] The tone in her letters had changed to that of an affectionate niece. Now her literary ambition, which Aylmer Maude had done so much to foster, had begun to take the central place in Marie's life. In the summer of 1915 she had sent the manuscript of the book that was to become *Married Love* to Blackie and Son, the firm who had published her first two books. This time, however, the subject was not ancient plants or scientific observations of travelling in Japan but a handbook on how to obtain sexual gratification and sustain romance in modern marriage, written from the woman's point of view. It was too much for Walter Blackie, who viewed the whole subject with some distaste. On 13 July 1915 he returned her manuscript, with a note:

Dear Dr Stopes,
Thanks. But the theme doesn't please me. I think there is far too much talking and writing about these things already. The world is suffering from too many physiologists and psychologists and it's not me that will lend a hand.[15]

Blackie suggested that she should delay publication until after the war. 'There will be few enough men for the girls to marry and a book would frighten off the few.'

Marie saw this rejection as a lapse on his part, not on hers. She replied:

Dear Mr Blackie,
I shall send you a copy of the book when it is out. *What* an idea of marriage you must have if you think the truth about it will frighten people off.

Yours sincerely
Marie Stopes[16]

Despite Aylmer Maude's shortcomings, in a daydream she had the two of them married and honeymooning in all the lovely places in Europe with Henry James. Then she made a perfect baby. Before she and Maude could marry, however, he would have to obtain a divorce from his wife and his attitude towards that is not clear. Also, Marie's own marriage was not yet nullified. (The decree was granted in May 1916.) At best they would not be able to become the perfect parents of her dreams until he was well over sixty and she almost forty. Marie was interested in breeding, initially through her botanical research, and she gradually realized that Aylmer Maude would not make the ideal partner to produce the best strain for the Race.

Sex, marriage, babies preoccupied Marie at that time. She was so concerned with herself and her sex that even the war and the terrible casualties of the British troops in France served only as a warning of the need to breed from the best stock – before it was too late. Even her doggerel described the longing for a man.[17]

> Won't you kindly leave 'old of me Tommy
> When you kiss me as 'ard as all that
> You do nothin' but ruin me temper
> And cockle the brim of me 'at.
>
> Yes I know you are going out fighting
> And risking an 'orrible death
> But is that reason I ask yer
> For crushing me all out o' breath?
>
> You're giving up football and freedom
> An' forgetting the last cricket score
> To save poor dear King George all the worry
> Of seein' them land on this shore.
>
> You're so tall and so fine in yer khaki
> You're a match for a 'undred wild Huns
> You're as cool and as straight as the guns that they 'ate
> And you'll silence their blasting big guns.
>
> But you, you're a Hun yourself Tommy
> Your arms squash me up like a vice
> Well – perhaps I'll allow that the squashin'
> You gives is rather nice.
>
> Yes, I'll marry yer Tommy me darlin'
> The day you come 'ome from the war

And I fancy if you was to ask me,
I even might do it before.

She sent two of her novels, 'A Man's Mate' and 'Winged Egoism' to Macmillan but their readers' reports reveal that Marie Stopes's writings made them feel uncomfortable. They wrote of 'A Man's Mate': 'it has been much shortened and a very objectionable episode, formerly treated at great length, entirely removed. But an extremely sensuous scene given in much detail remains.' And of 'Winged Egoism', written in 1915, 'It is all very unreal and unwholesome . . .'[18]

Immensely prolific, she wrote plays, poems and stories, all unpublished, but at the heart of her work was her non-fiction account of sex and marriage.

Early in July 1915 Marie Stopes went to Fabian Hall in London to hear Margaret Sanger, a birth control pioneer from America, speak of her fight to bring a knowledge of birth control to the masses in New York. In her former career as a nurse, Mrs Sanger had witnessed such misery among poor women weakened by constant pregnancies that, in defiance of the puritanical American laws which forbade publication of contraceptive knowledge as obscene, she had started a monthly magazine *Woman Rebel* with a series of articles on sex education for girls from fourteen to eighteen years of age and founded a National Birth Control League.

After the meeting Marie went up to the platform, fired by Mrs Sanger's courage, and invited the speaker to have tea with her at her Hampstead home to discuss the book about sex that she was writing, a book, she said, that would 'electrify England'. The letters that survive tell of a warm rapport between the two women: 'My dear Mrs Stopes,' Margaret Sanger wrote after their first meeting, 'It was a jolly talk and I felt that there was after all a real human-being in England . . . I'm sending you the Naughty pamphlet tomorrow . . .'[19] Mrs Sanger's pamphlet on Family Limitation proved useful to Marie for her own manuscript, and she invited the American visitor to dinner to meet Aylmer Maude.

According to Margaret Sanger's autobiography, she brought with her to this interesting meal the birth control devices she had with her, including a French pessary, since, she said, Marie knew nothing of the subject. Marie hotly denied such ignorance and, since the autobiography was written after the two women had quarrelled,[20] it cannot be regarded as reliable. A surviving letter from Margaret Sanger reveals that she discussed the criminal prosecution which threatened her when she returned home to America because of her birth control propaganda. A petition to President Wilson was suggested. In thanking Marie for the dinner, Mrs Sanger wrote:

Dear Marie Stopes – lovely one.
The draft to Mr Wilson cannot be criticized. It is clear and has the correct tone to reach him. I am certain. The evening with you was a delight. Mr Maude is most charming and it thrills me to meet a woman who has energy, control, decision and courage and such an abundance of strong characteristics and uses them. Your book will be a success in America no doubt.[21]

Mrs Sanger enclosed a list of American publishers and wrote to Norman Hapgood, the Editor of *Harpers*, suggesting that Marie should write a series of articles for him.

When Margaret Sanger returned to America in the autumn she found the criminal charges had not been dropped. Meanwhile in London, with Aylmer Maude's help, Marie got up a petition signed by Arnold Bennett, H. G. Wells and Professor Gilbert Murray among others, pleading with President Wilson to drop the charges against Margaret Sanger 'in the interests of free speech and betterment of the race'. The letter pointed out that only in the United States was it illegal to circulate information about birth control.

She also wrote a passionate covering letter to President Wilson:

Have you, Sir, visualized what it means to be a woman whose every fibre, whose every muscle and blood-capillary is subtly poisoned by the secret, ever-growing horror, more penetrating, more long drawn out than any nightmare, of an unwanted embryo developing beneath her heart? White men stand proudly and face the sun, boasting that they have quenched the wickedness of slavery. What chains of slavery are, have been or ever could be so intimate a horror as the shackles on every limb, on every thought, on the very soul of an unwillingly pregnant woman? And you have thousands of such slaves in your 'free' United States, many of them 'honoured' wives, forced to stumble through nine months of nightmare for want of the scientific knowledge which every grown man and woman has the right to know.

I pray that you, Sir, may be instrumental not only in rescuing Mrs Sanger, a tender and sensitive mother from injustice, but also that you will hasten the establishment of a new era for the white race, when it may escape the sapping of strength and disease that are the results of too frequent child-birth by overworn or horror-stricken mothers . . .[22]

The impact of the letter with the famous signatories was overwhelming and the newspapers blazoned it across their pages. A similar petition was organized in America and the case against Mrs Sanger was subsequently dropped.

This was the first public evidence of Marie's highly emotional style of writing and her effective propaganda won her friends and admirers among progressives on both sides of the Atlantic. Thwarted of marriage and children in her mid-thirties, Marie was preoccupied with what D. H. Lawrence termed 'sex in the head', and turned from the careful observation and meticulous recording of data needed by the scientist to the passionate partisanship of the propagandist. She recognized in herself something of this change and, in a letter to Aylmer Maude, written after she had mentioned the news of the sinking of the *Lusitania*, she commented:

> More and more intensely do I feel that the one thing worth bringing into and trying to increase in the world is love, love and its joy and beauty in every form and every possible expression. That is why I am beginning to revolt against so much of the so-called 'intellectual' work, the gloomy realistic novels, the problem plays – light, trust, joy, the palpitating burning beauty of simple things and greatly lived, simply lived lives, is what I should like to portray, if only God will give me the power.[23]

When she tried to portray 'simply lived lives' however, Marie, who was an exceedingly complex and unusual woman, succeeded only in creating heroines in her own image who mouthed her ideas, and heroes strong and sensible enough to adore her.

If thinking, dreaming and writing about sex took up much of Marie's energy, the need to make money came a close second. She always hoped that a millionaire would solve all her problems and in America in 1911 she had visited Rockefeller asking him to finance a scientific paleontological study of coal in the universities. Throughout her life she applied hopefully and without success to Ford, Nuffield and Cadbury to fund her in whatever work she currently considered of vital importance. By 1916 she had calculated that she needed to earn between £4,000 and £5,000 at least p.a. Winnie, a semi-permanent invalid, relied on her, and Charlotte, too, sometimes needed financial help from her daughter.

In the spring of 1916 Marie was trying, unsuccessfully, to obtain funds from the Royal Society, but her marital status as well as her gender made it almost impossible in wartime, although the British Museum (Natural History Department) had published her works, as had the Royal Society itself and the Government Geological Survey of Canada.

In wartime, educated women were increasingly employed in government offices and Marie was advised to apply to the War Office. She used her expert knowledge far more intelligently. A Home Office Experimental Station at Eskmeals in Cumberland was working on Coal Research backed by the Scientific and Industrial Research Department of the Government and Marie wrote to Professor R. V. Wheeler in charge of the Station suggesting that she should collaborate with him. 'I received a slight thrill reading that you have dissolved coal,' wrote Professor Wheeler, who knew her work. He visited Marie at her lab in University College and by July 1916 agreed to her pitching her tent near the Station. 'We so far honour you as not to fuss about you at all . . .'[24]

Whatever she was doing, however, her central mission, the manuscript of *Married Love*, was never forgotten. She sent it the rounds to sympathetic doctors, scientists and sex experts. In May, Edward Carpenter, the author of an earlier influential book, *Love's Coming of Age*, wrote to Marie encouragingly about her manuscript and suggested that his publisher, Stanley Unwin, should consider it.

I think the silly old British lion might be silenced from growling and even persuaded to wag its tail . . . you certainly put in a lot of important points – menstruation, positions, ejaculation without penetration, birth control, insemination, etc. – which will terrify Mrs Grundy; but, she, poor thing is in a very moribund condition already so this book may hasten her end!

He added cautiously, 'I don't want it to hasten your end (professionally) . . . is it possible you might like first to publish it in French . . . and after a year or two in English?'[25] Edward Carpenter was generously trying to save Marie from herself. But his comments reflected the hypocritical attitude of the English educated classes who wanted to ban sexual knowledge from the working class. Publishing her book in French would effectively restrict its readeship.

In his own book on the relationship between the sexes, Carpenter, a homosexual and a Communist, had preached revolution, calling for woman to rise up against her serfdom with the working man: 'he with no means of livelihood except by the sale of his bodily labour, she with no means of livelihood except by the surrender of her bodily sex.' What was wanted, he urged, was a love untrammelled by laws. Then, he proclaimed, the sexual would be 'transformed by magic into the emotional and spiritual'. Carpenter, a Cambridge mathematician who had held a curacy, had written a book in 1895, over twenty years earlier and had carefully avoided naming the sexual organs or referring to anatomy at all. His mystical glorification of sex appealed to Marie's romantic instincts, while her explicit language intrigued him. At his cottage at Millthorpe in Derbyshire, Carpenter went through the manuscript page by page, with Marie as his guest. 'He has made two or three useful suggestions,' Marie noted in a letter to Aylmer Maude on 8 June 1916, 'but mostly approves'.

Next month, she was camping at Eskmeals and occupied with the nature of coal, but the subject of sex was never far from her mind. Inevitably she spoke to scientific colleagues about her manuscript. Such frank talk from a woman was rare and exciting, even among intellectuals. As she beamed her gaze on them her colleagues were encouraged to confide their own sexual troubles to her.

A male scientist at Eskmeals and his wife, whose marriage was strained, asked for her advice on their sex life. 'But he is very puritanical, so I fear when my true character and mission is revealed it may shock him horribly. I have to go wisely and carefully as he is only ignorant; all his wife wants is in him, part dormant and part consciously repressed',[26] she confided to Maude in a letter. Soon after, the couple split up and Marie pressed a copy of her manuscript on each of them. After studying it assiduously and awarding himself marks, the husband wrote a letter to Marie marked 'private', asking her to destroy it after she had read it. She did not. 'The only mistakes for which I appear to be responsible are: a) Ignorance that immediately after menstruation was a bad time and, b) an avoidance of long continuance of connection from the belief that sex was not a matter to be played with . . .' If his wife did return, there was the problem of contraception:

As a Catholic I cannot make use of women's bodies for personal amusement, nor can I enforce suffering . . . I may say that I am unaware of any methods save the rubber appliances the use of which seems to me to savour of the Greek comic stage rather than of real life . . . Could you inform her of any form of protection that she could wear which, while preventing penetration of sperm to the vagina, would not produce the grotesque features of affixing a cover to the penis?[27]

Even before her book was published, Marie was using her research as a source of advice. As early as 1916 she presumed to lecture to a group of women doctors on the neglected subject of 'woman's spontaneous and natural sex drive'.[28] She emphasized to her audience the ignorance among the 'experts' in their profession. 'A leading London gynaecologist looked me blandly in the eyes and assured me that normal women do not have orgasms, even in coitus.' For centuries, she said, women had been trained to be reticent and guilty about their sexual instincts. But now the normal, spontaneous sex drive in women could be charted, independent of stimuli which affects only 'a) married women with children, b) married women without children and, c) unmarried women approaching and over thirty.' (Since she herself was only awakened sexually in her late twenties and since she still firmly accepted her father's strictures against early sex, Marie believed all her life that girls of a superior class developed emotionally and sexually very late.) She drew heavily on her own experience for her leaps forward and, although often wildly unscientific, her self-knowledge was valuable and original.

In her own love affair with Aylmer, Marie was not able to be so wise. The truth about their love remains a mystery. But whatever the complications, her relationship with Aylmer Maude remained her anchor. 'Dear', she wrote to him in August 1916 from Eskmeals, 'Even thwarted, spoiled and flawed as our relationship is by all the outward facts which keep us away from each other, it is very, very good that there should be a golden streak of love to outline life's pattern.'[29]

The outwardly strident and strong Marie Stopes retreated almost into infantilism in her love affairs: 'I should like to curl up in someone's arms and go to sleep for weeks, with just little tiny kisses now and then as I half wake up. I have just a few little puffsie kisses for you now, dear, dear old goosie', she wrote. And, the next day, in a letter which reveals more clearly than ever that part of Aylmer Maude's attraction for her was a longing for the paternal protection she still missed: 'Do sleep and rest and get strong for next year . . . it would be so nice to have someone to lean up against hard.' In November 1916 she moved to a small house in Leatherhead, partly because her expenses would be so much less than in Hampstead, partly because London was becoming smokier and more full of traffic and she wanted to breathe the fresh air of the country. Despite the journey to the city Maude moved to Leather-head too, her faithful lodger.

Marie had expected that Winnie would move out to Leatherhead with her. It would preserve the proprieties and save expenses; she intended to grow her own vegetables in the new garden and to keep bees and, although she did not articulate it to herself, Winnie could be a useful emotional fallback in her stormy life. She was openly jealous of Winnie's close friends. Winnie, however, saw differently and more realistically. She wrote to Marie from Hampstead of her decision:

> I never was a real companion to you because I hadn't the brains and more than ever when I am perfectly well aware that my mental capacity is failing very rapidly, that would be no real pleasure for you having me with you and is only a worry to you having the extra thought of the trivial details of an invalid's life. Poor old Bun (her pet name for Marie) I wish you had as good friends as I have![30]

Ailing and unsuccessful as she was, Winnie did have good and loyal friends and rightly suspected that, despite the public functions that Marie attended, scientific, academic and literary, and her membership of several clubs, Marie was terribly isolated.

Through all her moves and the chaos of her emotional life, Marie kept on writing, collecting rejection slips. In the grim years of war, audiences were looking for colour, escapism, frivolous diversion. Her works, even those she considered light, were too earnest and missionary in tone to appeal.

On a cycling holiday with the Fabian Society, Marie had at last met George Bernard Shaw. Years later, she was to say that Shaw went down on his knees to her and begged for a kiss – which she refused until he promised to learn how to waltz. Certainly he thought of her as an 'ardent dancing girl' with a remarkable brain.

A bantering friendship sprang up between the two and, soon after, Marie sent him her play, *The Race – or Ernest's Immortality*, an echo, like all her work, of her situation, her frustrations. The heroine, Rose-mary, a solicitor's daughter, falls in love with Ernest, a strapping young soldier off to the front, and becomes engaged, despite her father's dis-approval. After Rosemary hears of her fiancé's death in action, she is urged by her family to marry a more suitable man, a solicitor. Rosemary reveals to her horrified family that she is pregnant and, in a speech of passionate self-justification, pleads: 'Is it not more wrong that . . . all the fine, clean strong young men . . . who go out to be killed should leave no sons to carry on the race; but that the cowards and unhealthy ones who remain behind can all have wives and children?' On holiday in Kerry, Shaw ran his blue pencil through her work:

Dottisima

Short of re-writing this play, I can do no more with it than cut 20 pages just to shew you how you should cut the rest. You haven't used your brains on it one bit. Would you find me very interesting if I had nothing more to say than 'dowdy frocks, fiendish ideas, blue stockings and spectacles', and such-like reach-me-downs? . . . You think you can make a motor bicycle by tying a second-hand tool bag and an old poker together and hanging out a few ribbons on it; but you can't. You must cut everything that does not get your play along; and if you wish to convey that your hero's head is turning grey, you must leave that to his wig maker and make-up box and not spend pages of irrelevant twaddle on it. Until you take the stage more seriously than you take a coalmine you will never do anything with it. Or shall I say that until the stage interests you as seriously as fossils do you had better let it alone. At present you are doing nothing half the time but enjoying the amateurish delight of making-believe; it's so interesting to invent a room with doors and windows and furniture and a man named Smith, aged about forty-five, in it, that you imagine they will interest people who haven't invented them. They WONT. so there! . . .

Shaw also mentioned in his letter some photographs, evidently of her, which were 'no worse than it is in the nature of such things to be'.[31]

Other would-be dramatists might have been crushed by a trouncing from such a source. Marie, resilient as ever, took him to task instead: 'My dear Mr Shaw', she countered:

. . . I didn't set out to make a motor-cycle. I think that people who make motor-cycles can ride to the devil on them; the only possible destination for anything so superfluously stinking of intellect. I know intellect's ephemeral falseness . . . Don't you tend to over-rate it? I know I have much to learn about plays and at present I lie a meek valley at your feet, grateful for stones hurtling from down your steeps at me. But the day will come when I will arise as a peak also but the *opposite side of the valley from you* . . . I wish you were less famous then we might discuss our plays in minute detail without your charity being too ridiculously taxed and my impertinence being too evident.

Your meekly appreciative
Marie Carmichael Stopes[32]

Marie, always jealous of her image, begged him for the negatives back and promised a 'decent photo' in exchange. The six photographs Shaw sent back reveal a woman, no longer young, with enormous, burrowing eyes, kneeling and crouching in numerous kittenish poses. She wore a long dress buttoned from the neck to the ankles and buttoned at the wrist, waisted, with contrasting collar and cuffs.

The Race was never staged, but Marie did have a theatrical production put on during the war years — *The Sumida River* — based on one of the Japanese No plays she had translated with Professor Sakurai. Clarence Raybould had made an opera from the story and Marie was disgusted to see that the composer's name figured more prominently than her own in the poster advertising the Birmingham production in 1916.

In her thirties Marie was in the swirl of London society, a committee woman, a club woman, a regular and enthusiastic theatre-goer. She knew everyone and everyone knew her. When Beatrice and Sydney Webb were canvassing for subscribers for their journal, the *New Statesman and Nation*, they approached Marie. Lilian Bayliss appealed to her to join supporters of her new theatre, the Old Vic. Her activities fed each other and were to prove immensely useful to her in the future.

In 1917, she was nominated to represent the Society of Authors on the Cinema Commission of Inquiry set up by the National Council of Public Morals. Cinema was in its infancy in Britain in the First World War. The middle classes affected to disdain the Westerns or murder stories imported from America which made up the vast majority of the films shown. Marie was quick to grasp the potential of the new medium, both as an outlet for writers and as the 'most powerful instrument for creating opinions'. Keen to improve the quality of the films shown, she argued that since all the classics had been 'done', the best writers must be encouraged to work for the screen. She also felt that the cinema trade, 'frankly there to make money and not characterized by any popular idealism of deep culture',[33] was not the best body to control the cinema. And that, since the author's property was to be manipulated by the film industry, authors ought to be represented on Censorship Boards.

Her approach to problems was innovative and original. During a talk on the dirty, dusty atmosphere in the cinema by a representative of the Institute of Hygiene, she pencilled a note in the margin: 'suggest open-air cinema.'[34] Marie demonstrated her grasp of the educational possibilities of the films by giving a talk to the Cardiff Naturalist's Society on 21 March 1918 entitled 'The Cinema and the Naturalist'. In a brilliant exposition she outlined a brief history of the medium with illustrated slides in colour of rare creatures and/or plants under the microscope, prefiguring the wild-life programmes of today

In 1917, wanting a man, a husband, a baby, Marie flirted incorrigibly. Russell Wakefield, the Bishop of Birmingham, a widower with four sons, was President of the Cinema Commission and attracted to Marie's looks and vigorous intellect. From the Bishop's letters a tale of a painfully chequered romance emerges. In April he wrote inviting her to dine, but his next letter of 8 May suggests that Marie had rejected his advances:

> Dear Friend,
> I now know what you think of men – however though the opened chapter is now closed, still we will be friends, especially if I can be of use.
> God bless and keep you,
> Yours in all sincerity.[35]

His letter crossed with one from Marie, addressing him as 'My dear Lord Bishop'. With it, she sent him a copy of the manuscript of *Married Love*, asking him to be 'so dear and kind' as to read it: 'It may be the sort of thing that the Council of Morals [National Council of Public Morals] would like to see available for a well-meaning and pathetically ignorant public. If only I could have read it years ago . . .' Marie hoped that the Bishop's knee had healed and that 'life is as full of promise and beauty as my plum trees.'[36]

That June, Marie invited Russell Wakefield to dine at Leatherhead and stay the night. The slightly apologetic tone in his reply suggests that either his nerve had failed or that she had moved too quickly:

> I become more and more conscious that I have no longer the power to be more than a friend, i.e. I cannot give the vigour I once possessed. Whether even my counsel is as virile as it once was I question. But I can be a friend with sympathy and so you shall ever find . . . You are young, you have to be one of our greatest women. God help me and all your friends to help you to be what your gifts should make you.

And, in August, he told her the truth: 'You need a real man in your life'.[37] But, although the Bishop of Birmingham could not become that man, he remained affectionate and supportive.

All through 1917, Marie was desperately trying to get *Married Love* (called, at that stage, 'They Twain') into print. Her colleague, Professor

Wheeler, whom she liked and respected, was in two minds about it. On the one hand, he thought it was wonderful:

> some of the writing must live as among the finest in the English language. You can understand then how it is so appalling to be suddenly knocked down by a grisly word or a brutish sentence . . . the point you seem to hammer home is the '*medical* necessity for sex relations' . . . This is to reduce what has always been to me . . . a mystery of love to a business-like arrangement for keeping fit. And it is a tribute to the power of your writing that you have almost convinced me that man should model himself on other 'mammalia' – and so have disgusted me with the whole idea of marriage relations. It is true that you write beautifully of the spiritual side of the subject . . . My fear is that as it stands . . . your book would . . . establish among Englishmen that abominable calculating condition of mind where women are concerned that is characteristic of Frenchmen.[38]

Marie's manuscript contained an explicit description of sexual intercourse, which came as a shock even to publishers and academic colleagues, still influenced by Victorian attitudes to sex and to women. Despite the emergence of the New Woman and the avidly read sex scandals in the newspapers, the Englishman, as Professor Wheeler's letter reveals, liked to think of himself as deeply chivalrous. For decades, woman had been placed on a pedestal, her highest virtue her chastity, her purity, her essential sexlessness.

From Marie's childhood in the 1880s onwards, attempts had been made to alter the basis of sex morality. The repeal of the Contagious Diseases Act in 1886 (which had forced women accused by the police of soliciting to be declared 'common prostitutes' and subjected them to periodical medical examinations if they lived in military or naval towns) exposed the whole question of double standards. The year before, the editor of the *Pall Mall Gazette*, W. T. Stead, actually bought a thirteen-year-old girl for £5 and had her taken to a brothel overnight to expose the laxity of the law in a series of sensational articles.

Public alarm and outrage caused social purity organizations to produce a series of tracts on sex education for boys, pointing out the dangers. A popular pamphlet which, by 1909, had sold over a million copies, *True Manliness*, urged young men to 'wear the white flower of a blameless life. There are scores and scores of men all around you who are just as pure as any woman'.[39] No such literature existed for girls; they were to be protected from any guilty knowledge. Sex among the poor was seen as particularly dangerous, and high-minded women, the 'Snowdrop bands' of the Mothers' Institute, the female soldiers of the Salvation Army and the White Cross workers of the Anglican Church, regarded it as their duty to save and protect poor women from the lust of men and the depravity of sex.

By 1911, the National Council of Public Morals had recommended the teaching of nature study as an introduction to the facts of life. One or two of their tracts actually mentioned married life but always with the warning that too much indulgence could be dangerous. The Boy Scouts, the eugenics lobby and sections of the Women's Suffrage movement, alarmed at the scourge of venereal disease and at the assaults on women, supported the purity campaign. Now Marie Stopes, a self-confessed virgin wife, had violated her purity with a manuscript that claimed that women's sexuality was as powerful and therefore as dangerous as men's. So strong was the taboo on the subject that even in the sixth edition (1915) of T. H. Huxley's *Human Physiology*, no editor had dared to include a reference to the human reproductive system. In writing so openly about 'married love' Marie had taken an enormous risk.

Adverse reactions did not deter her from sending her text to a colleague from the Cinema Commission of Inquiry, the Reverend James Marchant, the Secretary of the National Council of Public Morals. She hoped, rather naïvely, that his Council would publish it. To his credit, Marchant considered the work carefully and recognized that she had said much that needed saying. But he was convinced that his Council would not agree to publish without considerable modifications. He also felt doubtful about the effect on young people if, as Marie wanted, the book were to be published cheaply. But he was sufficiently impressed to talk about it to the publisher, Stanley Unwin, in November 1917.

Unwin saw the sales possibilities but a colleague, C. A. Reynolds, disagreed, and by the end of 1917 Marie still had not found a publisher who would take the risk of prosecution by publishing such a 'dangerous' book. Professor Starling, a distinguished physiologist from her own college, had given her a measure of respectability by endorsing her work in careful terms: 'The need of such guidance as you give is very evident . . . At the present time it is of vital importance to the State that its marriages should be fruitful – in children, happiness and efficiency . . . If your book helps in securing this object, your trouble will not have been in vain.'[40] But she badly needed the moral authority of a Church of England dignitary to dispel the misgivings of publishers and printers.

Dean Inge, the Dean of St Paul's, the most progressive of the church's theologians, told her frankly that she would find it impossible to get any clergyman to associate his name with it and even her friend the Bishop of Birmingham could not be persuaded to write a preface.

In the end, it was Marie's own reputation that produced the desired result. Her courageous championing of Margaret Sanger had made her well known in the Malthusian League. In 1829, the Reverend Thomas Robert Malthus, an Anglican clergyman, had argued for a reduction in population since 'the constant tendency in all animated life is to increase beyond the nourishment prepared for it'. Malthus urged late marriage and 'moral restraint' as a means of curbing the population. Twentieth-century Malthusians, like Dr Binnie Dunlop, of the League, favoured contraception for economic reasons. Marie lent Dr Dunlop, a virgin of sixty, a copy of her manuscript in the autumn of 1917. He was fascinated by the arguments in her work although she had little to say about birth control. By chance, he had been in touch with a would-be philanthropist interested in birth control, a Mr Humphrey Roe from Manchester, who was anxious to find a means of helping poor mothers overburdened by bearing too many children. Humphrey Roe had offered to endow a birth control clinic at St Mary's Hospital, Manchester, but his scheme was turned down. He had recently joined the Royal Flying Corps and was due to go overseas shortly. On 5 November, Dr Dunlop wrote to him: 'A lady Doctor of Science in a good university position has just lent me the MS of a sexological study which would greatly increase the number of happy marriages. Her publisher said to her "you are a brave woman, too brave for me". She fears she will have to publish it herself.' Dr Dunlop added that he was considering selling about £50 of his own war loan to help finance the book.

By the beginning of 1918, no major publishing house had agreed to risk printing Marie's work. A small firm, Fifield & Co., had expressed an interest, but they would not publish without financial backing. Dr Dunlop remained enthusiastic. He wrote again to Humphrey Roe on 11 January, 1918, telling him that publication would involve raising £100. Both he and Dr Drysdale (a prominent advocate of birth control and later President of the Malthusian League) had promised £10 each, he said, and added in a postscript: 'if the book is not prosecuted . . . it will sell fast and guarantors will benefit.'

Dr Dunlop's support was generous and far-sighted. As Secretary of the Malthusian League, his interest was in promoting birth control and the book contained only two or three pages of vague and imprecise information on the subject. As for Humphrey Roe, he was in the mood for taking risks. He had recently resigned as managing director of his family aircraft business, A. V. Roe & Co. Initially a regular Army officer, Humphrey had fought in the Boer War and later run a more pedestrian family business, manufacturing braces. Before the First World War, Humphrey had decided to help his talented older brother Alliott, an aircraft designer, to found a pioneering aeronautical firm: Humphrey had invested £10,000 and became a partner. In 1916, Alliott was excited about a new two-seater fighter plane he had designed. Humphrey, he claimed, had spoilt the firm's chances by writing a long-winded report full of criticisms and he accused his businessman brother of being unable to delegate responsibility on technical matters. Humphrey's pride was hurt in the bitter quarrel; he left the firm and volunteered for active duty as a flying officer.[41]

By mid-January 1918, Humphrey, a Lieutenant in the Royal Flying Corps, had agreed to back the book. 'I do not see why I should not guarantee £10,' he wrote. Three weeks later, he came to London from the RFC station at Lympne to meet the author. Dr Dunlop had told Marie about the 'rich young man . . . who might be glad to be the means of launching such progressive work'.[42] He invited them both to lunch at the Lyons café at 213 Piccadilly on 6 February. Marie had expected an elderly gentleman, with a broad watch-chain on an expansive front. Humphrey had pictured Marie as a stout German *Frau*, a weighty and ponderous piece of goods. He met, instead, a youthful woman with softly waved chestnut hair, luminous eyes, immensely alive, dressed in flowing feminine clothes. She saw a tall, handsome officer in khaki in the uniform of the Royal Flying Corps looking younger than his thirty-nine years. In his diary Humphrey noted the lunch and a Director's Meeting where he sold all his shares and his brother's company bought all his debentures.

To Marie, he wrote from Manchester that evening: 'Dear Dr Stopes, I am very glad indeed you have allowed me to take a hand in pushing your book, it is very good of you.'[43] He added that he had not yet read the book and enclosed a cheque for £200, insisting that the money was sent to her anonymously and his name was not to be mentioned. Humphrey Roe's diary records laconically the course of events. The following day, Marie wrote thanking him for the cheque. She had managed to catch Fifield (the publisher) just in time for spring publication and together they took the manuscript to the printer.

Before he sailed for France, aware of the high casualty rates among fliers, Humphrey Roe, a committed feminist, made time to call on the Editor of the *Manchester Guardian*, who had suggested that a scholarship should be established at Manchester University to celebrate the adoption of Women's Suffrage, bringing a £500 cheque.[44] Lieutenant Roe insisted on remaining anonymous, although C. P. Scott wrote to thank him, assuring him that 'if the thing comes off it will be due to your initiative'. He managed to fit in tea and dinner with Marie Stopes and a visit to her home at Leatherhead before sailing on 20 February for the Front, his head full of the book he had sponsored and its author.

6

Fulfilment

When Humphrey Roe sailed to the Western Front aboard the *Princess Victoria* for Boulogne in 1918, he was already deeply interested in Dr Stopes. He sent her a telegram to say he was crossing to France and, as soon as he landed, wrote asking her for a photograph to add to his 'all-too-small' collection of celebrated people . . . 'I do hope you will favour me with a photo of yourself. Be a brick!' he wrote boyishly.[1]

Their letters crossed. She replied to his wire with a blithely optimistic letter: 'Dear Flying Man, . . . I do hope that you had a good crossing and that you will be safe through the wonderful times you will be having. Get leave as soon as you can and come for a day in the woods . . . Yours ever sincerely, Marie Carmichael Stopes.'[2]

A month before the long-awaited publication of her book, Marie was frantically busy, rushing to wholesalers trying to obtain supplies of rationed paper and correcting the 'complete proofs' from the publishers. Nevertheless, she sent off her photograph immediately and asked him for his photograph. Marie was beginning to care about her 'flying man'. She asked him to send her the name of his unit, if possible, so that it would be easier to read the casualty lists and 'for me to weave magic round you to make you safe . . .'[3]

Before the correspondence could develop further, Humphrey's plane crashed due to engine failure when he was returning from a night bombing raid over Germany. The doctors at the American Hospital in France diagnosed a broken ankle and a jarred spine and Humphrey was invalided home to England. From the ambulance train, he wrote asking Marie to visit him at the Royal Flying Corps Central Hospital in Hampstead as soon as she could. Humphrey arrived in England on 24 March, two days before the publication of *Married Love*. To the baffled fury of her publisher, she went to the hospital to visit Humphrey on the day of publication, 26 March 1918.

The wartime friendship ripened rapidly. Marie called three times to the hospital, the first time with a plant, the second time with a copy of *Married Love*. On the third visit, Humphrey was well enough to escort her to town to book tickets for '*Dear Brutus*'. On 3 April Humphrey managed to wangle a day's leave and spent it at Leatherhead, in the woods with Marie, taking tea at her home. Aylmer Maude, who was still lodging with her, had been given precise instructions for dinner that night. 'Dear Ducky, Please be home in time for dinner and *not late* (velvet jacket required) as I have an unexpected and important visitor, a "wounded" from France whom I am rather fond of. Please call me Una. Don't tell him I have never spoken of him! Yours affectionately MCS.'[4] (Una was Aylmer Maude's pet name for Marie, based on the Virgin in Spenser's *Faerie Queene*.)

Two days later, Marie attempted to have Lieutenant Roe transferred temporarily to her home to recuperate. She loved the sport of intrigue and, writing on University of London headed paper, sent compliments to the Commanding Officer of the Royal Flying Corps Hospital and suggested that a few days in the sunny open air of Leatherhead might speed Lieutenant Roe's recovery: 'Dr Stopes undertakes that Lieutenant Roe will lead a strictly disciplined life, be out of doors all day, go to bed early and touch no alcohol if the short leave is granted to him.'[5] Despite her assurances, the Commanding Officer refused to give up his patient to Dr Stopes's care. Marie had not, of course, revealed her sex or the nature of her doctorate.

Marie enjoyed the escort of a handsome wounded officer and friendship soon ripened into courtship. She appreciated Humphrey's considerate manners and his concern for women's rights, and he was clearly a man of means. At last, it seemed, her hopes might be fulfilled. Humphrey, in his turn, was thrilled by Marie's accomplishments, her air of authority, her vitality. The courtship took place almost in public; the couple whispered together in the ward and exchanged confidences sitting on a bench on Hampstead Heath or on the tube. They strolled to Well Walk to look at No. 14, Marie's old home. Within a fortnight they were in love, taking it for granted that they would marry. They had even decided on a name for the first born child, 'Margaret'. At last, Marie could see marriage and motherhood ahead. And then came the shock.

On 14 April, Humphrey's diary records: 'Go to Marie. Finally I propose, but I tell her about Ethel.'[6] Humphrey had allowed himself to be caught up in a whirlwind romance without first releasing himself from his engagement to his fiancée, Ethel Burgess, a clergyman's daughter from Manchester whom he had known for years. Marie had wanted to marry immediately so that she could be carrying 'Margaret', the child she wanted so desperately, before Humphrey returned to the Front. Only then did Humphrey reveal, haltingly, that he was already engaged.

Marie felt bitterly deceived yet again, but this time she was determined not to lose her man. Humphrey was abject, ready to do anything to make amends. He had intended to disentangle himself as gracefully as he could from Ethel and then propose to Marie. But the speed of the courtship, the excitement of Marie and her urgent desire to marry had driven such sensible plans from his head. He was just as keen to marry as she was.

On the afternoon that Humphrey proposed, they agreed that Marie would go to Manchester and confront Ethel Burgess. The following day when Marie visited Humphrey in hospital, they changed the plan. The luckless Ethel should come to London and go with her to the theatre in the evening. The following day Humphrey wrote a letter from hospital to placate Marie: 'Everything will be all right I am sure . . . but there is nothing very serious: it is much better that there is nothing hidden between us . . . You give orders as to what is to happen in future. Or, if you don't give "orders", you let me know your wishes . . .'

Ethel, however, was not to be put off so easily. She travelled from Manchester to visit Humphrey in hospital on his fortieth birthday, 18 April, and Marie was not present, although she sent birthday greetings. Ethel then told Humphrey she would visit him again on Sunday. He explained that he had arranged to see Marie that day but Ethel protested that she had a right to his company while she was in London. After she left, Humphrey dashed off a letter warning Marie that despite his objections Ethel might come with him and hoping, rather pathetically, that it would 'all end in a friendly chat'. He felt, he explained, that he wanted to know that he had done everything possible for Miss Burgess and asked Marie to be as patient as she could.

The letter did not arrive in time and when Marie opened her front door on Sunday morning she was 'hurt and surprised' to find Miss Burgess standing beside her fiancé looking aggressive, while Humphrey stood awkwardly by. Inside, there was a scene. Miss Burgess, aggrieved, mistrusted the whirlwind courtship and accused Marie of marrying Humphrey for his money. Marie defended herself angrily and loquaciously.

'You may tell [Ethel] that my power of love is not less than hers and that she need have no anxiety that you are being married for your money!' she wrote in an angry letter to Humphrey the following day. '. . . even if you settled on me half of all you possess it would be annually much less than I am securely earning for myself . . .'[8] If she had to stop earning while 'Margaret' was small, she added, she was worried that they might have to live in comparative poverty (an exaggeration since Humphrey was a wealthy man at the time). But she added in a postscript: 'I have just remembered I said "how lucky you are" about having your money . . . What I meant was having all your money in freely available capital and not, as I have it, tied as earnings because capital, when one is young means so much power . . .'[9] They met next day, both doubtful about Ethel: 'still we kiss, hers are very cold,' Humphrey noted.[10]

Although she was in love, Marie was cautious after her scorching experiences. She wrote to Professor Wheeler, who knew of Humphrey's family, for information about him and also to Councillor Ashton for 'references'. Then she received another blow. Ethel Burgess was not prepared to surrender her fiancé completely. She insisted on a promise in writing that Humphrey would wait six months before getting engaged to Marie.

Marie had hoped to marry by the middle of May. In six months' time she would be thirty-eight and, in all probability, she would not have her first baby until she was thirty-nine. The tension between the lovers grew. On 30 April, Humphrey spent the day at Marie's house in Leatherhead: 'Marie and I very happy until just before tea. Marriage mentioned. I say Ethel must release me. So there is trouble . . .'[11]

Ironically, Marie's book, *Married Love*, was proving more successful than she had dared to dream. Over two thousand copies were sold within a fortnight. In April, Marie wrote to Humphrey about it:

The Times Book Club has ordered over 50 copies!!! All sorts of papers are now bothering [the publisher] for review copies, also the Times newspaper has definitely, finally and absolutely refused an advertisement of the book, which seems rather comic doesn't it? (This is not exactly a romantic love letter is it? But love is stunned or hibernating till the storms roll by . . .)[12]

Humphrey wrote appealing to her to understand his position:

Please help me to keep up to the standard I have set for myself. As one interested in women's questions I have always maintained that the man must bear his equal share; now that I am the sinner I do not want to neglect Miss Burgess' feelings . . .[13]

Humphrey paid Miss Burgess £2,000 to compensate her and did his best to allay Marie's anxieties. She wrote him long letters with suggestions to cover the event of his death in action, leaving her with a young baby. They agreed finally that in Humphrey's new Will, Marie would become a beneficiary to the extent of £20,000 with £10,000 left for the advancement of birth control. Marie tried to explain her fears to her future husband:

> The worst (the unlikely) is that you die just when I was in the middle of having, perhaps, a second Margaret with the first Margaret quite young, and that something made me awfully ill; in that case I should need money at once. (It would be a pretty ironic farce to have you giving money to start girls at College and me starving!)[14]

Marie was referring to the £500 Humphrey had donated to promoting a scholarship scheme for women at Manchester University. Her feminist sympathies did not extend to promoting other women's interests at the expense of her own.

Meanwhile, Marie sent a letter to the Department of Scientific and Industrial Research to reassure them that her marriage would not affect her work or her need for a salary commensurate with it. 'As regards finance, I will be just as much (or more) compelled to earn my way and we both believe in woman's economic independence . . . my future husband gives his money mostly to all sorts of public work.'[15]

Humphrey was hurt by her materialistic attitude: 'All your plans are being made on the assumption (a cold, calculated one at that) that I shall be killed or maimed,' he wrote. Humphrey tried to delay their marriage as he had promised Ethel Burgess. But he was fearful lest Marie might have a nervous breakdown if she were balked again of fruitful marriage. Part of Marie's attraction for Humphrey was her forceful character, and in the end her will prevailed. They decided on a secret marriage, to take place at the Register Office, Hanover Square on 16 May, three weeks after Humphrey's pledge to Ethel that he would wait six months to marry.

Marie asked Aylmer Maude to be one of the witnesses, a role which he found hard:

> Oh my dear, you do not know how many conflicting thoughts and feelings rise in my mind and heart when I think of you and of our past, present and future friendship. I want you to be happy and to live a normal life with children and I am deeply grateful to you for

having befriended me in my loneliness from December 1912 onwards. Au revoir my dear one, it is such a joy to think of your cleverness, your sanity, your originality, your taste, your looks and when you please – your sweetness.[16]

Marie looked on Maude as her 'nearest relative', but he found it more and more difficult to reconcile himself to giving her away. 'I have never had enough of you, nor indeed could have,' he wrote ten days before the wedding.

Of course he was present at the Register Office on 16 May. Dr Binnie Dunlop, who felt proud to have made a match as well as having helped to produce The Book, was the other witness. Even Charlotte, who knew of the engagement but had not yet met her future son-in-law, was unaware of the little ceremony. The couple spent the night at Leatherhead. Rather cruelly, Marie wrote a note to Aylmer Maude about her married love: 'Humphrey and I were very happy last night and this morning – the marriage is consummated but naturally I haven't had it at its best yet . . .'[17] She also told him he had to give up his lodgings with her.

The couple went to Land's End on honeymoon where Mrs Roe was, for the first time in her life, blissfully happy. However, she was not content to keep their marriage a secret. After being baulked for so long, Marie wanted a proper church wedding and she called on all her men friends to play their part. At the last, two days before the ceremony, Aylmer wrote to her rather pathetically: 'My dearest Una, I have been bothering you with letters recently . . . Still, I cannot let the eve of your *third* marriage pass without sending you my most cordial good wishes and fondest greetings.[18]

The Bishop of Birmingham conducted the marriage service on 19 June (he had to coax her to promise to 'obey'). Aylmer Maude gave her away. As they came out of St Margaret's Church, Westminster, it was raining and Humphrey, tall and handsome in his RFC uniform, held an umbrella over the bride. Marie wore a round-necked gown of cream satin and silver brocade, with a veil of tulle fastened by a wreath of orange blossom, with orange blossom at her waist. An expression of mischievous triumph lighted her face, while in the background the white-haired Aylmer Maude looked on wistfully. Winnie was too weak to attend but Charlotte saved her a slice of the wedding cake.

Meanwhile her theoretical account of *Married Love* was exceeding even Marie's hopes. The runaway success of the book caused difficulties for its small, quiet publishing firm. The proprietor, A. C. Fifield, initially admiring of both the book and its author, was soon overwhelmed as sales outstripped the capacity of the firm.

The reasons for its success are complex. Writing from a woman's point of view, with an intensity of feeling with which her many readers would empathize, Marie had produced the first book about sex technique for women. In it she had dared to stake a claim for female sexuality, for women's sexual needs and sexual rights. Her views challenged the centuries of prejudice and superstition and the accretions of religious teaching which saw women's bodies and women's attractions as desirable but also dirty and corrupting and the lust for women as shameful and sinful. The wife's fate, therefore, was to be a passive, suffering victim of her husband's lust. Marie dismissed the idea that 'nice' women have no spontaneous sexual impulses and devoted a chapter, 'The Fundamental Pulse', to explaining women's sexual instincts through her own law of the 'Periodicity of Recurrence of Desire in Women', illustrated by two charts. Her records of her own and her friends' peak period in the month may not have been strictly scientific but they were immensely important, because they led women to understand that they had a right to sexual impulses and need not feel ashamed of them. Havelock Ellis described Marie Stopes's theory as 'the most notable advance made in recent years in the knowledge of women's psycho-physiological life'.[19] No less important was her advice to young husbands (to whom her book was dedicated), urging them to discover how to arouse and satisfy their wives, at a time when husbands would still demand 'marital rights' without considering their wives' feelings.

Then, the timing of the book could not have been happier. *Married Love* came out eight months before the First World War had ended, a war which transformed 'woman's place' in society. Because of labour shortages, women had been given a chance to prove their ability to take on 'men's jobs', working not only as doctors, nurses, landgirls and civil servants but also as plumbers, bus conductors, van drivers and factory hands and, latterly in the newly-formed Women's Corps of the armed services. By the end of the war they had far more opportunity to mix with men and, as Marie's play *The Race* had suggested, sex between a girl-friend and a soldier on leave from the Front became, if not acceptable, widespread, and casual sex without payment far more prevalent.[20] At the same time, a state of moral panic gripped the nation as the scale of venereal disease, highlighted by reports in the press and propaganda films, became known. By the end of the war, over 400,000 cases had been treated in the British Army, including the Dominion Forces.[21] This made good marital relations seem even more desirable, and Marie's book helped to point the way.

Even for well-brought up young ladies, the subject of sex could no longer be smothered. The ideas of Edward Carpenter, even of Freud, had begun to permeate the prejudices of the educated middle and upper classes. Above all, it was the work of Havelock Ellis, the most important sexologist in the late nineteenth and early twentieth century, who helped to open up the subject, with his massive seven-volume work, *Studies in the Psychology of Sex*.[22]

Ellis's own sexual experience was unusual. Impotent for most of his life, he was married to a lesbian and suffered from urolagnia (sexual excitement at seeing women urinate). Although he was helpful and generous to Marie, she disliked his concentration on the abnormal in his works. Reading him, she said, was 'like breathing a bag of soot; it made me feel choked and dirty for three months'.[23] Marie's book, by contrast was designed for healthy young men and women and was a celebration of sex. Her victory over Mrs Grundy in publishing *Married Love* can be gauged by comparison with the fate of D. H. Lawrence's novel of explicit sexual love, *Lady Chatterley's Lover*. The 'shameful' novel was first published in a small edition in Florence in 1928; the bowdlerized version appeared in Britain in 1932; and not until 1960, after a sensational court case which turned on the taboo sex words was the unexpurgated text of the novel published. Even given the obvious differences between the two works, Marie's triumph was remarkable.

By good fortune her book appeared a month after the enfranchisement of women (limited to householders, wives of householders and women over thirty). That the time was now ripe for a new attitude to marriage was sensed among enlightened women, but it took a Marie Stopes to give it tongue.

Marie was so abundantly feminine, so confident in her own womanhood, so conscious of her feminist pedigree that her tone was exactly right for her time. Like her readers, she had been brought up to be romantically idealistic and abysmally ignorant about sex. Many girls feared that they would have a baby if they kissed a man; they knew little, if anything, of the female anatomy and nothing of the male. Even Vera Brittain, who was to become one of the most liberated and militantly feminist women of her generation, gleaned her knowledge of sex through scanning the Bible and such novels as *Adam Bede* and *David Copperfield* for obstetrical details. As a débutante, just before the war,

Vera Brittain confessed that she was 'extremely hazy with regard to the precise nature of the sex act'[24].

Less privileged and less educated women derived their knowledge from sniggering remarks in the lavatories or playgrounds, glimpses into bedrooms, half-understood bawdy jokes or frightening stories. The popular romantic novels of the time in which the hero gathers up the heroine in his arms for a moment of 'supreme bliss' followed, in print, by a row of asterisks, were not much help. Nor could the bride-to-be rely on parents or doctors to give any guidance. (And her groom was often just as ignorant.) The result of this half-knowledge left many brides frightened and disgusted on their wedding night. Marie Stopes's book offered a 'contribution to the solution of sex difficulties'. In *Married Love*, she managed to combine the idealistic, romantic and mystical approach to sex with a clinically detached description of how to enjoy it.

Implicitly, her book promised rapture ever after. Her first chapter of *Married Love* contains nothing to alarm:

Every heart desires a mate ... neither man nor woman singly can know the joy of the performance of all the human functions; neither man nor woman singly can create another human-being ... and there is nothing for which the innermost spirit of one and all so yearns as for a sense of union with another soul, and the perfecting of oneself which such union brings.[25]

From the high aspirations of this first chapter, the tone changes to disclose very basic information couched in anatomical language in the fifth:

The woman's vaginal canal, which has an external opening covered by double lips, is generally of such size as to allow the entry of the erect penis ... After the preliminaries have mutually roused the pair, the stimulated penis, enlarged and stiffened is pressed into the woman's vagina ... when the woman is what is physiologically called tumescent (that is when she is ready for union and has been profoundly stirred), local parts are flushed by the internal blood-supply and, to some extent, are turgid like those of the man, while a secretion of mucus lubricates the opening of the vagina ... It can, therefore, be readily imagined that, when the man tries to enter a woman whom he has *not* wooed to the point of stimulating her natural physical reactions of preparation, he is endeavouring to force his entry through a dry-walled opening too small for it . . . It should be realized that a man does not woo and win a woman once and for all when he marries her: *he must woo her before every separate act of coitus*, for each act corresponds to a marriage as other creatures know it . . .'[26]

By providing women with a rational, factual account of sexual intercourse, and a language with which to describe it, Marie was rendering them less helpless and less dependent.

Her frank exposition, of course, shocked some readers. A former Australian MP, W. N. Willis, who wrote works with suggestive titles, *Why Girls Go Wrong* (1913), *White Slaves in a Piccadilly Flat* (1915), and *Should Girls Be Told?* (1917), professed horror at Marie Stopes's suggestion that:

'. . . it is not only a woman's arms which should embrace her lover'. In his view, she was encouraging stimulants to passion which 'ordinarily do not enter the head of a normal married woman . . . Let us . . . in the name of true normal manhood and womanhood and indeed of [sic] the name of the British Empire endeavour to keep the imagination down at all costs – never purposely call it into play as suggested by Mrs Stopes . . . the human imagination is the most deadly foe to the clean, wholesome methods of Nature . . .'[27]

Dr C. P. Blacker, a distinguished psychiatrist and member of the Eugenics Society, wrote disparagingly; 'her books are read extensively and secretly in girls' schools and by boys in the same spirit that indecent literature in general is enjoyed . . . They can, in fact, in one sense, be considered as practical handbooks of prostitution!'[28]

As writers on sex themselves, both of those critics had particular reasons for their objections. There were, of course, members of the public who found *Married Love* a great shock, like her neighbour from Leatherhead, a Mrs L. S. Marie received her protest four days before her own marriage.

The details into which you go are absolutely unnecessary . . . and are fit only for a medical treatise. Your book is written for married people but you cannot control its distribution . . . Personally much of the book simply disgusts me and spoils other parts. I also think the way you quote the opinion of men who have discussed the subject with you is a great mistake, as to my mind a man who discusses his marital relations with another woman is guilty of a gross breach of confidence . . . I feel deeply on the subject and feel it should not be ruthlessly and inartistically treated as you have done . . .[29]

Another wife and mother expressed herself even more forcefully:

> As a 30-years married and, I hope, broad-minded woman, mother of six children, I read your Married Love and was disgusted with the filth. Your two to three pages on contraception are, and have been, known to most of my acquaintances for years and all the other pages of muck demean you . . . You take upon yourself to teach us what surely nature herself does is an insult to all decent people and I fail to see the use at all except to excite people and cause a deal of immorality.[30]

Marie was usually morbidly sensitive to criticism from any quarter. But the surprisingly small number of 'disgusted' readers was vastly outweighed by the mail from Marie's admirers who sent hundreds of letters to her publisher. Her correspondents found her style so accessible, her expression so right for the subject that they came to look on her as a heroine, counsellor, doctor and friend:

> Will you let me thank you from the bottom of my heart for your pluck and congratulate you on putting into words so beautifully the great message of help and hope to us poor mortals who strive to make married life a success and to place love in its right position . . . !

wrote a Mrs M.B. of Felixstowe a month after Marie's book was published.[31] Her outspoken clarity gave her woman readers the courage to ask questions and to hope for improvement in their married lives: 'As a girl I was taught that it was really rather a misfortune to have a body, but that, as it was there, the best thing to do was to ignore it as far as possible', wrote a Mrs M.F. from Perthshire, who described herself at forty-two, after a good marriage, as without desire and with pleasure in love almost impossible. She asked Marie to write about the subject: 'It is books like yours . . . that are needed to clear away the old evil conspiracy of secrecy which has ruined so many women's lives.'[32]

Through personal advice as well as through published writings, Marie influenced sexual behaviour. 'I do not believe that the normal man's sex needs are stronger than the normal woman's,' she wrote to a Hampstead inquirer in December 1918. Men did have more urgent sexual desires at present, she went on, due to 'the false repression of the woman's and the utterly unnatural stimulation of the man's . . .' But if she courageously encouraged women to acknowledge their sexuality, she also distanced herself from lesbians. To a married woman who asked her to write a book about the subject she replied: 'I should be very pleased to write a book on what – don't be hurt – I consider the disease of uranianism. So any information would be recorded with that in view. You may find in me a doctor – a saviour – but *not* a champion . . .'[33]

In some of her readers Marie's book raised hopes long dormant: 'I have been married fourteen years to a man whom I love and who loves me. . . .', wrote a Mrs E.B., 'Like many other girls I knew little of sexual matters or of their importance in married life.' Mrs B's husband always wore a sheath and she added: '. . . never after all these years although we love one another, have I felt any *rapture* of love.'[34] Only once, when her husband had made love to her half-asleep without his sheath, had she experienced joy in intercourse. Marie advised her not to tell her husband of her lack of satisfaction all those years but to show him her book. 'I belong to that multitude of the grateful,' wrote A.J.C. of Muswell Hill on 7 August 1918, 'whom your book "Married Love" has called into being. After reading it . . . the thing has been transfigured. Especially do we love the way in which you have steered a course between arid science on the one hand and an unhelpful idealism.'[35]

For the young Naomi Mitchison, *Married Love* came out just in time. She was married in 1916 and when the book appeared in 1918 she found it such an eye-opener that she rushed out to buy a second copy to send to her husband, a liaison officer with the French serving in Italy with a note: 'read this before we meet again.' Apparently it made all the difference.[36]

After *Married Love*, Marie Stopes's name rang round the nation and she practically ceased to be a private individual and allowed herself to become public property. Readers besieged her for advice, sympathy, a listening ear. Many of them believed that her book should be given to every couple on their marriage. Her readership was by no means limited to women: about 40 per cent of her correspondents, who were to grow into many thousands, were men, grateful to be able to ask an expert about impotence or premature ejaculation, or even to 'chat' about the subject. 'I hope you will not think it impertinent of me to write to you on the subject,' wrote a Mr. B.B., engaged to be married. 'I once asked a doctor of my own sex who merely advised me to spend a night with a prostitute.'[37]

From France, a captain in the Royal Engineers asked Marie what to do about his urge to masturbate. She counselled him: 'to run a bath full

of the hottest water you can stand and to soak in it up to the neck.'
While a correspondent from the Carlton Club in Pall Mall, a Mr. H.
confessed that at the time he married he was quite ignorant although 'I
had knocked about at public school, Cambridge, the world of wholesome sport and London Society till I was twenty-six . . . I did not know
that a woman either required or was capable of having any decided
orgasm on having connection and when my wife had them which she
did freely when aroused, I was frightened and thought it was some sort
of fit . . .'[38]

Although the chapters on sexual love naturally provoked the most
interest and comment, Marie's attitude to freedom in marriage was just
as radical. She utterly refuted the idea of the wife as little woman:

> For too long men have been accustomed to look upon woman's views
> and in particular on her intellectual opinions, as being something
> demanding, at the most, a bland humouring beneath the kindest
> smiles. Even from the noblest man, the woman of sensitive personality
> to-day feels an undercurrent as of surprised congratulation when she
> has anything to say worth his *serious* attention outside that depart-
> ment of life supposed to belong to her 'sphere' . . .[39]

Marie advocated that both husband and wife should be free to go alone
on long trips, week-ends or walking tours 'without the possibility of a
breath of jealousy or suspicion . . .' and asserted that marriage could
never reach its full stature 'until women possess as much intellectual
freedom and freedom of opportunity within it as do their partners'. In
her marriage to Gates, Marie had assumed that freedom for herself, and
in her relationships with men became the dominant partner, since for
her the notion of equality between the sexes was almost impossible to
practise.

At the same time, in her book, as in her life, she looked for eternal
romance: 'For man is still essentially the hunter, the one who experiences
the desires and thrills of the chase, and dreams ever of coming unawares
upon Diana in the woodlands.'[40] Wives, she believed, should be always
escaping. She disapproved of married people sharing a bedroom because
it was impossible for the woman to keep her aura of mystery and
romance if her husband saw her 'during most of the unlovely and even
ridiculous proceedings of the toilet. Now it may enchant a man once –
perhaps even twice – or at long intervals to watch his goddess screw
her hair up into a tight and unbecoming knot and soap her ears. But it
is inherently too unlovely a proceeding to retain indefinite enchantment.'

Much of Marie's writing was autobiographical and in *Married Love* one can trace her desire for a mate who was both medieval knight and modern man. Her high ideals for marriage had proved disastrous to her personally. In her recipe for a happy marriage she omitted two ingredients that many people would consider vital: a sense of humour (which Marie largely lacked) and the ability to compromise. Nevertheless, for the flappers of the post-war period and the newly married, her ideals were beautiful. They enabled young women to dream of an unfettered existence, intellectual and physical freedom and ecstatic sexual union safe within the romantic bonds of marriage.

Ten days before *Married Love* was published, Marie herself had doubts about the value of the 'pristine purity' of the virgin state. In a draft letter to an unnamed correspondent, she pondered whether too much emphasis was placed on the woman retaining her virginity before marriage: 'in giving her body in love, a woman gives her "all" (while a man scarcely does as much).' This, she argued, divided women into three unhealthy categories:

a) The unmarried – never allowed any sex joy or relief however much they fundamentally suffer for lack of it . . .

b) The married (possibly burdened without limit with childbearing) with perhaps a normal (but often excessive sex) life.

c) The outcast – in order to balance the unhealthy percentage of unmarried, they are overworked to the point of sex machines . . . That a woman should never give herself save for love is an axiom; but it is outrageously violated in our social system . . .[41]

This plan for 'free love' and sexual equality, Marie sensibly kept to herself. Had she not insisted emphatically that the sexual knowledge that she had made available was intended only for married couples, her book would have been declared obscene and the author and publisher prosecuted. Instead she disarmed her critics with her aura of ultra respectability.

The press gradually acknowledged the importance of her new book, although *The Times* continued to boycott it. 'All medical men and women should read this,' wrote the *Medical Times*, 'they can't fail to glean valuable information . . .' The *Lancet* described it as an 'extremely sensible little book,' while the *English Review* commented that: 'the great revolution in women's position and attitude is shown in this frank physiological statement.'[42] 'Frank, straightforward truth finds no greater admirers than in the heart of Mayfair and this is the real reason for the success of Dr Stopes' book,' observed the *Book Monthly*.[43]

Sophisticated circles in the West End adored *Married Love* and the book was read in men's clubs and, more surreptitiously, in women's drawing-rooms. But grocers in Wales, deckhands on the high seas and women waiting outside pawnshops whispered and gossiped over a shared copy of The Book, wrapped in brown paper. Marie had once said that she wanted to appeal to all classes, and in *Married Love* she had found a topic of universal interest.

The readers who wrote to her after *Married Love* was published were predominantly the middle- or upper-middle-class book-buying public. At first, Marie answered every letter herself but the task was Herculean. Even those who wrote to congratulate her usually included a request for advice. The questions varied widely from how to effect intercourse, sometimes after years of marriage, to pre-marital etiquette. (Was it permissible, a young man asked, to kiss his fiancée on the breast? Better wait, Marie replied cautiously.) She would write long letters in reply, two or three if necessary. Occasionally she asked for a fee to stem the flow of post, two or three guineas for a postal consultation, up to ten guineas for a personal interview but since she was not qualified to practise medicine, it was dangerous to charge on a regular basis. As she explained to an inquirer: 'I do not practise medicine in the ordinary way but I have had forced upon myself an unofficial consultation sort of practice on sex, psychology and physiology.'[44]

She became the nation's first acknowledged, if informal, adviser on sexual and emotional problems. The Welsh Education Board asked her to give schoolchildren advice on sex that summer and the Oxford University Press invited her to write a book on the subject addressed to medical practitioners. The book she had decided upon to follow her sensational success was one she knew from her correspondence was badly needed – a guide to birth control methods. When overburdened wives or worried husbands wrote to her pleading for her help to prevent them from 'falling again', Marie advised them to wait for a few months! Her new book would have all the answers. 'I've been thinking of the title,' she wrote to Humphrey, who was enthusiastic, 'what about "Wise Parenthood"? That gives a positive suggestion that there should be children instead of the slight hint of a negative idea in birth control.'[45]

Her own opportunities for married love and parenthood, now that she could claim practical as well as theoretical knowledge of the subject, were limited, with Humphrey still in the Air Force as the RFC had now become. Marie desperately wanted him to stay in England, even visited Air Ministry HQ at the Hotel Cecil in London to try to persuade the authorities to find her husband a job at home. So long as he could be 'of more use to the country' Humphrey was only too happy to agree. They were often parted and wrote passionate love letters. 'Kisses from my soul will reach you if those from my lips don't,' Marie wrote to her husband. Humphrey tried gamely to attain her tone: 'Dearest Wood Nymph,' he wrote, 'I am in the train, passing through woods and trees but there is no Wood Nymph anywhere. Perhaps it is because they know I have left the Queen of the Wood Nymphs behind me . . .'[46]

On 5 August, they spent a night together at the Seaview Hotel, Hythe. 'My darling sweetheart,' Marie wrote to her husband the next day, 'I wish our first experiment on last night's lines had been in a big, beautiful bed in a pretty room and not so cramped and sordid.'[47] And, in a later letter: 'Your lips are awfully nice to kiss.'

By the end of August, Humphrey had been given unpaid leave from the Air Force and the couple snatched a second honeymoon near Land's End, anxious themselves to conceive, almost as if Marie wanted her life to keep up with her book list. She took the manuscript of *Wise Parenthood* with her, as well as a huge bundle of letters. 'My correspondence is getting utterly unmanageable,' she wrote to Charlotte. 'It is no sort of holiday to write letters all day and every day. I'm thinking of putting an announcement in the papers that no letters will be answered for a month!'[48]

By coincidence Helena Wright, a young woman doctor, was staying at the hotel with her husband and baby, and the two women enjoyed each others' company. Helena Wright remembered Marie as 'a graceful, attractive woman sitting on the rocks in a long white lace dress'.[49] Helena was breast-feeding her baby at the time and while the nurse watched the baby the two women would often swim together in Sennen Cove. Helena had read *Married Love* and Marie told her about her new work, *Wise Parenthood* and asked Helena as a doctor to read the manuscript. Helena Wright, who was seven years her junior, agreed provided she was given a free hand to 'take out all the nonsense'. To her surprise Marie showed '. . . a deferential attitude to a much younger, qualified woman. When I handed back the considerably mutilated script I was prepared for storms. None came.'[50]

In 1918 there was an air of excitement and of improvisation about her work. Before *Wise Parenthood* was published, she sent a copy of the manuscript to a husband on a submarine, desperate to avoid having a child when home on leave. He returned it within a month, grateful for the chance to 'thwart nature'. After all, thwarting nature was, as she pointed out, practised on every side to combat disease and preserve life against accident and the ravages of old age.[51]

She was not herself yet pregnant, but she had little time to brood. From the time *Married Love* was published she was in her element, in demand by a grateful public and courted by publishers and newspaper editors. Besides, throughout the war years she had continued to pursue her researches into the constitution of coal, to travel to the Home Office Experimental Station in Cumberland and to work in the lab at University College. She had also rigged up a makeshift lab at home, to save unnecessary travelling. In 1918, with Dr Wheeler as co-author, she had written an important paper, 'A monograph on the Structure, Chemical and Palaeontological, of Coal' for the Department of Scientific and Industrial Research. This work led on to her paper identifying the four ingredients of coal – vitrain, clarain, durain and fusain – which was published by the Royal Society in 1919. Her nomenclature came into international usage and the names are still used, with some modification.[52]

As for *Married Love*, it was praised everywhere: 'oh! Humphles,' she wrote, 'I could be a society *lion* if I chose to chuck coal work and roar . . .' Part of her wanted just to capture the delight of youthful love. 'I wish I were with you at this minute,' Marie wrote on 24 September 1918. 'I'd pounce on you and make you roll on the ground and I'd pull your hair and tickle you and behave altogether like a wild pussy kitten. So I'll send little scattering scurrying kisses instead to the great, big growly silky, curly Humphle Tiger . . .'[53]

At that stage, Humphrey needed all the scattering, scurrying kisses she could send him. He was floundering, not certain what to do. Whether through Marie's influence or not, he was no longer the glamorous flying officer. The RAF had seconded him to more humdrum war-work, assembling American aircraft at a government factory. The logical step would have been for him to go back to the family firm, Avro. Both his own hurt pride at their treatment of him and the desire to please his wife prevented him. In June, when he had visited his mother, he was offered a post as business manager in charge of production but turned it down. He would only go back, he insisted, if he were to become Chairman and Managing Director. 'I have added that I am doubtful whether you would approve of that,' he wrote to Marie but went on, in a pleading tone, 'Sweetheart, it would be really nice if I am Chairman.

There is much work for me to do in London. The position is an interesting one with plenty of scope.'[54]

Marie did try to heal the family rift and save Humphrey's position. In October she travelled to Manchester to visit her mother-in-law, who had a financial interest in the business. She met a cool reception, however, and came back complaining that her mother-in-law was not at all interested in her new daughter-in-law but only wanted to settle business affairs. Alienated from his own family, Humphrey transferred all his loyalty to his love for Marie. Unless the family made honourable amends before the Peace was declared, he told his mother, he would abandon them altogether even to the extent of changing his name. 'I will drop Roe and take on Stopes – because it is a name of which I am very proud.'[55]

At one stage, Humphrey devised a promising scheme to start a flying service between London, Dublin and Belfast but that, too, foundered. All his pride went into Marie's achievements and he was so engrossed in his wife's career, wanting to work with her after the war, that he made only desultory efforts to pursue his own. 'What about my Wood Nymph becoming an M.P.?' he asked her in October 1918, a month before the Act enabling women to be elected to the House of Commons was passed. 'I really think my best plan is to invest £5,000 in some business and so be free to play with my wife.'[56]

Humphrey's somewhat cavalier attitude to his money alarmed Marie. She had had to work hard to earn hers and she was pleased to be able to pay back 'to dearest Lieutenant Roe' the whole of the £200 he had lent her to launch *Married Love* with £100 interest. Nevertheless, she was afraid that the generosity that she prized might lead others to take advantage of him. 'There are plots afoot to get money out of you,' she wrote and asked Humphrey to trust her completely and sign a strange agreement: 'I hereby register to my wife Marie my inviolable promise not to part with or re-invest sums totalling more than five thousand pounds without previous complete and full discussion with her.'[57] The document was witnessed by their housekeeper, Alice Gertrude Heap. The very day on which she sent the letter she received further proof of Humphrey's generosity. For her thirty-eighth birthday he bought her a fur coat from Swan & Edgar. ' . . . it was what they call a model . . . it is very cheap.'[58]

On Armistice Day, 11 November 1918, while the country went wild with church bells ringing, fireworks lighting the skies and parties in the street, Marie and Humphrey spent a sober evening at the Birmingham and Midland Institute in Paradise Street where she was lecturing on the constitution of coal.

The following week the 32-page book, *Wise Parenthood*, a guide to the technique of birth control, was published. Marie had hoped to counter criticism of her very brave venture by stressing the positive aims of planned childbirth. The book opened with a sentence to which no one could take exception: 'A family of healthy, happy children should be the joy of every pair of married lovers.' But Marie's arguments as justification for birth control were more contentious. She took on the established church when she advocated that sexual intercourse was an 'act of supreme value in itself' in married life, 'separate and distinct from its value as a basis for the procreation of children,' although, forty years later, the Lambeth Conference of the Church of England was to make a proclamation on very similar lines. Her book was also open to criticism medically. She had advised that the cap could be left in safely for several days or even weeks. The *Eugenics Review* regretted her book, suggested that the cap might cause lacerations, even cancer, and disliked the intimate details: 'We think it a pity that this book has been published.' The *Practitioner* noted that popular handbooks written by women without medical qualification contained practical information of which medical men had been ignorant and 'a great deal of which they might legitimately disapprove'.[59]

Marie recommended a small, well-fitting, rubber cervical cap, preferably combined with a soluble quinine pessary or a small, wet sponge whose pores were filled with powdered soap, or a pad of cotton wool smeared with Vaseline. She thought the condom largely harmful, withdrawal detrimental to the nervous system of both sexes, douching and the 'safe period' unreliable. The first indications were that despite the snooty attitude of the scientific press, *Wise Parenthood* would sell splendidly.

To crown her happiness that year, ten days after *Wise Parenthood* was published Marie knew for certain that she was pregnant. 'How lovely it will be,' she wrote in an ecstatic letter to Humphrey, 'if we can really settle into a home and make it together and together do great work for the race! I hope my darling is being a very splendid and to-be-proud-of darling and will master everything except his little wife what loves him . . .'[60] They exchanged kisses in their letters (Humphrey sent a 'quiet splosher', Marie, a soft, fat kiss).

She would unexpectedly introduce a brisk broadside into the lovers' correspondence: 'Darling, I want you at once . . . carefully to fill a clean good-sized bottle with your water, label it with the enclosed label and send it to Harley Street.' Germs had appeared in Marie's urine and regardless of her husband's feelings she was convinced that Humphrey had infected her: 'I am *fundamentally* so sound and healthy! I haven't time to write a love letter but all my thoughts are love for you.'[61]

What worried her gynaecologist more than the germs was that Marie was constantly increasing her professional responsibilities. Besides lecturing on paleobotany, research into coal, publishing activities, travelling to meetings and heavy correspondence, early in 1919, as a recognition of the success of *Married Love*, she was appointed a member of the National Birth-Rate Commission.

The majority of members of the Commission (including her friend, the Bishop of Birmingham) was in favour of limiting the birth-rate but opposed to artificial contraception on what they described as 'medical grounds'. Marie wrote to them to ask for evidence to support their opposition to contraceptive methods but received no reply. In protest she wrote a minority report which was signed by three other commissioners. Dr Stopes's report was widely covered in the press and this in turn brought offers for her to write for the *Sunday Chronicle*. She accepted gladly, stipulating six guineas a thousand words, a high fee for the period, and used the opportunity to promote her new book *Wise Parenthood*.

The result of this open propaganda for birth control agitated her publisher to a panic. Fourteen hundred letters poured into his small office in Clifford's Inn in three days and turned it into an 'indescribable state'. The book was already out of print and Fifield had to take on two extra assistants to deal with the avalanche of correspondence. For years he had quietly published Fabian literature and was unprepared for the disruption or for Marie's overwhelming personality. They had agreed that *Wise Parenthood* was to be directed towards educated young married people. 'It certainly is disgusting to me,' he wrote reprovingly, 'to receive furtive letters from illiterate young unmarried girls asking me to send the book along "in plain wrapping".' Dr Stopes's activities, he wrote, were taking over his business, paralysing his other activities and bringing him into disrepute. Despite the sensational success of *Married Love* and now *Wise Parenthood*, Fifield, who was to retire soon, vowed he would not go through the ordeal of publishing Dr Stopes's books again for £5,000! Nevertheless, to show his gratitude for her work he had published two of her plays in 1918, *Gold in the Wood* and *The Race*.

Marie was gloriously unperturbed. If her readers had to wait because he could not keep up with demand, well: 'Let them wait, they have waited more than a thousand years.' She was on the crest that year and in danger of believing what the most flattering of her admirers and her adoring husband told her. Life for Marie was pleasanter and more comfortable than it had ever been.

Marie had written *Married Love* for women like herself, educated middle-class wives who had been left ignorant of the physical side of marriage. Her tone in her book and in the letters of advice sent to readers implied that they shared a community of interests and of income. She had no particular interest in the lower classes and in *Wise Parenthood* had written censoriously of the 'less thrifty and conscientious' who bred rapidly and produced children 'weakened and handicapped by physical as well as mental warping and weakness'. 'The lower classes were', she wrote in a letter to the *Leicester Daily Post*, 'often thriftless, illiterate and careless'.[62]

However, most birth control campaigners, including her husband, Dr Dunlop and the Malthusians, saw birth control as a crusade against poverty. Dr Charles Killick Millard, the Medical Officer for Health in Leicester, a leading campaigner, shared this view and in his letter congratulating Marie on *Wise Parenthood* pressed the point. Marie replied:

> I quite agree that the matter is most urgent among the very poor and ignorant and my publishing it first in a rather expensive form for the middle-classes is chiefly a matter of tactics, in order to establish the book firmly, so as to prevent, if possible, the rows that would follow if one went straight to the poor . . .[63]

She gave a similar answer to an Irish friend who raised the question.

When she came across individual or poor mothers whose plight moved her, she was horrified and tried to help. Once she realized that helping poor women to limit their families lay at the heart of the birth control campaign, Marie set about working for that aim with her usual energy. She condensed her short book to a sixteen-page pamphlet written in simple language: *A Letter to Working Mothers on how to have healthy children and avoid weakening pregnancies*. Her fastidious publisher was appalled by the idea. She hoped that the Ministry of Health would publish her pamphlet but eventually published it herself in 1919. Through a woman friend Marie attempted to get the pamphlet distributed house-to-house in the East End but with very little success. The poor families called upon instinctively mistrusted any lady who looked as if she came from 'The Welfare' and only a handful took the booklet.

Marie could not have advanced so rapidly without a ruthless streak in her nature. Since her marriage to Humphrey, she had relegated Aylmer Maude to the status of doting uncle, not unnatural in the circumstances, but Maude was deeply hurt. In November 1918, with his business affairs in decline, he went to Archangel, under the auspices of the YMCA, as lecturer to the Allied North Russia Expeditionary Force, hoping to be able to disseminate anti-Bolshevik propaganda to the troops after the Russian Revolution of 1917. 'From February 1914 until May 1918, you were the chief feature in my life – and you still hold a place in it which is profounder and more tender than that held by anyone else', he wrote to Marie before he left Britain. 'It would be a much greater wrench for me . . . if it were not that your marriage has cut us apart to a painful extent . . .'[64] They remained friends for the rest of his life but with none of the old intimacy.

Marie's attitude to Winnie, her invalid younger sister, was more calculating. Winnie herself had realized sadly that she could no longer be a companion to Marie because she 'had not the brains' and had wisely made her life among her own friends. Marie talked to Dr Jessie Murray and other doctor friends prepared to bolster her belief that Winnie was a hypochondriac. Humphrey too, under his wife's influence, was only too content to see his sister-in-law as a nuisance rather than an invalid. The couple had published *A Letter to Working Mothers* at their own expense and, with the baby coming, were very conscious of the need for caution in financial matters.

In mid-April 1919, Marie sent Winnie a cheque for £30 – with conditions attached:

1) That Winnie was not to take any money from or bother their mother;
2) That she was not to cadge from friends;
3) That she was not to go to faith healers or cranks of any kind at all;
4) That she was to make the money last as long as possible since Marie would not be able to repeat the offer.[65]

That month Humphrey and Marie held an At Home with Dr Killick Millard, to try to launch a Wise Parenthood League to distribute information, undertake research, promote discussion and helpful legislation about birth control. But their efforts, at that stage, came to nothing.

With her baby due in June or July, Marie showed no sign of retreating from public life. Although Humphrey had taken over answering the routine letters, she told a male inquirer that if he was very anxious for personal professional advice on psychological or physiological points and would send full details, she sometimes took a case.

Marie kept herself busy and her name in the public eye by writing letters to the newspapers on topics about which she felt strongly, the need to monitor the birth-rate among the mining communities, etc., and suggested to the Ministry of Health that she should publish a book on food and nutrition at her own expense.

She had calculated that the baby was due in June, but it was a month overdue when she went into a nursing home at Teddington on 16 July 1919. She arrived at half-past two in the afternoon with her husband, who had precise instructions to remain within earshot of the delivery room and to keep a diary of events. Against the advice of her gynaecologist, she had decided to use Twilight Sleep to dispel the pains of childbirth. Humphrey too was keen on the then fashionable analgesic. The doctor argued with Marie, saying she could not be starting just yet because she was suffering no pain, she was furious at being thwarted. Humphrey's diary records:

5.23   I leave the room.

5.35   The first injection . . .

7.00   I sit near M's room. All quiet.

7.05   M. asks for chloroform.

7.30   M. has second injection.

8.53   Very beautiful sunset from the seat outside M's room. During this time M. is sometimes quiet and sometimes she is sighing and moaning.

9.21   M. has another injection.

9.23   M. sighs now almost continuous.

9.40   Dr Brown said no more morphia.

10.35   M's voice: 'Give me chloroform for God's sake.' She is now moaning.

10.50   M.: 'I can't endure it. Oh, Nurse, do be quick.'

11.00   Bell and Brown come out, they tell me they cannot hear the child's heart.

17th July

12.30   Quietness broken by sighs from M. Oh! Oh! what is it? cries M.

12.44 'Fiendish – Oh! – ', cries M.

To any woman who had longed for a baby, the loss of a first child at the age of almost thirty-nine would have been a tragedy. Marie, by then a heroine to many women, regarded herself as something between a priestess, a prophetess and a model wife, and the tragedy took on epic proportions. Mixed up in all her histrionics was a genuine, terrible grief.

Recovering at home, she wrote distraught to her mother: 'it was so splendid, a little Hercules and the report [the post mortem] says perfectly formed without a germ or a flaw save incidental to nasty severance. It was "murdered essentially".' Marie claimed that she was 'wantonly tortured' during delivery. She wanted to be delivered first kneeling, then on her back, but the doctors ignored her. Every time she struggled to get into her preferred position:

> I was hauled round, my hands and wrists and finally my legs were held, till I felt like a trapped and frenzied creature . . . my unusually well-developed muscles were unable to work. Also as they allowed me no support, not even the bars at the top and foot of the bed, there was nothing to lever against . . .[66]

'I am the nearest thing to a physically savage woman that you have ever had the luck to meet in your life, and don't you forget it when it comes to the actual confinement,'[67] Marie had warned her doctor before she went into labour, but the medical profession demanded unquestioning obedience from its patients at the time, and Marie's attitude must have antagonized the nursing home staff. Today the Active Birth Centre promotes a 'more natural' posture and Marie could have found midwives and doctors to allow her to give birth in the way she chose. In her desire to have her child in the age-old kneeling or squatting position, Marie was paradoxically too far ahead of her time and consequently her experience of childbirth was devastating.

Dr Brown recorded that the delivery 'was quite natural, no forceps were used. She delivered herself of a male still-born child . . . the liquor was mixed with meconium and the placenta, which took a long time to deliver itself, was very large and almost typically white and greasy.' This report strongly suggested syphilis and, on hearing that opinion, Humphrey rushed the dead baby up to the London Hospital for a pathological report. No trace of syphilis was found and meanwhile the placenta had been destroyed. Demented with grief, Marie wrote violent accusatory letters to the doctor in charge of the nursing home and, in turn, was threatened with legal action by the Medical Protection Society unless she apologized. She would not.

A photograph marked TO BE KEPT showed the baby on his back, dressed in white baby clothes. The inscription reads:

Henry Verdon. 12.5 a.m. 17 July 1919
died just before birth

photograph taken 12 noon same day.

Although the first child, he was delivered naturally within 7 hours of onset of labour and would have been born alive but for the interference of the doctors.[68]

7

The Turning Point

The loss of the baby marred the rest of 1919. For months Marie was overwrought, subdued by a physical weakness she had never known before. She clung to Humphrey and when she had to go into a London nursing home again, in September, for a birth repair to her womb, insisted that he too was ill, suffering from jaundice. He was admitted to a nursing home in Mandeville Place, a few doors away from her, and the lovers sent kisses through the open windows. The doctors, however, did not confirm Marie's diagnosis of jaundice and for once Humphrey asserted himself: 'I am so glad you now leave my illness to the doctors and me to settle,'[1] he wrote, and left the nursing home, his mysterious illness unexplained. He was impatient to go home to Leatherhead to supervise a move to a new house. Humphrey now hated 'Craigvara', Marie's old home, and the couple had decided to move to a larger house near by. At his best when Marie was dependent, Humphrey tried to shield her from all the worry that he could.

Unfortunately two ferocious attacks on her work coincided with her post-natal illness and distress. The *New Witness* savaged her book *Wise Parenthood*, the author and Arnold Bennett, who had written an introduction to the fifth edition:

> . . . we have decided that a thundering attack would please this most unpleasant woman almost as well as ardent support . . . The peculiar horror of her book is that it is couched in pseudo-scientific terms and is addressed to the married woman . . . Mr Arnold Bennett bears an honourable name: he can hope to bear it no longer if he does not at once disassociate himself from Dr Marie Stopes and her rubber goods. The introduction he has written is a disgrace . . .[2]

Marie felt criticism deeply and, despite the sensational success of her books, always needed reassurance. She passed the second, private, letter to Humphrey to deal with: 'Is it a desire to put bank notes into your pocket that you wrote such stuff as "Married Love"?' wrote S.J.C. of London. 'Do you really think that my wife and I . . . are sadly in need of such dirty advice as you offer? . . . You deliberately misrepresent Malthus who advised moral restraint . . . really some of the things you propose in your book might have emanated from the brain of a Kaffir woman.'[3] The author signed himself 'a lover of Shelley'.

Humphrey leapt to her defence with a gallant, if not altogether logical, argument. '. . . my wife Dr Marie Stopes has shown me your letter. I am afraid you have written without considering "Married Love" seriously because the vast majority of people have nothing but praise for her . . .'[4]

By October 1919 they had moved to, if not settled in Givons Grove, a country house with stabling and a farm in the vast grounds which bordered on Lord Beaverbrook's estate at Cherkley in Surrey. Both Marie and her mother were anxious that the couple would be living above their means, since Marie was unable to work that autumn and the nursing homes and illnesses had cost 'hundreds of pounds'. Anxious to console Marie, Humphrey waved their worries away.

The married lovers spent the New Year apart. Marie was resting at St Ann's Hotel, Buxton, while Humphrey, now discharged from the RAF, was involved in industrial relations and had meetings to attend. 'Poor little sweetheart was left alone with the rain. I wish I had been with you to cuddle you,'[5] he wrote on New Year's Eve. After the cruel year they had been through, she wished him:

> A good New Year
> A Lucky New Year
> A Happy New Year
> To You
> And me.[6]

Marie visited a Dr Cox in Buxton, to consult him about her lacklustre love life after the birth of her stillborn baby; that may well have been the reason for her stay there.

Dr Cox wrote on 26 January 1920:

Dear Dr Stopes, You must really try to take matters more easily . . . Can you tell me if there is any change in the disappointing nature of the orgasm as yet? I had hoped that it was simply a passing phase due to all the nervous worry you had so recently passed through. Have you considered about the advisability of conception again . . .[7]

In the New Year Humphrey and his 'little wife' wrote longing letters to each other when they were apart. In the face of the devastating loss of her baby, Marie's courage was nothing short of heroic. By March 1920 she was appearing on public platforms again, writing polemical articles in the press and giving advice on sex, marriage and birth control to the hordes of correspondents who sought it.

Aylmer Maude, just back from Russia, came to call on her that month and was charmed to find his hostess looking well in her 'stately home'. Maude, of course, had lodged with her in the cramped rooms in the Hampstead semi-detached and in the suburban house at Leatherhead. Marie enjoyed showing him round her spacious rooms. One was converted to a forty-foot laboratory, another – the music room with parquet flooring – was large enough to accommodate an orchestra and cabaret when Marie held a dance. In the drawing room, 'in corner cupboards fronted with trellised gold wires', Marie displayed the china and other treasures she had collected in Japan. Givons Grove now served as a useful base for entertaining and week-end house parties, dinner parties, dances and At Homes were held for colleagues, press people, politicians, publishers, anyone who might prove useful.

Aylmer Maude was greatly impressed and in his letter of thanks implied that he was as fond of her as ever. He was delighted, he said, that neither success nor prosperity had spoilt her and congratulated himself on behaving 'very nicely, in that I suppressed as far as I could any external signs of my very warm admiration for you . . .'[8] And, he remarked wistfully, that he had heard that there were good smart dances at the Piccadilly Hotel.

Dancing still appealed to Marie, but from the gracious atmosphere of Givons Grove she plunged into more pressing social concerns. During the war, the nation had been startled into awareness of venereal disease and the troops had been issued with free condoms. In the post-war years, medical and moral opinion was divided as to how to treat the 'scourge'. The National Society for the Prevention of Venereal Disease advocated providing any man at risk with a packet of condoms and self-disinfecting equipment. They were bitterly opposed by the National Council for Combating Venereal Disease, who held that the offer to make unchastity safe was 'a blow at the nation's morals'. Dr Mary Scharlieb, consultant gynaecologist at the Royal Free Hospital, prophesied that 'masturbation à deux' (contraception) would lead to degeneracy and effeminacy. She called 'for drill halls and tea-gardens to be established to divert the men's minds from drink and women'.[9] On the opposing side, Sir W. Arbuthnot Lane, Consultant Surgeon to Guy's Hospital, firmly ranged on the side of prevention, took Marie to lunch and suggested that as an expert propagandist, she should write a booklet on the prevention of VD.

She agreed and was eagerly welcomed to the crusade by the energetic Ettie Rout, Secretary of the New Zealand Volunteer Sisters. With one in five of the troops in the Army infected, soldiers were asked to sign a health pledge, promising to abstain at best, or at least to disinfect themselves immediately and seek medical help. They were also 'earnestly advised' to purchase a copy of the 1/6d. booklet *The Truth about V.D.* by Dr Marie Stopes. Her work enhanced her reputation among those doctors interested in prevention but also made her enemies. In 1920 the Federation of Medical Women warned that if condoms were made available, 'promiscuous intercourse would be looked upon as free from the risk of infection and to a great extent free from the risk of conception . . .' This would introduce a phase of society, 'as vicious and degenerate as any of which history has record . . . moral degeneration and sex excesses would rot the very foundation of society . . .'[10]

In Humphrey's copy of the booklet, Marie's dedication on 21 January 1921 read: 'With true love to the man who swore he had not got it; and so got love on the Leatherhead River Meadow. HVR MCS.'

In her fortieth year Marie was concerned not only with women's sexual and emotional lives, but also with their economic inequality in the post-war world. With thousands of demobilized men looking for work, promised by Lloyd George 'a land fit for heroes', public opinion assumed that it was natural to restore the men to their pre-war jobs and turn the women workers out. Early in 1920 the Rhondda Valley Education Authorities had sacked all their married women teachers and Marie fought a furious campaign to restore their rights. Despite her efforts the campaign failed but the publicity brought her back into the public gaze, with more requests from newspapers to write articles and more letters from the public.

Although in many of her ideas she was extremely progressive, Marie believed that progress was dependent on the class structure. She knew from personal experience that freedom for educated women depended on the servitude of their 'sisters' from the working class. 'How long would civilization as we know it today last if every woman of marriage age was married and bearing children with no domestic help? Civilization as seen today would fall to pieces . . .'[11]

When the Skilled Employment and Apprentices' Association wrote asking for her support she replied indignantly that she strongly disapproved of their aims: 'apprenticing girls to such work as the furnishing and leather trades and not training them as they should be trained in household occupations.'[12]

Marie was an élitist, an idealist, interested in creating a society in which only the best and the beautiful should survive. Brought up on the ideas of Darwin, she responded enthusiastically to the view that his theory of natural selection argued for the need to create a super breed of humans. She was in sympathy with the aims of the Eugenics Society, founded in 1908 by Darwin's cousin, Francis Galton, to encourage the prevalence of the more suitable races or strains of blood over the less suitable. Like writers of the calibre of Shaw and H. G. Wells, Marie was inspired by the simplistic notion of human perfectibility. Personally she was convinced that theories derived from research into the plant and animal kingdom could be applied to the complexities of the human situation. Her attitude to the problem was entirely academic, reinforced by her own studies into the evolution of primitive plants. The First World War had advanced the cause of the Eugenics lobby, since it had revealed widespread disease and disability among the lower classes. Marie believed passionately that if such people could be persuaded not to breed, society would benefit. She told the National Birth-Rate Commission in her evidence in 1919 that the simplest way of dealing with chronic cases of inherent disease, drunkenness or bad character would be to sterilize the parents.

To our ears, in the aftermath of Hitler, there is something bloodchilling in her fearless quest for excellence, sacrificing ordinary humanity on the altar of The Race. But at the time, the notion of suppressing weaker members of the next generation, reducing the need for institutions such as prisons and hospitals, and relieving the burden on taxpayers was immensely attractive to many members of the wealthier classes. Since wartime recruitment had drawn attention to the large numbers of physically lowgrade 'C3' people in the population, they could no longer be ignored and, rather than improve general standards of health, housing and hygiene, a preferred solution was sterilization or birth control. Marie was singular only in the zeal and lucidity with which she expressed those ideas. She even went so far as to personally hound the deaf and dumb father of four deaf children who had appealed for help to get his son admitted to the Royal School for Deaf and Dumb Children at Margate for irresponsibly 'bringing more misery into the world'.[13] But she was full of compassion for individual poor mothers who sought contraceptive advice: they were on the road to salvation.

Marie expounded her ideas on the class system in her book *Radiant Motherhood*, published in 1920 by Putnams, a larger firm than Fifield and better equipped to handle her books. She believed that 'the middle and superior artisan classes', who had to pay taxes, were reduced by circumstances into 'the position of the ancient slave and allowed to rear but one or two children as the result perhaps of a lifetime of valuable service ... while on the other hand society allows the diseased, the racially negligent, the careless, the feeble-minded, the very lowest and worst members of the community to produce innumerable tens of thousands of warped and inferior infants.'[14] In that same book she also revealed a very modern and humane approach to sex education, believing that it should start very simply and naturally in infancy.

In the two eventful years since they had met and married, Marie and Humphrey had discussed birth control, and looked for a way to work practically in that field. Tired of the delays and timidity of other birth controllers, the couple decided to open their own clinic, and by 1920 they had begun to look for suitable premises, both passionately involved. When her American 'sister in arms', Margaret Sanger, turned up in London, announcing that she had decided to open a birth control clinic there, Marie was distinctly peeved. 'Mr Roe and I have long been planning to found the first Birth Control Clinic in England as a memorial to our marriage,' she wrote icily. 'We were introduced and first met over this issue.'[15] Marie pointed out that although they had not yet found the right house, when they did they would open a birth control clinic at once.

Margaret Sanger had tried to work in her own country, actually opening a clinic in a seamy area of Brooklyn in New York in 1916. After nine days Mrs Sanger was arrested. Released on bail, she promptly reopened her clinic but was rearrested and sentenced this time to thirty days in a public workhouse for 'maintaining a public nuisance'. Since she could not work in America she had decided to transfer her plans to England. After visiting Marie and Humphrey however she agreed to abandon her plan. Since their meeting five years earlier both women had become famous. Even across the Atlantic they were potential rivals and their friendship was tested by the strain.

Despite Marie's great success (and *Wise Parenthood* too was selling thousands of copies) none of her grand plans for racial improvement was developing as she had hoped. That summer an important conference of Anglican bishops was to be held at Lambeth Palace and Marie was particularly anxious that the eminent churchmen should acknowledge the legitimacy of birth control. Hers was a strange temperament, a streak of mission and mysticism fused with her driving ambition for the limelight and luxurious living. For years she had sensed herself to be a priest or prophetess, bearing God's message and those under the spell of her personality accepted her visionary gifts.

One afternoon in late June, while sitting under the shade of a yew tree in the hills behind her home, Marie received, she claimed, a message from God: 'Say to my Bishops,' she was told. Marie got up and hurried home, sent for her secretary and re-dictated the words to him. She had the message printed privately and called it *A New Gospel to All Peoples: A revelation of God uniting physiology and the religions of man*. By July it had been sent to each of the 267 bishops present at the Lambeth Conference.

Marie's 'New Gospel' began: 'My Lords, I speak to you in the name of God. You are his priests. I am his prophet. I speak to you of the mysteries of the union of man and woman . . .' In it she refuted the teachings of Paul on the married state: '. . . if they cannot contain, let them marry: for it is better to marry than to burn.' (1 Cor. 7:9), saying with breathtaking certainty, 'Paul spoke to Christ nineteen hundred years ago. God spoke with me today.' The document proclaimed to the mainly unmarried bishops that without 'due balance of the subtle internal secretions of the sacred organs of sex neither child, nor unmated man nor woman can be whole individuals . . .' And it went on: 'No act of union fulfils the Law of God unless the two not only pulse together to the highest climax but also remain thereafter in a long brooding embrace without severance from each other . . .' Sexual union was not, Marie's 'New Gospel' asserted, as the Christian Churches had mistakenly maintained, designed solely for the purpose of creating children. God commanded that couples should use the best means of birth control 'placed at man's service by Science'. Above all, the Bishops must teach their flocks that 'the pure and holy sacrament of marriage may no longer be debased and befouled by the archaic ignorance of centuries . . .'[16]

How the bishops received this extraordinary document is not recorded. But they certainly did not act on the advice in it. Resolution 70 of the Bishops' Report of 1920 emphasized the 'grave physical, moral and spiritual perils incurred by the use of contraceptives'. Rather more pointedly they condemned 'the teaching which, under the name of science and religion encourages married people in the deliberate cultivation of sexual union as an end in itself.'[17]

Other earlier women reformers, Elizabeth Fry, Florence Nightingale, Josephine Butler, had claimed the prompting of faith, an inner voice which inspired them in their work. But none had received such an inflammatory and political message as Marie Stopes in the 'New Gospel'. The document made her bitter enemies among churchmen. The Roman Catholics in particular were deeply offended and a Father F. M. de Zulueta described the 'New Gospel' in a letter to the author as 'a most profane compound of imaginary mysticism and pornography'.[18] Her book, he went on, might serve the purpose of 'that type of young medical student who "needs a veneer of religiosity to dignify his sexual pruriency, but could only revolt anyone with a real sense of religion. . ." '.

The enmity of the Roman Catholic Church was to prove costly in the future. Neither did the book endear her to her free-thinking birth control allies. Even her friend, Dr Killick Millard, found it 'very didactic'. Two years later, when the book was published for the public, another colleague regretted that Dr Stopes, who had popularized the cause of birth control admirably, should have 'abandoned the scientific attitude and discredited herself in scientific circles by publishing a volume in which she makes the explicit announcement that she is a prophet and claims to have received a direct revelation from God . . .'[19]

Whatever Divine inspiration Marie may have had, she was not neglecting worldly means of furthering her work. In March 1920 she sent a copy of *Married Love* to Queen Mary, with an accompanying letter informing Her Majesty that the book was written 'in the interest, primarily, of your subjects, the British, but ultimately for the whole of Humanity'.[20]

The following year she favoured the Queen Mother, Queen Alexandra, with her birth control literature and told her of her desire to help 'desperately poor and ignorant mothers'. Neither the Queen nor the Queen Mother was able to accept the books. As Queen Alexandra's Private Secretary, Colonel Henry Streatfeild replied on 23 February 1921: 'It is Her Majesty's invariable rule never to allow her name to be associated with any movements which might prove to be of a controversial nature.'[21] Times changed, however, and when, a quarter of a century later, Marie sent her book to the then Princess Elizabeth and Prince Philip as a wedding gift for them to read together, the lady-in-waiting, Margaret Plymouth, replied thanking the author for the gift 'which Her Royal Highness is most pleased to accept'.[22]

The clergy and the professionals might sneer at her but through her articles in the popular press poor mothers knew her and were grateful. 'I think your work is splendid,' wrote a Mrs G.K. on 23 October 1920. 'The bishops don't have to have the children . . . they are not the people to judge whether birth control is right or wrong . . . You are doing more for humanity than all the churches. I am only a working woman myself and had two children in twenty months through ignorance.'[23]

With the Prime Minister, Lloyd George, Marie had more luck in 1920. She must have met Frances Stevenson, Lloyd George's secretary (who was also his mistress and later his wife) because she wrote directly to her, not to Lloyd George. On 30 September Marie sent Miss Stevenson a copy of her new book *Radiant Motherhood* as well as *Married Love*. In the new book she drew attention to the chapter on eugenics in which she commented on the tens of thousands of 'stunted, warped and inferior infants, who would invariably drain the resources of those with a sense of responsibility,' knowing that Lloyd George was privately sympathetic to the eugenists' arguments.[24]

> I hope so much you get Mr George to *read* the books and get him to realize that they can do an immense deal to help him to get this country fit for heroes to live in, and bring along the crop of actual heroes too.
>
> They will help him far more in real fact than a dozen Ministries will ever do.
>
> I have already a huge public you know – but I want to help still more widely. I want Mr George to know I am helping him, and to get him to help me to help him.
>
> Yours very truly
> Marie C. Stopes[25]

Marie was not exaggerating. By now her ideas were widely known, more through her newspaper articles than her books, and her face, through press photographs was beginning to be recognized. Every post brought in bundles of letters. For some time Humphrey had sent out a standard printed letter, telling correspondents that Dr Stopes could no longer answer letters personally because of the great volume of mail she received. She had been reluctant to take the step, but pressure of work was taking its toll on her health. Humphrey therefore felt obliged to take upon himself 'my duty as a husband and insist that she must give up answering these letters.'[26] Standard replies were devised to cover the more usual sexual problems and Humphrey and a secretary dealt with them. Nevertheless, Marie often wrote postscripts on the standard letters to questions that intrigued her.

Her answers to complex problems were sometimes eccentric. To a Mr G. I. of India who wanted to awaken his wife's dormant sexual instincts, Dr Stopes suggested first that he should give his wife her books and added:

> I presume that you would not wish another man to give her instruction to arouse erotic feeling in her: this, of course, apart from morals, would be the best way, but the results would otherwise be so disastrous that I expect you would not hear of it.[27]

She advised an all-round tonic and plenty of oysters. She often recommended oranges, eggs, whitebait and oysters as the best diet to promote sexual appetite.

Husbands and wives wrote for advice on sexual satisfaction, frigidity, impotence, premature ejaculation, masturbation. As she became known as a birth control expert, the majority of letters asked for advice and help on birth control and, despite her strict rule against giving abortion advice, many desperate women asked for help, which was almost invariably refused. Apart from the letters from the prurient, the majority of her correspondents were plainly relieved to be able to air the subject to an understanding 'expert'. The bulk of her replies were sensible and helpful but she was asked impossible questions: how frequent intercourse should be, the desirable duration of erection (some men manage up to two hours), the ideal age difference between the partners in marriage. Her advice frequently stemmed from her own experience (that after all was the source of her work) and sometimes reflected her state of mind.

In 1920, after the loss of her own baby, a Mrs A.F., pregnant by a man other than her husband, wrote to her for advice. Marie replied with a fine disregard of science:

> I am sure that if you are fortunate enough to be pregnant that is a very good thing and . . . you can make the baby so much what you think it is. Try and get some of your husband's photographs when he was young and look at them every day and make your baby just like him, then it will be . . .[28]

Marie learnt from her correspondents all the time and altered her books in later editions accordingly. In early editions of *Married Love* she had advised inquirers to refrain from intercourse for six months before the birth of a baby. But after her own experience of pregnancy, she felt that unions might be possibly beneficial during pregnancy. Refreshingly frank, she asked her correspondents to help by giving their age and full details of their lives as she discovered that different types of women had different needs.

She had no false modesty, and when a correspondent asked for her advice on where to find sound information about married life, she replied: 'The only sound source of sex information is my books. You should read all four.' Very few doctors were knowledgeable about sexual practice in those days and even fewer would give advice. Medical students were not taught about contraception. Marie Stopes's four books, *Married Love, Wise Parenthood, A Letter to Working Mothers* and *Radiant Motherhood*, factually flawed as they might be, were, in truth, the most useful guides to sex for the ordinary man and woman, and they created a desire for knowledge among both laity and professionals.

After *Married Love* and *Wise Parenthood* were published, Marie received a large number of letters from clergymen and their wives hoping for advice to enhance their love-making. A vicar from Newark suffered from premature ejaculation (a common complaint) and from a wife he considered prosaic:

> After the poetry of your book what actually has happened? We go to rest, my wife always lies with her back towards me, I make a 'tender advance' and suggest that she turn round so that we may chat and cuddle – the end of the poetry is 'I do not like your breath in my face!!!! . . .[29]

Many letters revealed a depth of ignorance: 'A young woman of twenty-two admitted to her fiancé that until just before her wedding last year, when her prospective husband lent her a book, she had always thought that children were secured as the result of prayers offered at the marriage ceremony,' wrote a clergyman from Derby.[30]

And a touching stoicism: 'There has been no consummation of marriage which is a byword for happiness – but my own share is not even now easy for . . . sexual life is still vigorous with me,' a thirty-nine-year-old vicar's wife wrote anonymously. '. . . my husband, affectionate and quickly moved, had so severe a training in chastity as to amount to inhibition. The doctor who knows me best is distressed at the state of affairs but though I envy women to whom the night brings more than rest I have much for which to be proud and thankful. But there are times when the false position and my husband's ignorance of the nature of my suffering are very trying . . .'[31]

Intrigued by these responses, in November 1920 Marie initiated what may well have been the first survey of sexual habits. With breath-taking nerve she sent out a questionnaire to 2,000 Church of England clergymen, chosen at random from Crockford's *Directory*, asking them about their married life, the age of husband and wife on marriage, the number of children born, the dates and intervals between births and/or miscarriages and whether any form of family limitation had been used. She listed:

a) Total abstinence
b) Safe period
c) Use of withdrawal – coitus interruptus
d) Use of quinine or other pessary
e) Use of rubber cap or occlusive pessary
f) Use of sheath
g) Other means

A number of respondents were predictably disgusted and sent back the questionnaire unanswered or with scathing comments. A few replies were prurient. It is difficult to take straight-faced the clergyman from Yorkshire who described his method of contraception as '. . . rubbing out "stuff" out of erect penis by hand – self – wife – and middle-aged cook in absence of wife'.[32]

Others used the questionnaire to air long-felt grievances: 'My husband would have considered all these suggestions absolutely criminal,' wrote a vicar's widow from Bath. 'He religiously confined himself to once-a-week unions but was quite rampant during the month of abstention during childbirth and I always thought, inclined to be "off his head" – I never felt any "orgasm" but he didn't seem to notice that.'[33]

The responses revealed that many of the clergymen knew nothing of the later forms of contraception listed. Many simply abstained for years or practised coitus interruptus. Ignorance was widespread and although the results of Marie's 'survey' were hardly scientific, her questionnaire helped to make the subject approachable.

The avalanche of work created by the response to her books left Marie little time to devote to Paleobotany, her original field of work. Since the spring of 1919, Marie had been battling to raise the status of the subject – and, coincidentally, her own – in the University of London. She wrote a detailed memorandum calling for a Department of Paleobotany to be created, attached to the existing Botanical Department, with a Professor in charge who would earn from £800 to £1000 a year, responsible both for directing and carrying out research and teaching, with a lab assistant with an Honours degree, and a lab boy to clean. This would, of course, have raised Marie's standing even further. She was already highly regarded by colleagues. Funds, however, could not be found and at the end of 1920 Marie resigned from the University. At her home in Leatherhead, she still worked in the laboratory occasionally and collaborated with Professor Wheeler.

Her literary reputation was high, her books were selling well, yet motherhood still eluded her. Now, ironically, she concentrated all her energy on the opening of a birth control clinic and the launch of her great crusade. She and Humphrey were very close at the time, for it was principally through her husband that she had found a worthwhile mission to fill her life.

For years Humphrey Roe had taken a personal interest in birth control, convinced that this was the means to solve most of society's problems. Several of his family were doctors – his father, grandfather and an uncle – and as a boy, accompanying his father on his rounds, he had come to know the back streets of Manchester and had witnessed the suffering of the poor mother, burdened with thirteen or fourteen sickly children, living in a slum. Nevertheless, the problem of birth control was a strange preoccupation for a well-to-do and eligible bachelor.

Humphrey's diary before he met Marie reveals a sympathy with the working classes:

February 16, 1914. All mill girls have tea with us.
February 17, 1914. Palace Theatre with girls.
September 1915. Overdrawn at bank.
April 16, 1916. Visit bank re overdraft, four or five thousand pounds.
Summer 1917. Nine girls from Brownsfield Mill come for a tea party at Windsor Road [Humphrey's home in Manchester]. Then we go to pictures.
October 24, 1917. Visit St Mary's Hospital [Manchester] Give the Secretary my report on birth control.[34]

These terse accounts of his activities suggest a warm-hearted, generous young man, fond of women and thoughtless about his money. In her papers, Marie copied out two entries from his diary which show her rival, Ethel Burgess, in an unfavourable light:

June 27, 1914:
Ethel out by side door.
June 27, 1914:
Ethel sleeps with another man.[35]

Perhaps Ethel became pregnant, which would have explained Humphrey's intense interest in birth control, or perhaps he himself had an entanglement with one of the mill girls, or possibly the interest was purely altruistic.

His interest in birth control was far from casual. He was not in the least concerned with status-seeking or political gain – in fact he preferred to give help anonymously. But he had thought out the requirements for a birth control clinic very carefully in 1917 before he met Marie. The arguments he summarized in favour of founding a birth control clinic were:

1) that most people would welcome it [that was questionable at the time].
2) that it would help to redress the food shortage.
3) with the housing shortage at the time (1917) it was 'almost murder' to introduce more children.
4) bringing children into the world reduced the labour force.
5) parents who were consumptive and disease-ridden could be instructed not to have children.
6) parents should space their families for the sake of their health. [The illhealth affected the woman, not both parents].[36]

Humphrey suggested that male doctors should treat male patients, female doctors the females and that the medical staff for the future clinic should visit the Netherlands where, in 1882, Dr Aletta Jacobs had opened the world's first contraceptive clinic. Dr Jacobs gave free advice to poor women, promoting a large rubber vaginal cap, or diaphragm, actually developed by Dr Mensinga, a German, but known as the 'Dutch cap' because of its widespread use in the Netherlands.

Many of the rules that Humphrey suggested to St Mary's Hospital were to be adopted in the new clinic. For example, Humphrey insisted that 'his' clinic should advise married people only and that clinic workers would have to swear on oath not, in any circumstances, to perform an abortion. That had to be made clear to the public and the police, since there was great confusion as to the difference between the two; abortion was seen as a form of birth control.

The logo of a lantern with the slogan, 'A safe light in the darkest of places', envisaged by Humphrey, was adapted by Marie to: 'Joyful and deliberate Motherhood, A Safe Light in our Racial Darkness', and she drew the logo of a lantern herself. Humphrey had even drawn up a list of furniture needed and considered the notepaper necessary for the clinic and a name too, 'The Humphrey Birth Control Clinic'. Scant tribute to Humphrey's part in the planning was ever made and, although, in the beginning, Marie usually talked of the clinic 'founded by my husband and myself', very soon his name was dropped from the enterprise and his contribution has been written out of history.

If Humphrey had drafted the scheme for opening a clinic before he met Marie, only her energy and instinctive ability to sense the mood of the public could have brought it to life. They purchased a house in an impoverished area of North London, No. 61, Marlborough Road, Holloway, sandwiched between a confectioner's and a grocer's shop, and converted the shop and rooms into a Clinic. Marie made the premises as friendly and welcoming as possible. The walls were covered with a white distemper and paint of Botticelli blue. Bright blue curtains hung in the windows and photographs of beautiful babies decorated the walls. A jar of fresh flowers stood on an old Jacobean table.

The Mother's Clinic had four aims: to help the poor (and advice was given free); to test out the attitude of the working class towards birth control, hitherto considered hostile; to obtain first-hand data about contraception in practice and to collect scientific data on the sex life of women. The Clinic was kept deliberately simple to demonstrate that birth control advice could be given to the 'poor and ignorant' in a small institution without spending large sums of money. This was necessary since Humphrey and Marie had bought the house, renovated it and equipped it themselves and would pay for the staff and upkeep. The running costs for the first year were approximately £1100. The only expense for the users would be contraceptive devices, sold at cost price.

The Clinic was opened quietly and without ceremony on 17 March 1921. Only the *Daily News, Daily Sketch* and *Daily Graphic* reported the event. Family newspapers considered the subject 'inappropriate for discussion or publicity'.[37]

Marie's original and brilliant idea was to staff the clinic with women, a qualified midwife to examine the women and make recommendations and a woman doctor attached to the Clinic as a consultant to whom any unusual or abnormal case was to be referred. She was convinced, rightly, that women would feel more comfortable with trained nurses than with male doctors, although the medical profession was hostile to a clinic run without a doctor.

Nurse Hebbes, a suffragist and the midwife in charge, had worked in the East End with mothers and babies during the war and was an ardent supporter of 'Voluntary and Joyous Motherhood'. The Clinic, the patients were told, was 'For Beauty' as well as for birth control; mothers would be considered not only as the producers of mere babies, but the creators of splendid babies. To mothers who had never been considered at all, the reception was delightful and helped to overcome their fears of the new contraptions. Nevertheless many patients were fearful and reluctant to give their names.

The Clinic was open every day, and after tactful questioning about their personal history, Nurse Hebbes made a vaginal examination, fitted the women with a pessary and showed them how to use it.

Any patients the nurse was worried about were referred to Dr Jane Lorrimer Hawthorne, the Harley Street doctor who acted as honorary medical consultant to the Clinic. Marie insisted on using a small check pessary, a high-domed rubber cervical cap that she had designed herself based on French models. She called it the 'Pro-Race' cap. She disliked the larger rubber Dutch cap, with a watch-spring rim, invented in the 1870s, because she believed it stretched the vagina. At the Mother's Clinic the Dutch cap was used only in cases of abnormality.

Although Marie's clinic was not the first in the world, as she sometimes claimed, it was the only one devoted to a scientific consideration of birth control. Records were kept and, although the publicity exaggerated the clinic's progress the records did not. Despite claims that patients poured in, during the first year a timid trickle of three women a day on average rang the bell at No. 61. It was scarcely the spectacular success Marie boasted, but it was a significant advance in the face of the prejudice that represented birth control as unnatural, unhealthy and unappetizing.

At the end of March 1921 Marie sensed another opportunity to save the country. Lloyd George had promised 'a nation fit for heroes' and a brief, spectacular post-war boom had seemed to promise a brighter future for the working man. But by the spring of 1921 Britain was sliding into depression and unemployment, with demobbed soldiers home from the war increasingly disillusioned.

The coal mines, taken into public ownership in wartime, were about to be returned to their peacetime owners and the Miners' Federation was dissatisfied with the new terms offered. They would have to accept a substantial wage cut and revert to differentials in pay, depending on the yield of the pit. The Federation refused the coal-owners' offer and the railway men and transport workers threatened to come out in sympathy.

Marie felt the matter personally. She had been going down the coal mines for years to search for her fossils. On 31 March, the last day of negotiations, she rushed up to London and went first to the Scientific Research Department of the Government. Dissatisfied with the answers to her questions, she then went straight to No. 10 Downing Street and offered her services as a mediator. From Downing Street, Marie hurried to the Miners' Federation Headquarters where she saw H. Smith, 'a huge bully', and 'the other beastly delegates just before their return north . . .'[38]

In an extraordinary note to Lloyd George, Marie observed that she had been the last person to meet the delegates after their decision to strike. She did this, she claimed, by forcibly barring the door with her bare arm, despite the threats of men with pistols in their pockets! She begged the Prime Minister not to yield to the threats of the miners' leaders but to insist on ensuring the safety of the mines. (On 1 April the Federation officially refused the coal-owners' terms, the angry miners, locked out of their pits, refused to operate safety measures, and the mines were threatened with flooding.) If Lloyd George would send 'a few wiry strong men to come with me with pistols in their pockets', Marie would lock the door of the Miners' Federation and make the miners send out notices to all the safety men to go back to work.

> I know publicly you would have to repudiate my behaviour or even know nothing about it but I'm willing to go to prison to save the mines of the country . . . Bullies are cowards and I won't hurt the creatures at all, but if they are shut in and *made to listen to me* it would only be a question of hours before they yield.[39]

It was a suggestion that even the histrionic Lloyd George could not take seriously. A polite note from Frances Stevenson in April acknowledged her offer of help: 'Mr Lloyd George is very much obliged for your suggestions in the present crisis, but he fears that it is not a practicable one and I am sure you will understand the objections to taking such a course.'[40] The following day, 15 April, the other two big unions called off their suport and the miners' hopes of defeating the capitalist system were dashed.

What is notable in this bizarre incident is Marie's frightening belief in her own powers. One might charitably consider that the tragic loss of her baby the previous year had temporarily disturbed her judgement,

1   Marie with her nurses at the Mother's Clinic, Holloway, the first Birth
     Control Centre in Britain, in the early 1920s.

2 Charlotte Carmichael Stopes, Marie's mother. Later she was to discard the frills and bustle in favour of 'rational dress'.

3 Henry Stopes, Marie's father, architect and archeologist.

4 The Stopes sisters in their rational dresses.

North London Collegiate School for Girls,

SANDALL ROAD, CAMDEN ROAD, N.W.

3rd term 1894

295

Fee for Registration of Application, Half-a-Crown.

APPLICATION FOR ADMISSION.

Christian Name, Surname, Age, and date of birth of the pupil, to be written in full.	Marie Stopes, aged 13½ born 15th October 1880
Profession or occupation of Father (if living) or Guardian.	Architect & Engineer 11 Queen Victoria Street
Has the pupil been to school before? If so, where, and how long?	Two years in Edinburgh High School for Girls 5 Melville Street.

SIGNATURE OF REFEREE.

(1.) *To the Parent or Guardian of a pupil already in the School: or*
(2.) *To a Householder.* Mrs Maxwell, Allendale, Green Lanes N.

I recommend ~~Margaret~~ Mrs Marie Stopes
for admission to the North London Collegiate School for Girls.

× *Signature in full* Margaret Maxwell

Address Allendale
Green Lanes
N

I hereby agree that if my daughter be admitted to the School, I will abide by all the regulations, made or to be made, for the government of the School, or in regard to its Scholarships, Prizes, or other Endowments.

Signature in full of Father (if living) or Guardian Henry Stopes
Date 28th July 1894
Address Mansion House Swanscombe
Greenhithe. N.

5   In October 1894 Marie enrolled in North London Collegiate, a prominent and progressive school for girls.

6   Clothilde Von Wyss, pupil–teacher at North London Collegiate.

7   On a field trip from London University,
    c. 1902–3.

8   Marie studied in Munich from 1903–4,
    where she gradually grew aware of her
    femininity.

9 In her laboratory. In 1904 Marie became the only woman lecturer in botany at Manchester University.

10 Professor Fujii in Munich, 1904.

11 Reginald Ruggles Gates, Marie's first husband.

12 Aylmer Maude.

13   Marie and Humphrey Roe at their wedding, 19 June 1918.

14   The National Birth Rate Commission's deputation to the Home Office, 1919. Marie (in white wings) with her friend the Bishop of Birmingham, president of the commission (with top hat).

15 Humphrey and Marie gardening at their home in Leatherhead. It was quite uncharacteristic for Humphrey to be giving the orders.

16 An adoring mother, holding three-month-old Harry, June 1924.

17 The ideal family, Marie holding Wuffles, Humphrey cuddling little Harry.

18 October 1939 at Norbury Park. Left to right: Keith Briant, Marie Stopes, Humphrey Roe, Lord Alfred Douglas.

19 Off Portland Island with Avro Manhattan in 1957. He had just rescued Marie from being swept away by a strong tidal wave.

and yet in August 1914 she had written to Aylmer Maude in similar terms: ('I shall come to you at once, dear, if you get too worried and depressed or if London is in danger.') During the war itself, she seldom referred to the suffering of the troops or the huge casualties, and it never crossed her mind to volunteer for service overseas. Marie was inspired when a leader was needed, when she could step in to head a campaign. Without her urgent day-dreams, she might never have headed a great movement.

She decided to hold a public meeting about birth control at the Queen's Hall and planned her campaign with consummate skill. A galaxy of famous people had already agreed to become patrons of the movement, among them Arnold Bennett, Dame Clara Butt the singer, J. R. Clynes, MP and Lady Constance Lytton. Marie always claimed that Lloyd George had advised her to 'make birth control respectable' and helped behind the scenes to make her great Queen's Hall Meeting a success. He would, after all, have every reason to be interested in the subject. Frances Stevenson accepted an invitation to sit on the platform, although she declined the invitation to dinner at the Ritz beforehand: 'I fear it will not be possible for me to join you at the dinner, as it is difficult for me to get away from the office so early . . .'[41] She also mentioned a Mr Sawyer in her letter, who had apparently been helpful to Marie, possibly a politico from the Prime Minister's office.

The organization was superb. The hall was booked for 31 May 1921. Keith Prowse sold tickets all over London and sandwich men paraded up and down in front of theatre queues with bills advertising the meeting. Tickets were priced at five shillings and half-a-crown, but welfare workers, midwives, health visitors and nurses were offered free seats. Over 2,000 people packed the hall; some were standing at the back; and for half-an-hour before the speakers arrived, Dr Bromley Derry, the organist of the Chapel Royal, gave a warm-up recital.

Promptly at 8.30 p.m. Marie entered, dressed in a short, *décolleté* evening dress of white muslin, to sit in the centre of the platform among the potted palms. The first speaker, G. H. Roberts, MP, a former Minister of Labour and Chairman of the Meeting, stressed the unfairness of a society in which 'women of the well-to-do classes have the benefit of knowledge of birth control' while 'the class to which I belong, grovelling in their ignorance, are still producing in excessive numbers and producing a race which is not fitted for the Empire which we have to govern'.[42]

Two doctors followed, first Dr Jane Hawthorne, consultant gynaecologist to the new Clinic, who described one or two of her cases:

> . . . one woman who has had fifteen children, five of whom are living . . . said she was afraid that she was going to be a mother of another . . . I asked if her husband was not anxious to help her in any way. She looked rather surprised and all she said was: 'When I tell him there is another baby coming, he kicks me downstairs.'[43]

Dr Killick Millard, the Medical Officer of Health for Leicester for twenty years, confirmed his experience of the need for birth control: 'The whole welfare of humanity may be said, without exaggeration, to be bound up with it,' he stated, and welcomed the patriotic action of Dr Marie Stopes and Mr Roe in starting the Clinic. Representing the Navy, Admiral Sir Percy Scott, KCB maintained the patriotic note: 'We only want A1 men for the Navy, not wastrels.'[44]

Among all the dignitaries, Humphrey had only his title as Councillor (he served on the local council in Leatherhead). His own conversion to birth control, he explained, had come through seeing the slums of Manchester, while Marie had been drawn to the cause through her scientific work. Today, the workers were rebelling against the misery in their homes and it was a case of birth control or Bolshevism. 'At last,' he said, 'our dreams and hopes have materialized in our simple little clinic in Holloway.'[45]

Looking fragile and feminine Marie stood up to speak to tremendous applause. She had allocated each speaker ten minutes but permitted herself unlimited time. She spoke superbly, in a mellifluous voice, deliberately keeping control of herself and the audience in a speech of rising emotion. She emphasized the positive element in birth control, the help for the childless wife who longed for a baby. 'Let it be made clear that by birth control I mean not merely the repression of lives which ought not to have been started but the bringing into the world of healthy, happy, desired babies.' At the climax of her speech, her voice stronger, Marie demonstrated what an eloquent propagandist she was:

> . . . the evolution of mankind in the past has been blind and blundering: our race has been recruited by accident, by chance, by misery, by crime; but from today we who are here may go forth as missionaries . . . who will make a feasible and possible thing, this great era of humanity.

She envisaged an era in which the race would be recruited only when love and knowledge combined for the conception, when men and women:

> ... will bring forth an entirely new type of human creature, stepping into a future so beautiful, so full of the real joy of self-expression and understanding that we here today may look upon our grandchildren and think only that the gods have descended to walk upon the earth.[46]

Thunderous applause greeted her as she sat down, and a bouquet of lilies-of-the-valley was presented to the bride of birth control.

Charlotte sat in the front row, proud and pleased at her daughter's success, yet unable to withhold a note of criticism from her congratulatory letter: 'Thank the Lord your meeting has passed over satisfactorily. You looked very pretty although your scarf was rather illusory.'[47] 'The audience', wrote Mrs Zangwill, 'looked the same as at a Shaw play, a Chaucer lecture or any progressive, little-known society ... the women were largely of the Hampstead type, sallow and soulful and badly gowned!'[48]

Despite Marie's forceful campaign and the articles submitted by her journalist women friends, press coverage of the undoubtedly impressive meeting was disappointing. Birth control was far from respectable in the England of 1921 and Marie and her supporters came in for criticism and derision. Aylmer Maude, whose name was on the list of Marie's supporters, received a warning letter from Mrs Humbert Barclay, the Central President of the Mother's Union. Did he realize the grave danger of the teaching and practices advocated by Dr Stopes? she asked. Such teaching, she feared 'must ultimately lower the moral tone of the whole nation'.[49] Even in Hampstead, Marie's work was not universally admired. The Medical Officer of Health, Dr Mary Kidd, wrote to Nurse Hebbes at the Clinic, strongly objecting to requests to her Health Visitors and nurses to send patients along. 'I entirely and utterly disapprove of Dr Marie Stopes' action in setting up this Clinic both as a doctor and as a woman and a Christian ...'[50]

Critical letters also began to appear in the Catholic journal, the *Universe*, condemning Dr Stopes, signed by Catholic professional women. Nurse Hebbes was warned that spies might try to ferret out information at the Clinic. She should answer 'little or nothing to anyone you suspect of being R.C.' Marie wrote,[51] and should refer them either to Marie herself or to Dr Hawthorne.

By now, she did occasionally offer medical advice through her midwife. For a mother who had undergone several abortions and become pregnant, anxious this time to keep the child, Marie recommended her to stay in bed for two or three days around the period, take Chloride of Potash lozenges, and purchase *Radiant Motherhood*.

Through the post that poured in Marie had become increasingly aware of the reality of suffering. Sometimes she received as many as a thousand letters a week. She had to employ four secretaries but still added a postscript or a personal message to a particularly moving appeal. A tubercular ex-nurse of thirty-seven with four children and an out-of-work husband, asked for her help:

> I am so afraid of conception that I cannot bear for my husband to even speak kindly to me or put his hand on my shoulder for fear he wants his rights and it causes a lot of anger and misery. It is two months since I allowed him intercourse . . .[52]

Marie sent her names of helpful welfare workers in the district, pessaries at cost price, and her *Letter for Working Mothers* at a few pence, which she had published at her own expense.

In July Marie and Humphrey escaped for some weeks to her beloved Cornwall, staying at Great Lizzen, near Polperro, and carving themselves a house out of the rocks in a tiny bay with glorious views of the Lizard and Land's End. She was cutting a staircase down the steepest slope, so that her mother, who had shared in her triumph, could come to stay: 'we can cook a chop and cocoa and give you strawberry jam, so it will be all very comfie.'[53] Both she and Humphrey were 'utterly happy' and for once she was prepared to give up the Annual Meeting of the British Association. While the couple were so blissfully on holiday, the enemies of Marie Stopes were preparing an onslaught.

8

Conflict

As the founder of a Birth Control Clinic, Marie now possessed new authority as a social reformer: 'Dr Marie Stopes and her husband Mr Roe have rendered a real service to the community,' wrote Harold Cox, the economist in the *Woman's Leader*. 'This is a practical piece of work that is worth a million speeches about a new world.'[1] He was one of the few to mention Humphrey Roe in describing the new Clinic. And Marie soon made it her own.

Writing in the same paper, she expounded her strikingly modern views on the place of birth control in the fight for the Women's cause:

> Great though women's political freedom is and well worth the struggle which all thoughtful women have been waging to win it, it is less to each individual than her personal and bodily freedom; and without control over her own motherhood, no married woman can have bodily freedom . . . To me, steeped in a realization of the unspeakable agonies of myriads since the world began who have been deprived of this elementary power . . . it seems incredible that there should be still any left to argue against giving the mother her due place as guardian of The Race.[2]

For educated and moderately well-to-do women to obtain the necessary knowledge was easy enough, she argued. They could either consult their own doctors or gain the information through *Wise Parenthood*, Marie's book. Although, she added, she had heard that some of her middle-class readers had been advised by their doctors that birth control could be harmful. Poor women, however, were still at the mercy of ignorance and prejudice.

Marie Stopes openly defied the medical profession by appealing to all those women who had been fobbed off to write to her direct, giving the precise reasons for their medical advisers' objections. She would fight their battles. 'I may say that so far, in every case which I have followed up, I have found simple ignorance on the part of the medical practitioner.' Marie offered to debate the subject with any competent medical practitioner and to supply addresses of qualified and suitable doctors to any woman wanting help.

For a lay person, and a woman, to denounce the august medical profession openly and make public her own favourites among them was gloriously rash. Her self-assertion did not go unnoticed. Though she had rightly assumed that editorially, the *Woman's Leader* would be sympathetic to her cause, not all the readers were supportive. In July 1921, Edith Eskrigge of the Liverpool Women's Christian Association wrote expressing regret on behalf of her committee for the 'undue prominence' given to the subject of birth control. Dr Marie Stopes's views had been given 'more prominence than opposition'. More predictably, Isobel Willis of the Catholic Women's Suffrage Society, also expressed misgivings at finding advertisements for Dr Marie Stopes's Clinic and the Malthusian League in the *Woman's Leader*. They were 'assisting in the spread of their immoral doctrines'. From Aylmer Maude, Marie heard of petitions circulating for Catholic women to sign. Most significantly, the medical profession fought back in an attack which contained a strong sectarian element.

At a meeting of the Medico-Legal Society in Chandos Street on 7 July, Anne Louise McIlroy, a Professor of Obstetrics and Gynaecology at the Royal Free Hospital, told a distinguished audience that the consequences of married life should be left in Divine hands. In the debate that followed, the views of the 'don't muck about with nature' school were represented by Dr Bernard O'Connor, who regarded those who killed germs (his euphemism for sperms) as no better than those who murdered children, while Earl Russell, the second earl (from whom Bertrand Russell, the philosopher, later inherited the title), argued against the indiscriminate breeding of children who would one day become cannon fodder. George Bernard Shaw, too, supported the birth control lobby, but less enthusiastically. In the audience, listening intently, was Dr Halliday Gibson Sutherland, a recent convert to the Roman Catholic Church. A thirty-nine-year-old physician who had specialized in the treatment of tuberculosis, Dr Sutherland argued that the poor woman with a large family of children in his own practice was, in a sense, more fortunate than 'the Society woman who is losing her looks and her excitement and who has not got the natural happiness that comes from the child.'[3]

Summing up, Professor McIlroy spoke of the joy of Irish peasants with large families. She referred briefly to the medical effects of using contraceptives, admitting to knowing nothing of the damaging effects of quinine, but she did say that 'the most harmful method of which I have had experience is the use of the pessary'. At Marie Stopes's Clinic, the small, rubber, check pessary was the method most commonly recommended. It would seem that Professor McIlroy intended her paper to discredit Marie's Clinic, as it turned out later that the Professor had never treated a woman who had worn one of the check pessaries she condemned. Her damning words did not go unremarked. Dr Sutherland was deeply hostile to birth control and mentioned the debate to his Catholic priest, who first asked Dr Sutherland to write an article for the Jesuit magazine, the *Month*, on the subject. When the article was written, the priest, Father Keating, S.J. suggested that Halliday Sutherland should expand his article into a book. On holiday in Invernesshire, Halliday Sutherland began to write his book, *Birth Control*.

'I want you to notice . . . the brilliance of our list of Patrons,' Marie boasted in a letter to Margaret Sanger.[4] 'They are all names of worldwide significance and a great triumph for the cause in this country. They all responded to my personal invitation . . .'

In August, when she held an inaugural meeting for the support organization, The Society for Constructive Birth Control, Marie was appointed President. H. G. Wells was one of the Vice-Presidents and Humphrey was the Secretary. Determined to prove that she was not a crank, Marie emphasized that her Society was promoting healthy children as well as preventing the unhealthy and adopted the motto: 'Babies in the right place'.

While camping in Cornwall the previous month Marie had received an invitation to visit America to speak to Mrs Dennett's Voluntary Parenthood League in New York. She agreed, provided that a number of stringent requirements were met. First, she asked for 'the biggest and best reputationed hall or theatre in New York' which was easy to speak in acoustically. Second, she wanted a big press campaign. Third, she required to be taken care of, 'for I'm fragile'. A strong man must be found, she insisted, to meet her, carry her grips, see her through the Customs. Finally, she demanded a nice hostess in a good private house right in the heart of things . . . where she could be 'safe and comfy'. The only exception she would make to 'racketing about': 'I might go to the White House in Washington if you can fix up an invitation for the President to give me a private chat . . .'[5] Humphrey was always on hand to puff up her self-importance. He fussed over her, arranged bookings and on board ship, made sure that she had a seat at the Captain's table.

Marie sailed for New York on 15 October 1921, her forty-first birthday, aboard the *Aquitania* and arrived in New York ten days later, to discover that Margaret Sanger, who had organized her own American Birth Control League, was furious at what she considered Marie's disloyalty in speaking to a rival organization and was 'too busy' to see her.

The Voluntary Parenthood League, formed to change the law, disapproved of Mrs Sanger, who had been gaoled for breaking the law by opening a clinic in 1916.

Marie reminded Margaret Sanger that it was she who had organized a protest to President Wilson, imploring him to drop criminal charges against Margaret in 1915, while Margaret Sanger reminded Marie, in reply, that she had 'borne the brunt of insults from publishers because I tried to get "Married Love" published'. Margaret Sanger had, it is true, taken the manuscript to America and after great difficulty found a publisher, a Dr W. J. Robinson of The Critic and Guide Co., to accept it. For Marie the arrangement had never been satisfactory. To her disgust, Robinson had insisted on editing and toning down her manuscript, which was still declared 'obscene' by the Court of Special Sessions in New York in 1921. She did not succeed in getting American royalties for the book until she changed publishers.

The quarrel between the two great pioneers of birth control was never fully healed and the lack of co-operation was to prove damaging to Marie. The stress of the situation made her long for home: 'I'm getting starved for love and want of you – I wonder if you feel the same?' she wrote to Humphrey. 'I don't want ever to be in a city again – not ever – I'd like to be a private person and only love you and the flowers and a babykins and the squirrels and not to be mixed up in all these horrid, horrid businesses with Sangers and Drysdales.'[6] (The Drysdales, Neo-Malthusians, were advocates of birth control in England and close friends of Margaret Sanger.) 'Well, I'm not cut out for public life and I shall retire into private life on my return and not budge again. I can't bear being so disillusioned about people . . .'

Within three days Marie's appetite for applause was revived by the audience of over 1,000 people who packed the newly-opened Town Hall in New York to hear her speak on the evening of 27 October. Marie charmed and thrilled the American audience as she had charmed the English, although she inveighed against their barbaric laws on obscenity and volunteered to rewrite the Declaration of Independence to include

the right to control their unborn children 'in the interests of the Race'.
Immediately it was over, Marie wrote to Humphrey to tell him of her
success: 'Yes, sweetheart, a real success. I got quite five times more and
more intense clapping than either the chairman or the other speakers . . .
and they clapped and clapped and clapped till it rang when I got up to
speak.'[7] Nevertheless, she was glad to get away from New York with
its breakfasts of 'cold prunes and beastly white maize' to the civilization
of bacon and eggs.

On board the SS *Cedric* Marie, whose name was spelt as 'Mrs Stokes'
on the passenger list, was 'spotted' by a young man. His name was Noël
Coward and Marie found him an intelligent and charming conversation-
alist. 'He is a dear, a dramatist, full of youth and enthusiasm and yet
sanity . . . He told the people at my table . . . that I am one of the
greatest living intellects which made them sit up . . . [8] The next day she
wrote about the twenty-one-year-old Noël Coward again.

'I have read two of the plays of this interesting young author-actor;
one very good and one very bad. I told him it was putrid and he took
it ever so nicely . . . He is both interesting and sound and young. In
this ghastly, down-trodden, middle-aged-ruled world it is good to get
a young live power who cares about drama exactly as we do and
more. I'm sure you will like him . . .'[9]

For his part, Noël Coward found Dr Marie Stopes 'of definite interest . . .
She had appropriately, the eyes of a fanatic but the rest of her was
dim, excepting her conversation. This was surprisingly vivid and almost
exclusively concerned with the theatre. Naturally this was a comfort to
me and we discussed plays for hours in a small rustic tea-room aft of
the promenade deck.'[10]

Marie kept in touch with Noël Coward for years and plied him with
invitations, including offers to collaborate with him in writing plays.
He always declined. He did, however, dash off some verses on board
ship:

> If through a mist of awful fears
> Your mind in anguish gropes
> Dry up your panic-stricken tears
> And fly to Marie Stopes
>
> And if perhaps you fail all round
> And lie among your shattered hopes

> Just raise your body from the ground
> And *crawl* to Marie Stopes.
>
> If you have missed life's shining goal
> And mixed with sex perverts and Dopes
> For normal soap to cleanse your soul
> Apply to Marie Stopes.[11]

At the time, she felt the meeting with Noël Coward was providential; he was, she gushed to Humphrey, 'sent to re-open my interest in my dear old love, the drama'. She would invite him home to Leatherhead and he would be able to put on her plays.

Back home in England Marie was caught up almost immediately in less agreeable business. A new book *Wise Wedlock* by a Dr 'Courtenay Beale' plagiarized Marie's *Married Love* so blatantly, and offered advice by correspondence, that she wasted a good deal of time trying to trace the pseudonymous author only to discover that no 'Courtenay Beale' appeared on the Medical Register. She suspected that the pseudonym concealed a syndicate but could prove nothing.

Emulation from another quarter worried her even more. Since 1913 Dr Drysdale of the Malthusian League had advocated that birth control clinics should be opened. Lack of funds and a timid fear of opposition from the clergy, the medical profession and the poor themselves held the League back. Dr Drysdale, now the President, whose parents, both doctors, had been pioneers of birth control, was stung into action by Marie's 'takeover' of the birth control movement.

Open-air meetings were held in the Old Kent Road during the summer, to noisy barracking. Women brave enough to ask for help were referred to a gynaecologist who had a tiny room locally. Just as Marie landed back in England, the Malthusian League opened a clinic at 153a East Street, Walworth, behind the Elephant and Castle. Staff, volunteers and patients had to face rowdy protest at the euphemistically named Walworth Women's Welfare Centre in the early days. Rotten eggs, apples and stones were thrown, windows smashed, the clinic doors battered and graffiti ('whores') scrawled on the walls. But inside the centre, which was open two afternoons a week, all women were seen by a gynaecologist. Thanks to Marie's genius no such odium attached to her Mother's Clinic, although occasionally, the police were called in to defend the Mother's Clinic against the threat of violence.

By now Marie Stopes felt that hers was the only legitimate voice in birth control. She wanted to stamp the movement with her image and disliked rowdy methods and references to the trials and imprisonment of early reformers. Her aim was to persuade the local authorities to allow advice on birth control to be given at existing maternity welfare centres, modelled on her Mother's Clinic. To found more voluntary clinics seemed superfluous to her. Marie resigned from the Malthusian League that autumn and regarded Malthusians as potentially dangerous rivals.

However, the real danger lay in the growing opposition of the Roman Catholic Church. That year the Catholic Truth Society began to publish a series of pamphlets denouncing birth control. In the *Catholic Times* of 17 December 1921, Father Vincent McNabb described the literature of Marie's Society as 'almost incredibly obscene'. Criticism still wounded her pride and she discussed the question of litigation with her friends and solicitors. In April 1922 the Editor of *John Bull* launched a two-page broadside at Marie Stopes entitled 'The Bunkum of Birth Control.' Lord Dawson of Penn, the King's physician, had spoken up for birth control at the 1921 Church Congress the previous October, and the sanctimonious *John Bull* professed the greatest respect for his views. The Malthusians too, escaped rather lightly but it was Marie 'the high priestess' of birth control who came in for the lash of *John Bull*'s lascivious indignation. The article in *John Bull* is worth quoting at length since the journal reflected so much of the contemporary humbug and hypocrisy it purported to attack:

in the sacred and austere name of Science, Dr Stopes has unloaded on to the market a series of books – 'Married Love', 'Wise Parenthood', 'Radiant Motherhood', and the like – which contain the frankest and most intimate discussion of sexual matters that has ever been permitted in this country. I write not as a prude or a puritan, but as a man of the world with a fairly easy tolerance in matters of this kind . . . The whole tendency of this raging, tearing propaganda . . . is profoundly mischievous. Its sole practical effect, as far as I am able to judge, is to impart a knowledge of 'birth control' methods to people who ought to have no use for them . . . and while I cannot possibly gauge the feelings of this gifted author as she sees her scientific works paraded for sale in the company of pornographic French novels and other accessories of vice, I should be wanting in candour if I did not point out the plain moral implications of these things.[12]

By the time *John Bull* appeared, Marie had already read Dr Halliday Gibson Sutherland's book *Birth Control*. Since it was written by a

Roman Catholic doctor, bitterly opposed to birth control, it was potentially more damaging than a newspaper article. Sutherland admitted himself that the book was intended to be controversial. The tone was provocative:

> During the decline of the Roman Empire, men gorged themselves with food, took an emetic, vomited and then sat down to eat again. They satisfied their appetite and frustrated the object of which the appetite is intended. The practice of birth control is parallel with this piggishness.

Marie read with horror that, according to Dr Sutherland, she was among those perverting the ordinary decent instincts of the lower classes and 'exposing the poor to experiment'. But the passage that convinced her that she must challenge Halliday Sutherland was a snide reference to Marie, her work and her Clinic:

> In the midst of a London slum a woman [Dr Stopes] who is a Doctor of German Philosophy (Munich) has opened a birth control clinic where working women are instructed in a method of contraception described by Professor McIlroy as 'the most harmful method of which I have had experience'. It is truly amazing that this monstrous campaign of birth control should be tolerated by the Home Secretary. Charles Bradlaugh was condemned to jail for a less serious crime.[13]

Charles Bradlaugh, a powerful and pugnacious lecturer and pamphleteer in the nineteenth century, was prosecuted with his associate, Mrs Annie Besant, in a notorious trial in 1877. The two had formed the Freethought Publishing Company and had published *Fruits of Philosophy*, a tract on birth control deemed to be obscene. They were sentenced to six months imprisonment and fined £200 but an appeal was allowed and Bradlaugh and Besant republished the offending pamphlet. By coupling Marie Stopes's name with Charles Bradlaugh, Halliday Sutherland had attempted to criminalize her by association and by mentioning her Munich degree he played on the post-war mistrust of foreigners and of Germans in particular. She was seething with anger and wanted to sue Halliday Sutherland immediately. Her medical friends and her solicitor urged caution and, initially, Humphrey wrote to Halliday Sutherland challenging him to a debate. A month later, when no reply was received, a writ for libel was issued against Dr Sutherland and his publishers, Messrs Harding and More.

Marie's Society for Constructive Birth Control was a useful forum for keeping her supporters in touch with her work; she held monthly social events and liked to strike a chatty, informal note with fellow members. At a nine-course dinner held in the Hotel Cecil in May 1922, the month she issued the writ for libel, Marie served up an unexpected tenth course: the first issue of her newspaper *Birth Control News* (sub-titled, oddly, 'The Statesman Newspaper'). The journal, written and edited almost entirely by Marie herself, emphasized the 'constructive' aspects of birth control and separated itself 'explicitly and emphatically from the many cranks with whom the public may confuse us'.[14] Marie wrote a swingeing review of Dr Sutherland's book in her first issue:

> Dr Sutherland's book will impose only on those who are more ignor-
> ant than he is. It is nicely calculated to encourage the biased in their
> prejudice, for now when speaking against birth control they can say:
> A Doctor says so. They will probably forget that he is a Roman
> Catholic Doctor . . . The omissions from the book are quite as remark-
> able as its lies . . .[15]

The review was an opening shot in the battle to come.

Nine months elapsed before the case was heard and in that time Marie and Humphrey were inseparable. Humphrey was involved in the running of both the Clinic and the Society for Constructive Birth Control. Marie had marked him down in her speakers' notes as being particularly sympathetic in handling workers and Humphrey spoke to clubs and trade associations up and down the country about their new Clinic. When she spoke, she preferred to have her husband at her side. The Hardwick Society invited her to second the motion: 'The Victorian Age has been discredited.' Marie agreed but in a curiously Victorian gesture asked for an extra ticket for her husband: 'for I do not go about without him.'[16]

When Marie felt insecure she could transform into a clinging little wife without realizing the contradictions in her behaviour.

They both enjoyed entertaining and in Givons Grove they could play host in style. In the spring of 1922 guests were invited to view the primroses and daffodils in the grounds, or dance to an orchestra in the music room if it was wet. A private bus was provided to ferry the garden party visitors from Leatherhead Station. There were hints that year, however, that Marie was tiring of public life. In the autumn a Doctor Hance from the Indian Medical Service wrote to her, asking whether he could send a friend of his along for a private consultation. Marie wrote back irritated, pointing out that she was not a doctor of medicine but of science: 'I have been inundated by cases seeking my personal help and advice, but I am *not* and do not desire to be a professional consultant. Without doubt I could make a future should I choose to do so. I have devoted four years of my life and pay four secretaries to answer letters from people who do not send even a stamped addressed envelope!' Marie added that she had founded a clinic and helped thousands of people but the burden was growing intolerable; 'I am a young married woman of the social class who would naturally be enjoying herself and doing nothing at all . . .' Curiosity and professional pride caused her to add: 'I am incurably scientific in my attitude and if there is any new problem or case that completely baffles the doctors, I devote my time to it . . . but without any fee.'[17]

Whether Marie really believed that she would enjoy living the life of a moneyed hostess seems doubtful, and she was equally unrealistic in describing herself as a young married woman. By the standards of her time, and even today, a woman of forty-two can scarcely be described as a 'young married'. She and Humphrey desperately wanted a child. Alone and at leisure she indulged in a little weep for 'babykins', her stillborn child and hoped 'he would send a little brother'. The friendly gynaecologist she had consulted wrote from abroad with concern:

> Is he [Humphrey] in any degree more vigorous? There are cases in which the special function of which you wrote to me becomes feeble at a much younger age than normal. I would like very much to learn that the strong wish of you both to possess a healthy infant should be gratified, for your child ought to be normal in every developmental way and to have a fine brain. It would be well if the entrance of the seminal fluid to the vagina could be managed and if you have little or no excitement, you might arrange to bring that about and possibly the spermatozoa might find their way to the uterus . . . H. should not be too anxious about his condition and should not try too often, but when anything is attempted, he and you should do all possible to arouse him thoroughly . . .[18]

Married Love, even at the second attempt, seemed as elusive as ever. Fortunately Marie had great challenges ahead which would tax even her effervescent vitality. In the country generally in the early 1920s a trade depression, unemployment and strikes led to a period of disillusion and the Conservatives withdrew their support from Lloyd George's Coalition Government, causing an election. Marie once said that she was 'naturally a Conservative' but in the cause of birth control was ready to support any candidate who would back her crusade. In November 1922, before the election, she sent out a questionnaire to parliamentary candidates asking them to sign a rather curiously worded declaration:

> I agree that the present position of breeding chiefly from the C_3 population and burdening and discouraging the A_1 is nationally deplorable, and if I am elected to Parliament I will press the Ministry of Health to give such scientific information through the Ante-natal Clinics, Welfare Centres and other institutions in its control as will curtail the C_3 and increase the A_1.[19]

She received 150 replies, the majority from Labour candidates. By no means all of them approved of the 'selective breeding' she proposed; many preferred to put their faith in economic and social reforms and Marie failed to make birth control an election issue.

Politics on a local level took up her attention in December when Nurse E. S. Daniels, a Health Visitor employed by Edmonton District Council, was dismissed from her post for giving birth control advice at maternity centres. She had undertaken not to provide such information but 'the tragedy of the poor mothers she visited' had proved too much for her and she referred many of the women to Marie's Clinic. She naturally appealed to Marie for support and also to the New Generation League (formerly the Malthusians) of which she was a member. Marie temporized, sympathetic but cautious, while the New Generation League rallied to Miss Daniels's side with a large protest meeting where Mr F. A. Broad, the Labour MP for Edmonton, had his call for public clinics for instruction in birth control overwhelmingly endorsed. Five hundred women signed a petition demanding Nurse Daniels's reinstatement. The publicity of the case provoked the Ministry of Health to rule that birth control information should not be given at maternity centres. This annoyed Marie, who withdrew her support on the legalistic grounds that Nurse Daniels had ignored the orders of a doctor and transgressed against the professional code. Perhaps, with her impending libel case, she balked at further clashes with authority.

That winter, her mother, now over eighty, was still writing on Shakespeare and getting her books published and her literary contacts were occasionally useful to Marie. In December she asked Charlotte to meet her at the British Museum: 'I want you to introduce me to Mr Pollard [of the Museum] as I want to see the shelf of sex books shut away from the general public and not in the catalogue.'[20] She and Humphrey spent Christmas at Worthing, where Humphrey read novels to his wife to amuse her.

In January 1923, a month before her own lawsuit, Marie was put to the test again. Guy Aldred and his wife, Rose Witcop, both Communists, were prosecuted at West London Police Court for selling Margaret Sanger's pamphlet *Family Limitation*. The magistrate found the publication obscene and ordered copies to be destroyed. Marie spent the day in court, anxiously awaiting the outcome and was relieved to hear from the bench that the prosecution was not directed at the birth control movement as a whole but only at that particular pamphlet. She was desperately anxious to ensure that her work should be regarded as respectable, and when Bertrand Russell, a Vice-President of Marie's Society, asked her for help in organizing the Aldred's appeal she refused. She detested the 'Bolsheviks' and had always disliked the suggestion in the Sanger pamphlet that abortion was occasionally justifiable (although she herself had once or twice sent a woman to a doctor when she felt the case was urgent). Perhaps to distance herself from the American propaganda she wrote privately to the Director of Public Prosecutions, condemning Sanger's pamphlet as 'prurient' and the diagrams in it as obscene.

Her refusal to help lost her important friends in the birth control lobby. Bertrand Russell, who less than a year earlier had pronounced himself 'very proud' to be a Vice-President of the Society for Constructive Birth Control, now resigned. He and others felt strongly that those who believed in birth control should stand together. Marie, by contrast, had convinced herself that she alone should head the battle to save the race. Communists, anarchists, those earlier pioneers who had challenged the existing laws, were all bad for the cause. She saw herself as the spotless saviour, the only one who could persuade public opinion.

The case of the Aldreds attracted the support of the Labour Party and of working-class groups, and drew attention to the need for information on the subject. The medical profession was still lamentably ignorant about birth control. 'The doctor is not familiar with the scientific aspects of contraception and there is no easily accessible literature,' the *Lancet* commented in 1921;[21] medical students were still not educated in birth control methods. Marie herself had sent out questionnaires to doctors in the autumn of 1922 and the 128 answers that came back reflected the deep division in the profession, and the need for her work. The replies varied from the surgeon in Stockport who told her that her writings were 'more in the interests of pornography than science,' to the London doctor who wrote: 'you are undoubtedly doing a public service. I have read your books and entirely agree with them.'[22] Professional medical opinion at that time was based, like the public's, largely on hearsay, personal bias and ignorance.

The case of Stopes *v.* Sutherland opened in the High Court before the Lord Chief Justice of England, Lord Hewart, and a jury of twelve on 21 February 1923. There were no legal restrictions against the practice of birth control so the case for birth control, which was, of course, at the root of the trial, rested on the views of moralists and medical men. Since the Plaintiff (Marie) and the Defendant (Dr Halliday Gibson Sutherland) invited equally eminent members of the medical profession with opposing views to testify, the outcome depended largely on the summing up by the Judge. Marie's solicitors had briefed Mr Patrick Hastings (later, Sir Patrick), the famous KC, with Sir Hugh Fraser and Mr Herbert Metcalfe. Counsel for the Defence was Mr Ernest Charles, KC, and Sergeant Sullivan acted for the publishers, Harding and More.

Many of the distinguished colleagues who supported Marie's work and testified on her behalf had misgivings. Sir William Arbuthnot Lane, consultant surgeon at Guy's Hospital, warned her in three separate letters against the 'uncertain luxury' of a lawsuit: 'If I had been as sensitive as you are to criticism I should have spent much of my life in the law courts . . . you and your work are too big to mind paltry criticism.'[23] That, unfortunately, was untrue. Marie could not bear even a hint of criticism. Nevertheless, Sir William and other distinguished supporters of Dr Stopes and her work came forward to testify.

The trial attracted enormous publicity. For over four years, Marie and her publishers had mounted a massive advertising campaign for her books and her birth control clinic. Through billboard advertisements, placards on the omnibuses, even leaflets on theatre seats, the name of Marie Stopes aroused and titillated public curiosity. Most notoriously in the sleazy 'rubber shops' in Charing Cross Road, in which medical appliances, pornographic novels and pills of dubious efficacy jostled for attention, an advertisement with a pointing finger signalled pessaries 'as recommended by Dr Stopes.' Unauthorized advertisements like that disgusted Marie, since they undermined her insistent bid for respectability. Although *Married Love*, the most explicitly sexual of her books, contained only a page or two on birth control, the defence concentrated on the steaming passages in that book, maintaining that since it referred to *Wise Parenthood*, all her books were part of the 'monstrous campaign' of birth control.

In 1917, Marie had been far-sighted enough to send the manuscript of *Married Love* to a Jesuit priest, Father Stanislaus St John, SJ. Her counsel read the priest's response out in court:

> As a piece of thoughtful, scientific writing I find it admirable throughout and it seems to me that your theme could not have been treated in more beautiful or more delicate language or with a truer ring of sympathy for those who, through ignorance or want of thought, make shipwrecks of their married happiness. Your clear exposition of the rhythmic curve of sex feeling and of the misinterpretation on the part of so many husbands of what they call their wives' contrariness, arising from their ignorance of its existence, should bring happiness to many married couples whose lives are drifting apart through want of knowledge ... So far we are in complete agreement but our ways part when you treat of birth control.[24]

Marie included the letter with her reply in the early editions of the book but Father St John must have been censured by his superiors when Marie's birth control activities intensified, for the letter was withdrawn in the seventh edition in 1919.

Sir James Barr, Consulting Physician to the Liverpool Royal Infirmary and for some time Vice-President of the British Medical Association, appeared as a witness for Marie Stopes. The Counsel for the Defence, Mr Charles, seeking to shock, quoted from a passage in *Married Love* on artificial insemination:

> I have received an interesting series of papers and correspondence from Australia, where under the name of "Scientific Motherhood" some high-minded women have been endeavouring for some time to found an institute for the scientific insemination of women war-deprived of mates, so that though husband-less, they may have the joy and sacrifice of child-bearing under properly protected conditions. What do you say, Sir James Barr, as a doctor to obtaining – it is almost too horrible to talk about.[25]
>
> MR PATRICK HASTINGS: Really, I do not want to object again but my friend must not keep on making these interpositions of his own; asking a question is one thing but he must not tell us at this stage whether it is horrid to contemplate.
>
> MR CHARLES: Now my friend has completed his observation –
>
> MR PATRICK HASTINGS: It was not an observation, it was an objection which I hope you will pay attention to.

Class bias was introduced in cross-examination with Mr Charles, Counsel for Dr Sutherland, suggesting to both Nurse Hebbes, the midwife in charge of the Clinic, and Dr Jane Lorrimer Hawthorne of Harley Street, Honorary Consultant to the Clinic, that the poor were unsuited for birth control because of their dirty personal habits. 'Do you not think,' Mr Charles asked Dr Hawthorne, 'that it is a very dangerous thing with poor people that they should feel about themselves?'

A. Dangerous, in what way?

Q. From the point of view, to begin with, from poor people of cleanliness; I mean to say, one is saying nothing against poor people but in say, a district round Holloway, the hands of women that you would see would not be very clean, would they?

A. Well, I think they would know that this was a very special occasion in which they had to wash their hands very carefully.

Q. Of course, they would be advised to by anybody but do you think they would be likely to do it?

A. Yes, I think so.

Q. Do you not find that poor people are very careless?

A. I have found on many occasions that the poor patients are very nervous about their own anatomy, and rather reluctant; and that would lead them to be very careful about washing their hands under these conditions.

Q. I do not think I need pursue that further. You agree with me that the dirt in the nails and so forth of very poor people in a slum area or a very poor area would be very dangerous machines to be working with on a business of this sort – dangerous, not machines, but articles, whatever you like to call them, to be feeling a way in the vagina with, and so forth?

A. Well, I cannot say I think it would be very dangerous.

Q. Supposing, for example, you know how broken women's nails are with the poor people?

A. Yes, they are generally very short, are not they?

Q. Sometimes.

A. Well, worn down.

Q. And very dirty?

A. Well, if they are very short, they will not have a chance to be dirty.

The defence tried hard to prove that Marie's books, particularly *Married Love*, were an incitement to immorality among the young. She stood up well to cross-examination, looking fresh and defiantly pure in a dark dress with white collar and cuffs. Sergeant Sullivan asked her whether she considered that fear of pregnancy might deter the young from sex. Marie replied that she considered the suggestion insulting to womanhood.

Q. I want to know have you considered that among young people apprehension of the possibility of parenthood has acted as a restraining influence in favour of propriety?

A. I consider that an insult to womanhood; we are not moral because we are afraid, we are moral because it is right and intrinsic in our nature to be moral.

Q. Are you able to answer the question?

A. You ask me: have I considered that question. I have considered it, and I consider it an insult to womanhood.

Q. Will you answer the question?

A. I understand the question to be: Have I considered that possibility, and I say, Yes, I have considered it.

Q. In your opinion?

A. Might I have the question explained. I do not understand.

Q. Perhaps you do not, and your answer suggested to me that you did not understand it, though I thought it was clear. Have you ever considered that the apprehension of resulting parenthood may be a restraining influence on the conduct of young people towards one another?

A. My answer is I have considered that, and I consider it an insult to womanhood.

Q. Very well, that is formal and I pass from it.

THE LORD CHIEF JUSTICE: Do you mean unmarried people?

SERGEANT SULLIVAN: Yes, unmarried people.

DR STOPES: He means, does he not, that women are moral because they are afraid, and I say no.

THE LORD CHIEF JUSTICE: I do not think he means that.

DR STOPES: Would you explain to me what he means?

THE LORD CHIEF JUSTICE: I should put it the other way round. Do you suggest there are not some cases, perhaps many cases, in which persons refrain from fornication because they do not want to produce illegitimate children?

A. I do not think so, except in very rare cases. I think that women are moral because it is right to be; it is insulting to suggest that we are only good because we are afraid.

Q. That is not suggested.

A. It is implied to me.

Q. It is not suggested that is the reason, but that in some cases it may be, and in many cases, it is the reason.

A. I do not think so, no.

Q. In other words, to put it another way, I am sure you will perceive that a criticism will no doubt be made which I think you ought to have an opportunity of dealing with. If you are to teach in a book, married people how to avoid the generation of children, notwithstanding the sexual act is performed – are not you also teaching unmarried people the same thing?

A. My Lord and the Jury, since 1823, these methods of various sorts have been taught. In my books for the first time, I distinguish between what is good and what is harmful, and the method I teach cannot be used by an unmarried girl.

Such exchanges made marvellous copy for the newspapers, although the press omitted the most sexually explicit passages cited in court, which tended to make the trial seem even more exciting – and to sell more copies of Marie's books. The twelve jurors were all men and Mr Charles in his cross-examination baited her for her feminism.

Q. I do not know whether you would like me to call you Dr Stopes or Mrs Stopes or Mrs Roe, I will do which you please.

A. I am Dr Stopes, if you please.

Q. Dr Stopes, if *you* please . . .

Throughout the trial, *The Times* ignored her title and referred to Marie as Mrs Stopes.

There were two main weaknesses in Marie's writing about birth control which the defence seized upon. First, in *Wise Parenthood* she had written that the cap (the rubber check pessary) could be left in safely for several days or even weeks. 'Some women put in the cap when the monthly period has entirely ceased and leave it in for three weeks. I am not sure that to leave the cap in so long is quite advisable.' When pressed on the point, Marie repeated that she was not sure. 'You are not sure whether it is advisable or not, but you advise people to use them: is that pretty nearly experiment?' asked Mr Charles.

Marie turned to the Judge to explain. 'You see, my Lord, these caps were invented in 1881 by a medical man and they have been used under supervision since 1881; that is over forty years they have been used and used successfully; and to ask me now if it is an experiment to suggest using what has been in general use for over forty years, I can only answer it seems a ridiculous suggestion.' Marie acquitted herself well in that exchange.

But, as her medical friends had feared, her initial enthusiasm for the 'gold pin', a wishbone-shaped pessary inserted into the uterus, an early form of the coil, proved more damaging. She was enthusiastic about the device used in America, since she believed it could be safely left in place for a month or two. Marie considered it a useful substitute for sterilization for the 'undesirable' mother, liable to produce diseased or degenerate children. She wrote about it in *Wise Parenthood* as a 'method of the greatest possible racial and social value if its further use proves it to be satisfactory.'

In February 1921 Norman Haire, an Australian gynaecologist working in London who admired Marie's work, visited her Clinic. She spoke to him about the gold pin and early in June wrote to ask him if he would take on two or three cases which he would 'watch carefully'. Meanwhile, Dr Haire had been making his own inquiries about the new method and was alarmed to learn that the gold pin was unreliable, that if conception did occur it was always followed by abortion, usually within two or three months and that the device caused irregular and profuse menstruation and sometimes inflammation of the cervix and body of the uterus. He warned Marie that since the pin 'sometimes, at least, acts as an abortifacient, I cannot try it without risking my professional reputation and rendering myself liable to criminal prosecution'.[26]

When asked in court by Mr Charles whether Dr Haire had told her that he would not use the gold pin because it produced an early abortion, Marie replied: 'On the contrary, Dr Haire came to my Clinic personally and asked me to send him subjects for the gold pin.' Although Haire *had* visited Marie's Clinic at his own instigation, she had lied to the court. The defence subpoenaed Norman Haire, and annoyed by her claiming that he had canvassed for patients, he read out her letter:

I hear from American women it [the gold pin] is entirely satisfactory. I should therefore like very much for you, if you do not mind, to take on two or three cases which you could watch carefully and if these yielded unsatisfactory results, we will then drop it. On the other hand, if it does have, as reported, so many advantages, I should be sorry to discard it without proper investigation. I have now on hand two or three people who desire its insertion. May I send these to you definitely . . . In corresponding with these two women, I have stated as follows: I would warn you that the method being a new one, we are not yet quite sure whether the result would be entirely satisfactory, but Dr Haire will watch the case carefully and remove the spring if it seems advisable and recommend some other method.[27]

The two patients, who were not from the Clinic but inquirers by post, turned up at Dr Haire's practice in New Cavendish Street to have the pin inserted and in both cases Dr Haire explained that he could not conscientiously recommend the method and sent them to the Mother's Clinic to have a check pessary fitted instead.[28]

By now, Marie's assumption of infallibility had led her to reconstruct the truth. Early in 1922 Dr Haire had become honorary medical officer to the Walworth Centre, giving lectures on sexual anatomy, hygiene and birth control to local men and women. Since he was with a 'rival' organization and advised the Dutch cap rather than the smaller check pessary, Dr Stopes regarded him with suspicion. His evidence was extremely damaging to her. But that did not prove that Marie had 'experimented' on the poor. In fact, no 'victims' were produced to substantiate Halliday Sutherland's claim. What was even more striking was that the defence's star witness, Professor Dr Anne Louise McIlroy, whose remarks about the check pessary had prompted Sutherland to write his book in the first place, was discredited by Marie's counsel. In the cross-examination of Dr McIlroy, Patrick Hastings endeavoured to extract an admission from the witness that she had never treated a woman who had worn one of the check pessaries which she condemned so roundly:

Q. Now, I want to deal with the question of the particular contraceptive for the moment. Have you ever had a case of a woman who has worn one of these pessaries?
A. I have never met a woman yet who was able to fit on the pessary.
Q. I wonder whether you could answer my question: have you ever met a case yet of any woman who has worn one?
A. No.
Q. So that all you have been telling us at some little length in answer to Mr Charles about the dangers of this, is based upon practical experience which does not include one single case of that being worn?
A. My remarks have been based on the experience of occlusion of the womb.
Q. Quite; but was my question accurate, that it is all based upon

experience which does not include one single case where it has been worn?

A. It is not necessary to have a single case.

Q. The answer is that my question was accurately framed and the answer would be yes?

A. It is not necessary to have a single case.

Q. When I say it would be yes, perhaps I may say it should be yes?

A. I do not know.

Q. I do not think that I will trouble you any more about that.

THE LORD CHIEF JUSTICE: But I understand the witness to say, Mr Hastings – I am sure you want to deal with the point of the answer.

MR PATRICK HASTINGS: Certainly.

THE LORD CHIEF JUSTICE: I understood her to say: 'True, I have not met a woman who wore a check pessary and had an occlusion of the womb from that cause, but I have had a large experience of occlusion of the womb and it is upon that experience, not upon my experience of the check pessary, that my evidence is based.' Is that what you say?

A. Yes, my Lord.

MR PATRICK HASTINGS: I am much obliged to your Lordship. I quite accept that, but that was not, if I may say so with respect, the point of my question. My question was, let me see if I am quite right, Miss McIlroy, that you had never had a case of a woman who has worn one of these check pessaries?

A. No.

Q. That is all I want.

In the event, the Lord Chief Justice's intervention had unwittingly helped Marie Stopes's case, although by now it was clear where his sympathies lay.

But, to Marie, Professor McIlroy's attacks rankled. When she heard, four years later, that at the Royal Free Hospital Dr McIlroy herself was inserting the very vaginal caps she professed to find so harmful, Marie determined to find out. She first disguised herself as a 'work-grimed charwoman', then went along to the out-patients' clinic. 'When Professor McIlroy examined the grimy Marie Stopes, she did not even glance at the sex organs or, even by a momentary view, examine the labia or vaginal orifice for discharge. She made no examination for venereal or other germs . . .'[29] Marie left the clinic with a cap and later wrote to the Royal Free Hospital demanding an apology and a retraction from Dr McIlroy. The Secretary replied stiffly that the Hospital had considered her letter and believed her to have abused the privileges of the Hospital by obtaining advice under false pretences. She received no apology.

In the trial, whenever the defence tried to demonstrate that Marie Stopes's teachings about sex and contraception threatened the young, the family, the life and morals of the nation, Lord Hewart, the Lord Chief Justice, seemed to be endorsing their accusations. Since medical evidence could only be inconclusive about the effects of contraception, the defence went to some lengths to produce a doctor who would swear that reading *Married Love* could cause ill-health. Dr Agnes Forbes Saville, a general physician, was asked by Mr Charles whether she had had any experience of a patient suffering evil effects from reading the book *Married Love*.

A. Yes, that particular one.
Q. What evil physical effect?
A. Shall I tell the case? Sleeplessness and nerves wrecked; thin, loss of health and self-abuse.
Q. How old was the patient?
A. Twenty-five . . .

Cross-examining Mr Patrick Hastings asked:

Q. What makes you suggest that a woman of twenty-five suddenly reads *Married Love* and it has this effect upon her?
A. Because I had known her for many years as a friend. She came to me suffering from sleeplessness and run-down nerves. I used all the usual methods of treatment for a month. There was no result and, therefore, in the usual way which one does in one's profession, I taxed that girl with some grave worry. I said: 'You have a love affair on your mind or some business financial loss?' Bursting into tears she told me she had read *Married Love*; she could not get it out of her mind day or night; it had been such a horrible revelation to her.
Q. In what way a horrible revelation?
A. She had been brought up in a nice, clean home; this is not a nice, clean book.

In his summing-up of the case, Lord Hewart made no secret of his dislike for birth control, 'copulation without consequences' as he termed it.

. . . the check pessary . . . has become something like a talisman, a goal or a standard, a panacea for social ills, both public and private.

It is not spoken of in any tone of diffidence or apology, not in the least; it is spoken of with boldness and, indeed – the phrase has been used again and again – enthusiasm.

Nor did he hide his contempt for Marie's books.

What can be the legitimate purpose of the insertion in these books, to be read by married and unmarried, young and old, persons of both sexes . . . passages which describe the male organ in quiescence and in erection, which describes the encouragement which a man should give to a woman and a woman should give to a man before the act of intercourse is entered upon and which analyse the successive phases and sensations of the act of sexual intercourse? Obscene!

As to Marie Stopes herself, Patrick Hastings in his closing speech had spoken of her philanthropy and the generous way in which she devoted her money to the cause of birth control. This, said the Lord Chief Justice, had caused him to do a little sum. By the time the case came to court, *Married Love* had sold 191,000 copies at six shillings net, £57,300 in all, and *Wise Parenthood* had sold 165,000 copies at three shillings and sixpence, £28,875. So that, allowing for printing costs, Marie would receive something in the region of £80,000. She had said that she devoted her money to the cause. Her influence, he implied, would be proportionate to the wealth so that through these sums of money 'one begins to see what the dimensions of this propaganda may be or may become'. Lord Hewart had, of course, miscalculated, since most authors received a royalty of 10 per cent, or a maximum of 12–15 per cent, not the full published price of the book. But that was only one illustration of his bias. At the conclusion of his summing-up, Lord Hewart made it clear that although there had been no criminal prosecution against Marie Stopes's publications that was not because they were blameless necessarily but might be because 'launching the matter into the public and the press' could do more harm than good. 'I speak of what I know,' he added ominously.

The special jury retired for four hours and came back with the answers to the four questions they had been asked to consider:

1 Were the words complained of defamatory of the Plaintiff? – Yes.
2 Were they true in substance and in fact? – Yes.
3 Were they fair comment? – No.
4 Damages, if any? – £100

A confusing verdict on a confusing case. Despite the Lord Chief Justice's hostility towards Marie Stopes and her works, the jury seemed to have awarded the victory to the Plaintiff. Certainly that is how the press interpreted the case, the next morning, 1 March 1923. The Lord Chief Justice, however, who had deferred his verdict until the next day, entered judgment for the defendant with costs.

The *Daily News* the following day published an editorial backing Marie Stopes's decision to appeal:

A High Court common jury has declared that the statements made by Dr Sutherland in his attack on the birth control crusade of Dr Marie Stopes, though true in fact, were defamatory and constituted unfair comment. This the Lord Chief Justice interprets as a verdict for Dr Sutherland! The question of law involved in this decision is to be the subject of appeal, till that is heard the decision must be taken as a correct interpretation of the law. But whatever the law, the fact is that Dr Stopes has been signally vindicated in the issue she sought by her action to raise. Lord Hewart himself declares that no one doubts the ability, sincerity and honesty of purpose of Dr Stopes. The jury declares that the attack was injurious and unfair. We have nothing to say here as to the rightness or wrongness of birth control. What we do say, and what the jury says by implication, is that Dr Stopes and anyone else who thinks that the welfare of her patients and of the public is served by a certain recognised medical procedure has the right to advocate it, unhampered by palpably false attacks upon her character and professional standing. We cannot pretend to be satisfied at the position in which legal technicalities as interpreted by the Lord Chief Justice leave the case and we regard the decision to appeal as one taken in the interest not merely of the plaintiff but of the public generally.

Sympathy for Marie Stopes, admiration for her courage in the witness box poured in: 'whether you win or lose, you have done an immense service to womanhood by bringing the case', a woman friend wrote;[30] indignation on her behalf came from her patients at the Clinic, her correspondents, and fans of her writing. Shoals of letters arrived at her publisher's office, the Mother's Clinic and her own home. A standard reply went out to unknown sympathizers:

Dear . . . The result of the trial is indeed remarkable but I feel absolutely vindicated as I obtained a clear finding for damages from the

British public as represented by a Jury, though this is withheld as a legal technicality . . .[31]

Her birth control campaign enjoyed a boost and Marie travelled the country to speak in town halls and medical schools. In Stockport the Labour Party organized a meeting and thousands turned up. In Edinburgh, a branch of the Society for Constructive Birth Control was founded, and packed meetings were also held in Liverpool, and in the Battersea Town Hall in London. In Oxford, where she had been scheduled to speak at the Town Hall, the Vice-Chancellor decreed that he would not give his consent for 'any public meeting of undergraduates addressed by a lady on any problems connected with sex or the birth-rate'. But the undergraduates smashed the glass case and removed the notice banning the meeting and transferred it quickly to Ruskin College, outside the university's jurisdiction. When Marie appeared, the undergraduates cheered themselves hoarse and the young – and as yet, unconverted – Evelyn Waugh presented her with a bunch of mimosa.[32]

The opposition was active too. Catholic societies throughout England held large meetings, often addressed by Halliday Sutherland, and Catholic bishops all over the country endorsed the crusade against birth control. From this time in her life onwards, Marie developed a deep and sometimes deluded mistrust and fear of Roman Catholics plotting against her. At hotels she always booked in under the name of Mrs Roe. But not all of her fears were imaginary.

She reported that scurrilous notes kept arriving at her home in Givons Grove. Certainly when the Court of Appeal heard the case on 20 July 1923, Lord Justice Scrutton remarked that both he and other members of the Court had been 'pestered by anonymous communications, all proceeding from and advocating the side of the defendant'. The appeal was allowed by Lords Justice Bankes and Scrutton (Lord Justice Younger dissenting) and the judgment reversed. Marie received £100 damages, half the costs of the action and the costs of the appeal.

But her triumph did not last long. The Catholic Church was not prepared to accept defeat and, with the support of Cardinal Bourne, Dr Sutherland and his publishers decided to make a final appeal to the House of Lords. A Committee was formed to support Dr Sutherland and a fund started to aid his cause, backed by the Catholic press. 'Every right-thinking person' was invited to contribute. 'By the immediate success of the Fund it is hoped to give the country a lesson of the solid Catholic determination to stem the flood of Pagan ideas which threaten the future of the Nation and of Christianity,'[33] thundered the *Universe* on 23 May 1924.[33]

On 21 November 1924, the case of Stopes *v.* Sutherland was heard for the third time by Viscount Cave (the Lord Chancellor), Viscount Finley, Lord Shaw of Dunfermline, Lord Wrenbury and Lord Carson. The Law Lords upheld the original verdict and entered judgment for the defence. No new trial was to be allowed. Only one of the Lords, Lord Wrenbury, who held that the jury had been misdirected, dissented.

Marie Stopes had to pay the defendant's costs in the Court of Appeal, also costs of the original and cross-appeals to the House of Lords and to repay to them the damages and costs paid to her by the defendants under the order of the Court of Appeal. All in all, Marie estimated the cost of the litigation to be about £12,000. Her publisher from Putnams, Charles Huntington, sent her a cheque for £1,325, for the trial had been magnificent publicity for her books. The case had cost Dr Sutherland about £10,000, mostly paid for by the Catholic fund.

George Bernard Shaw, who had a soft spot for Marie, considered the final outcome a perversion of justice, and wrote to her sympathetically:

My dear Marie Stopes
The decision is scandalous; but I am not surprised at it: the opposition can always fall back on simple taboo. The subject is obscene: no lady would dream of alluding to it in a mixed society: reproduction is a shocking subject and there's an end of it. You may get a temporary success by luring the enemy out of that last ditch where there is no defence but argument; but the only result is to drive them back into the ditch; and then you are done; the taboo is impregnable . . . And WHAT has this business cost you?

Ever
G.B.S.[34]

9

Private Life?

Marie had pushed aside her private worries to cope with the trial. Nine days before the hearing began, her mother wrote with news that she could not ignore. Winnie was gravely ill in St Michael's Home of Rest, a private nursing home near Kettering where she was staying. The sisters were worried as dropsy had set in as a result of her heart condition. Winnie's breathing was laboured and she needed special nursing. Did anyone from Marie's clinic know of a suitable person?

Marie felt irritated at having to bear the anxiety of her sister's illness on top of her trial, 'when I can't scarcely get the strength for all I have to do'.[1] She was sorry to hear about Winnie but reassured her mother that dropsy was a disease that progressed slowly. Even bad cases sometimes lasted for twenty years and Marie could not take on the charge of paying for a special nurse indefinitely. The proper course was for the sisters to apply to a hospital. Meanwhile, Charlotte should not worry and 'on no account speak to anyone at the Clinic connected with my work about it.'

Since she had gone to Munich twenty years earlier, Marie had always tried to keep her private life distanced from her work, embarrassed by her family. Now that she was a public figure she felt the need was even greater.

The day after the trial opened, 22 February, Winnie's physician wrote for the second time, warning Marie that her sister could not survive much longer. By Saturday 24th Marie had received the letter; the court did not resume until Tuesday. Over the week-end she thought over her response carefully and on Monday 26th wrote a defensive letter to the doctor:

Dear Dr Robinson,

I am sorry she is in this state, but I feel with her marvellous vitality, one not used to her may underestimate her powers of recovery. It is over ten years ago when we were told she could live six weeks and for years she kept us at a daily strain of expecting her to die that day 'till my mother's and my health simply broke down ... as you can imagine I am under a very great strain of urgent work this week.[2]

On Tuesday 27 February, just before the trial ended, Winnie died, as thoughtless of her family in death as they considered she had been in life.

Both Charlotte and Marie had received telegrams from St Michael's and Charlotte, just turned eighty-two, a little grey-haired old lady in a bonnet, had rushed down to the nursing home in time to arrange for her younger daughter's funeral. Marie had not managed to see her sister before she died, but she dutifully paid £10 for her funeral expenses, just as she had paid for her upkeep at the nursing home for years. 'Poor Winnie,' she wrote in a note to Charlotte, 'it is rather awful all coming at one with the case.'[3]

Marie felt no great sense of loss at her sister's death. Even before her marriage the sisters had had little contact. She simply felt responsible for Winnie and disliked the idea that her younger sister should have to depend on her friends for support. Marie had behaved badly at the end, but under that kind of pressure anyone might have failed. Her own ideals demanded nothing less than perfection of herself and she could not bear to admit any weakness.

After a gruelling ten days in court and a death in the family, her own powers of recovery were really remarkable. Controversy and publicity acted as a stimulant. Three weeks after her ordeal she appeared as combative and bumptious as ever. Writing to Sister Marjorie of the West London Mission, an organization for young business women from all over London, to discuss a lecture, Marie had no qualms about meeting dissent: 'an audience which disagrees with me would be of great interest. I have never yet met it and should much enjoy it. At any meeting hitherto that I have had, my opponents keep silence or get converted!'[4]

Despite her air of supreme self-confidence, however, Marie was still wounded by the slightest hint of criticism, still driven by an insatiable desire to win public approbation. She did not dwell on motives and had little time for Freud's new psychological insights. 'Don't please think about your subconscious mind,' she advised an inquirer, 'all the filthiness of this psychoanalysis does unspeakable harm.'[5]

The publicity of the trial, Marie recognized, had increased enthusiasm for her and she was in demand to speak and to write newspaper articles. As well as accepting almost every invitation, she attended daily at the Clinic whenever she could.

She was now so well known that she was sometimes recognized in the street. Her fame had even spread to the playground. In the 1920s schoolgirls chanted with glee:

> Jeanie, Jeanie full of hopes
> Read a book by Marie Stopes
> But to judge by her condition,
> She must have read the wrong edition.

Marie considered writing a book about the trial but abandoned that idea in favour of writing a film script. Ever since she had worked on the Cinema Commission of Inquiry in 1917, she had realized the immense possibilities of the new medium. Knowing the film censor, T. P. O'Connor, to be a Roman Catholic opposed to her ideas, she wrote a tear-jerker which, she claimed, was *not* about birth control. *Maisie's Marriage* was originally titled *Married Love* when the film was made but the censor objected to the association. The melodrama, a thinly concealed birth control message, unfolded the story of a young girl from Slumland seeking to better herself. It was '. . . full of convincing situations, dramatic contrasts, startling and soul-gripping incidents,' wrote a fan from Katoomba, in New South Wales, who saw the silent movie in 1928.[6] Marie's captions were 'a stroke of genius' he enthused and the mysteries of birth neatly explained.

BOY: But where are the kitten babies now mother?
MOTHER: Safely tucked away near a mother's heart, where naughty boys cannot pull their tails.
BOY: Was I a kitten baby once, Mama?

In brief, the plot revolves around Maisie, the beautiful heroine who refuses to marry the nice boy next door because she wants to escape from Slumland and a life of poverty and hungry children. Maisie runs away to Piccadilly Circus, where warm-hearted prostitutes introduce her to a night-club. Inside a dark den, a tired businessman attempts to seduce her but the virtuous Maisie bolts again, this time to fling herself into the Thames. Mr Sterling, an honourable bystander, dives in to save her and takes her back to his affluent and well-ordered home where his equally honourable lady, Mrs Sterling, agrees to train the stray girl as under-parlourmaid. Her mistress points out helpfully to Maisie that rearing children is like growing roses, prune them and you produce beautiful blooms, let them grow wild ... At that point the camera reveals a rose gradually changing into the face of a baby. The shot was cut out by the censor who considered it too explicit.

Maisie is left in charge of the nursery one night when one of her wastrel brothers breaks in to plunder. The children hide a lighted candle near the nursery curtains and the house catches fire while our heroine is seeking help. 'Black despair, death and disgrace now face our heroine ... What will happen? See the picture and then take off your hat to Dr Marie Stopes.'[7]

The censor tried to achieve a nationwide ban of *Maisie's Marriage* by sending out a letter marked 'Confidential' to every Chief Constable and local Watch Committee. But outside London, many towns decided to show the film in the summer of 1923. It received valuable publicity from the reports of Marie's successful appeal in her libel case and she travelled throughout the country making personal appearances. Her life was extraordinarily full that summer and in June she gave a paper in French to a three-day Conference on fuel held in Paris. In buoyant mood she wrote to Humphrey: 'All the men here are hideous and you are splendid ... You are much more unique as a man than I am as a woman. A big fat kiss from your own little Marie, the wood-nymph.'[8] At that stage in their marriage Marie was trying hard to boost her husband's confidence by making light of her own achievements with uncharacteristic modesty.

Humphrey drew strength from her letters. By now he was totally in the shadows, keeping Marie's engagement diary, answering correspondence himself, dealing with difficult callers, reading proofs, acting as chauffeur, always in a subordinate role. He was interested in industrial reform, particularly in the wage structure, but his interests, his committees, took place in private, and he was known to the public as Dr Stopes's husband, a title he had at first resented but latterly had grown proud of. That the famous Clinic had been at least as much his idea as hers, funded with some – perhaps most – of his money, was almost forgotten. He adored Marie and was painfully eager to be of service. Even when they were gardening Marie (who as a botanist was much more knowledgeable) gave directions. On quiet evenings she would sit and sew by the fire while Humphrey read to her from novels of her choice.

In the autumn after the court case Humphrey was re-elected as Councillor for Leatherhead Urban District Council. In his election address he declared that he was standing 'principally in the interests of women'.[9]

At last it happened: Marie became pregnant – in the summer of 1923 in the romantic setting of an old lighthouse on Portland Bill she had acquired as a holiday home. More than ever that year she seemed to be living in an animated dream. Her baby, she wrote, was conceived:

> in a stone tower high above the sea, with the sea all round it and the brilliant blue sky above, in a blaze of sunlight he was called into being. There, as the night fell and the blue darkened into a purple curtain spangled with great stars, his mother lay under the sky, high above the world all night.[10]

Less romantically, in July 1923 the medical paper the *Practitioner* devoted a special issue to contraception. Eight physicians, all of them hostile to birth control, contributed. Sir Maurice Abbot-Anderson MRCS prophesied that contraception would produce sterility and might 'finally land the victim in a lunatic asylum'. Professsor Anne Louise McIlroy described the 'rubber shops' as a grave moral danger and called for their closure. Contraception, according to other learned doctors, would destroy the glamour and romance of marriage, lead to race degeneration and deplete the flower of the nation's manhood. Three of the medical writers had been witnesses for Sutherland in Marie's case and she might have been forgiven for thinking that the issue amounted almost to a retrial.

Nothing but complete vindication would satisfy her. She asked her faithful follower Aylmer Maude to rush out a biography of her. Having written the life of the 'cleverest man of his age' (Tolstoy), Maude said, he was now to write the life of the cleverest woman. Still dotingly fond of Marie, he agreed to impossible conditions. He was not allowed to mention any previous birth control campaigns and, although at the time *The Authorised Life of Marie Stopes* (her title) published by Williams & Norgate, appeared on the bookshelves, his subject was forty-four, he was not permitted to mention her age! Expecting a runaway success, Marie paid for all the costs, including the advertising. The critics saw through the puff and wrote scathing comments.

The biography came out at Christmas 1924 and by December 1925 only about 500 copies had sold.[11] Marie, of course, did not recoup her outlay and the book helped neither her reputation nor Aylmer Maude's.

In November, just before the biography came out, Marie achieved her ambition to see a play of hers produced. *Our Ostriches*, a drama of undisguised propaganda with an element of autobiography, was staged at the Royal Court Theatre. The heroine, Miss Evadne Carrillon, struggles to convert the Birth Rate Commission to birth control but only one of the Ostriches lifts his head from the sand. Dr Verro Hodges, 'on the sunny side of thirty', signs the minority report dissenting from the Commission's disapproval of birth control and gets the girl. Evadne, of course, breaks off her engagement to the aristocratic Lord Simplex. The names in her pieces are almost as entertaining as the plot.

The play ran for three months and, at the opening, Marie offered Lord Cromer the Lord Chamberlain, and his wife, a box. Marie's motives in entertaining were often transparent. She badly wanted to be presented at Court, but in her own name, and she wrote personally to the Lord Chamberlain to ask if it was possible. On 14 January 1924, from the Lord Chamberlain's office in Buckingham Palace, came a reply marked 'Private':

> Let me now say that, although I appreciate the fact that you prefer to be called by your own name rather than that of your husband, there is a strict rule at Court that married ladies must be presented under their husband's name. There are several cases of ladies coming to Court having to conform to this rule. The case of Lady Rhondda which you mention is hardly analagous as, being a Peeress in her own right, she is entitled to be summoned to Court under her own title, which is in no way affected by the fact of her being married.
>
> In the circumstances I am sure you would wish to conform to the rule I have mentioned, especially as I am unwilling to raise the question of your authority to style yourself 'Doctor' in this country.[12]

Marie's reply four days later was quick and very pointed:

Dear Lord Cromer
It was kind of you to write personally when you must have been so very busy – I do hope you won't be cross if I say that the last paragraph of your letter positively shocked me. You see I have always felt a proper contempt towards the large numbers of medical practitioners who impudently usurp the title of 'doctor' for which they have no right and I rested assured that all who mattered *knew*. Now to find that you, supreme authority in the country, evidently do not realise. The only persons legally entitled 'Doctor' in this country are the learned Doctors of the various faculties of our universities. (The majority of medical practitioners have not this high degree.) We who

are so entitled are a small body of learned people who, with heads in the clouds, have not bothered to protect our ancient rights and privileges . . . As a learned doctor of London University, I have by Act of Parliament the right to bear that title at all times.[13]

Three weeks later Lord Cromer wrote again, suggesting rather wearily that she should come to see him: '. . . when I can explain the circumstances which oblige married ladies to come to Court under their husband's name. You could then tell me what you suggest as regards inserting or omitting the title Dr on presentation.'[14]

But by now Marie's interest was focused on having her baby. In February she suffered from bronchitis and pneumonia and, advised by her gynaecologist, Dr Harold Chappel, consultant at Guy's Hospital, she went into hospital two weeks before the child was due. She still retained a professional and, she believed, detached interest in the event. She was making 'some interesting scientific observations on contractions in the womb,' she told Charlotte, amazed to discover that 'apparently the medical profession don't know when contractions of the womb start or how they work. The trouble of course is, that most women don't have the faculty of medical observation . . .'[15] Five days later at 10.15 a.m. on 27 March 1924, her baby, a boy, was born by Caesarean section. The infant weighed eight and three-quarter pounds and was an 'excellent child', nineteen inches tall. Marie explained to her mother that she chose the word 'tall' in the birth card because her baby 'stretched out, feet firm, like a soldier at attention, before he was a day old.'

Marie and Humphrey were overjoyed with their healthy little son, Harry Verdon Stopes-Roe, but a birth controller giving birth caused comment. W. S. of Berwick-upon-Tweed inquired snidely whether her child was intended or 'was it a failure of your preventative?'[16] 'I consider your enquiry about our son incredible,' Marie replied. 'Of course he was planned and arranged for.' The Times, always hostile, refused to accept the announcement: 'ROE: on the 27th March to Dr Marie Stopes, wife of H. V. Roe of Givons Grove, Leatherhead, Surrey – a son.' But both the Daily Sketch and the Daily Express featured the arrival of Dr Stopes's baby on their front pages. Interviewed by the Express, the proud father explained that they would have liked a twin sister for Harry. '. . . People imagine we do not want children simply because my wife advocates birth control . . . We do want fine, healthy children, as many as we can afford to bring up properly . . .'[17] Three weeks later photographers were invited to Leatherhead. The Daily Sketch displayed a photograph of Marie in a lace cap, cuddling her little son, while the *Express* showed the baby by himself. Early in June Marie received the 'Command' card she had coveted for years.

The Lord Chamberlain is commanded by their Majesties to summon
Mrs Humphrey Verdon Roe
to a Court at Buckingham Palace
on Friday the 27th June, 1924 at 9.30. o'clock p.m.
Ladies: Court dress with feathers and trains.
Gentlemen: Full Court dress.

In a dress of cream net, sewn with crystal and iridescent pearl over satin, with a matching train fringed with shaded orange and flame-coloured ostrich feathers, Marie was presented.

By now she had a taste for luxury, dinner at the Ritz or the Savoy Grill, with literary or medical men, evenings at the theatre in the best seats, holidays in top-class hotels.

The public work she was doing was magnificent, travelling from meeting to meeting, spreading her gospel, giving advice. By August that year some 5,000 women had been seen at her clinic and she published a report on *The First Five Thousand*.[18] In 1925, her Clinic moved from Holloway Road to premises in Whitfield Street, in the centre of London, where there is a Marie Stopes Clinic to this day.

That year too, she began to train nurses and to hold demonstrations of the fitting of birth control appliances for medical students and doctors. Marie originated the idea of a motor caravan clinic which would move from place to place, with a nurse and apparatus to give practical help and literature to spread the knowledge into the community. To put the idea into practice took almost two years and then the nurses discovered that in rural districts the women were afraid of ridicule and would not come near the caravan. The travelling clinic fared better near a town.

Marie's own experience of motherhood made her even more sympathetic to the harassed mothers she heard from. A Mrs F. of Kilburn wrote to the nurse at the Clinic on 25 February 1925:

I am a married woman of 35 and have had a family of 9 children of whom 7 are living. I have 2 daughters married and who are expectant mothers attending school still and I myself go in daily fear of contracting another . . . I have never experienced the pleasures of married life, I have had only miseries of bearing and rearing a family. I think Dr

Marie Stopes work glorious and wish it every success. Why should not the working class mother be enlightened?[19]

The year Marie's baby was born, thanks largely to her spectacular activities, birth control became a topic for public discussion and both the Labour Party, and to a lesser extent, the Liberal Party, as well as voluntary groups, began to press for advice to be given to women at Local Authority maternity and welfare centres. To Marie's horror, the new Minister of Health in the 1924 Labour Government was a Catholic, Mr J. Wheatley, and when it became clear that the Government barred birth control advice, voluntary groups began to set up their own clinics. In April 1924 the Walworth Women's Welfare Centre adopted the name the Society for the Provision of Birth Control Clinics. Marie had always believed that her clinic should serve as a model for the state and saw the others as rivals. Her refusal to co-operate with the 'upstarts' lost her a lot of support. 'I wish the various Birth Control organizations would not spend so much time scrapping with each other. It tends to sap confidence in all of them alike,' J. M. Keynes wrote later in a letter to her.[20]

When the General Strike broke out in May 1926 Marie felt drawn, once again, to try to resolve the nation's social and economic problems. The miners were still at the heart of the struggle against the wage reductions for all workers demanded by the Conservative Prime Minister, Stanley Baldwin. This time Marie's knowledge of the hardships of working-class families made her more sympathetic to their case and she held informal talks with their Federation. Lack of security, she argued cogently, was the main problem and in a letter to Baldwin, she suggested a minimum uniform wage of £3 a week for all miners.

At the present moment, it is no exaggeration to say that some men . . . are by piece work, odd day shifts etc., incapable of earning more than 25s to 30s per week. In these days this is sheer cruel starvation . . . May I say personally that I think your insistence on the miners accepting 'without any reserve' the report of the Coal Commission is misguided . . .[21]

The Prime Minister had welcomed her efforts but neither side would budge, and her intervention failed. Within ten days, the General Council of the TUC called off the strike, leaving the miners to fight on until November, their position weakened.

Balked of a political role, Marie turned her attention to the growing 'competition' in the birth control movement, and to fighting off the Catholics' vigorous and personalized attack on her since she had identified herself with the cause. In the mid 1920s Marie was using up too much of her energy on defence against her enemies. As early as December 1924 she was employing a National Detective Agency to discover if a Catholic organization had been responsible for the publication of Dr Sutherland's book. From then on, she engaged a series of lapsed Catholics to ferret out Roman Catholic activities.

Convinced that a Roman Catholic conspiracy was threatening civil liberty in Britain, particularly the liberty to publish birth control literature, by 1927 she re-defined her objectives in a paper marked Secret & Confidential: 'To retain our established but threatened liberties in Great Britain and to initiate a new era of human life by spreading a sound and responsible racial ideal among the people and rendering it practically effective by a knowledge of contraceptive measures.'[22]

Meanwhile her own literary output continued unabated. In 1923 Contraception: Its Theory, History and Practice, written principally for the medical and legal professions, appeared, as well as a pamphlet Mother, How Was I Born? With the birth of her baby, her interest in sex education grew. She was understandably proud of her text book The Human Body and Its Functions which she said 'was the first popular book to put sex organs in their proper place. Until [1926] popular books on human physiology had no sex organs.'[23]

At home in Leatherhead Marie found great joy in her baby son. She fed him herself at first and then watched over his diet (honey, not sugar, and wholemeal flour for his rusks). She kept a critical eye on the nursemaids and changed staff several times, convinced that no one but herself could take care of her baby properly. At nine months she claimed her beautiful, intelligent little son could distinguish between flowers and weeds; at eighteen months he could safely hammer a nail into a stair carpet by himself; at two he looked like a 'dewy rose'. Marie was a possessive mother and sometimes even Humphrey felt excluded.

Her breathless adoration for the child was echoed in the adoration one or two women friends felt for Marie. Molly Wrench, who wrote a corner in Woman's Friend and was able discreetly to direct some of her readers to Marie's clinic, wrote: 'Three times I've seen you and baby in dreams in a field of yellow flowers – I was there talking to your husband and we all laughed . . .'[24]

Baby Buffkins profited from his mother's ability to weave fairytales. For years Marie had written for publication, scientific papers, articles, poems, novels, plays. During the war she had written fairy stories too, under the name of Erica Fay, and those had sold better than her other writings. Although she rarely spoke of them, her fairy tales read like daydreams of a childhood denied to her. In 1926, when her son was two, *The Road to Fairyland* by Erica Fay appeared, published with a frontispiece by Arthur Rackham. One of the stories in this collection, 'The Tiger and the Wood-Nymph' uses the pet names Marie and Humphrey called each other in the title and hints at Marie's view of sexual encounters. In her tale, the great roary tiger bounds up to the little wood-nymph, snarls and bares his teeth. But the gentle, intelligent little creature does not flinch. Instead she swings her legs on the branch of a great oak, flatters and tames the tiger and binds up his teeth with blue ribbon. The moral: '... the way creatures behave depends very much on how they are treated.'[25]

Marie had tamed Humphrey to the extent that he was now completely involved in her world, with no paid work outside his administrative duties on behalf of the Clinic and of her. At Givons Grove their way of life was expensive. The large house and grounds needed gardeners and outdoor workers as well as the household staff. By 1927 *Married Love* had gone into its eighteenth edition, translated into twelve languages, including Afrikaans, Arabic and Hindi; her other books were selling well too. But the expense of their new son, of running the Clinic, of Marie's lawsuit and the biography of herself she had financed (the publishers, Williams & Norgate, went bankrupt the following year) had all taken their toll of the family coffers. Reluctantly, in late April 1927, the family moved from their splendid country mansion to 'Heatherbank', a far more modest suburban house in Hindhead.

Years later Marie complained that after making the gesture of buying Givons Grove, Humphrey had never given her any money for the upkeep of the house and left it to her to pay for staff, the food bills and even for extra furniture. All she asked him, she said, was never to mortage Givons Grove, and to keep at least £30,000 invested in war bonds.

She was obsessed still with her conviction that the insidious influence of the Roman Catholics was blocking her work on birth control, and that obsession proved expensive in 1927. There is no doubt that to some Catholics she represented the devil incarnate and her fears of Catholic suppression of her work had a basis in reality, especially in Ireland. In 1926, the Catholic Truth Society had published a report on 'evil litera-ture' and that was to herald a rigorous Censorship law. Marie also believed that the banning of advertisements of her books and meetings was a result of Roman Catholic manipulation of the English press. That was more difficult to prove. With the aid of a Mr J. H. Guy, Marie attempted to find out the number of Catholics working in the English press. His first findings led him to believe that it was Roman Catholic journalists employed in sub-editorial posts, 'quite out of proportion to their number',[26] who were used as a weapon in the anti-birth control campaign.

The controversy and the headlines 'No Stopery, No Popery' which Marie claimed originated in the Catholic press, caused wry amusement and made good copy. G. K. Chesterton attacked her weekly in his magazine, and R. A. Walker, sub-editor and manager of the *Print Makers' Quarterly*, put his spoke in:

> A wit with initials G.K.
> ran a mag neither clever nor gay.
> But he founded his hopes
> on attacks on Miss Stopes
> And solatiums from Rome made it pay![27]

In February 1927 the *Morning Post*, which had accepted advertisements for the Clinic since its inauguration, suddenly refused to accept them any more. Marie had no doubt as to the source of the trouble and wrote an ingratiating note to the Chairman of the Board of Directors, the Duke of Northumberland:

> 'My dear Duke of Northumberland, I am sure you would just hate to feel that a very small handful of Roman Catholics were manipulating your paper, the *Morning Post*, unknown to you . . .'[28]

The Duke forwarded the note to his editor, H. A. Gwynne commenting: 'I do hope we shall keep off this subject of birth control as I feel sure it will do us a lot of harm to advertise it.' Gwynne was offended by Marie's letter and took it as a slur on his professional conduct and, although she apologized, he sued for libel. In January 1928 Marie had to admit in Court that she had no evidence whatsoever of a Catholic plot. She lost the case and was ordered to pay £200 damages and costs. Marie decided to fight back on her own behalf. She took lessons in court procedure and conducted her own case in the Appeal. In court she wore a brown velvet coat trimmed with fur and a brown toque adorned with pink ribbons. Although she tried to exploit her femininity by standing on a seat to address the Court because she was so small, Marie lost her case. Even more damaging to her was the virtual boycott of her activities by the *Morning Post* after the case.

The Fates seemed to plague Marie that year, for her beloved black chow, Wuffles, whom she had had since he was a pup of six weeks, was in trouble with the law as well as his mistress. This was not the first time that Wuffles had bared his teeth. Three years earlier a neighbour had accused the dog of 'wantonly attacking' his spaniel, 'tearing its hip and making it bleed profusely'. In 1928 the Farnham Magistrates' Court ordered her to keep Wuffles on a lead. Marie felt the indignity. With Wuffles chained it gave the opportunity 'to a number of yapping, scurrilous curs to glory over him and to attack or attempt to attack him and say unforgiveable things.'[29] Wuffles continued to offend, the maid seemed unable to restrain him and, after further incidents, the court ordered Wuffles to be destroyed.

Marie was distraught. Wuffles was a member of the family; she had had his portrait painted by a Royal Academician and it hung on the walls. Like her father she adopted an anthropomorphic attitude towards her pets. When she was away, she placed the letters she wrote against her neck and told Humphrey to give Wuffles the letters to sniff. Naturally, Marie adopted a fierce defence of her 'watchdog and friend'. She wrote to MPs, to the Home Secretary, with a demand for a Bill to 'save innocent dogs and their owners from suffering the injustice of unfair condemnation without any power to appeal', sent a donation to the National Canine Defence League and a petition to the Lord Chancellor for a reprieve for Wuffles. Convinced that the Farnham magistrates were Roman Catholics, she employed a detective to find out the religion of the bench. All the magistrates were Protestant.

The affair ruined her Christmas. Marie was fined a pound a day for failing to destroy the dog but in January 1929, when a policeman was sent to her home to find out if the order had been obeyed, she refused to answer his questions and the baffled constable went away. The Farnham Magistrates' Court too decided to adjourn the case, since they could not decide on whom lay the proof as to a dog being alive or dead. In the end she lost her beloved Wuffles.

Even on the literary front 1928 had proved disappointing. For years Marie had been working on a novel, and in spite of her vast output had not yet succeeded in publishing in that form. In 1928 *Love's Creation*, her first novel, finally appeared. Like most of her fiction, the book serves principally as a vehicle for her ideas, with the sympathetic characters incorporating much of Marie Stopes.

In *Love's Creation* Kenneth, the scientist hero, first marries Lillian, a fellow scientist, an earnest, rather glacial young woman who conveniently loses her life in a cycling accident soon after the wedding. Kenneth's brother-in-law Harry next falls over a cliff, leaving the hero free to mate with his wife's younger sister, Rose Amber, a softer, more feminine creature. This gentle, loving partner is able to release in Kenneth the creative spring and to develop what Marie described as 'large cosmic theory . . . a development of geological and paleontological research'. Unfortunately Marie advised most of her readers to skip the revelatory section of the book: 'This chapter does not carry on the story and should only be read by those who *think*.' H. G. Wells wrote her a patronizing note on it.

> Dear Marie Carmichael
> [she had written the book using her mother's maiden name]
> Congratulations on your birth (Love's Creation) so far as it has gone. But writing a novel is a business even more subtle and delicate than making love and it has to be learnt.
>
> You are still but half-delivered from that pamphlet-writing woman, M. C. Stopes. The most difficult form of the novel is the novel of ideas and your little hands have still to master most of its technique. When you have, you will not put notices to tell people not to read particular chapters unless they *think*.
>
> Tut. Tut!
Yours,
H. G. Wells.[30]

Marie must have been furious at that dismissal, and the novel's reception in the press was disappointing too. The *Spectator* dismissed it as 'old-fashioned' and the *Morning Post*, a little more friendly in spite of the recent court case, summed up *Love's Creation* as 'a mixture of sex, science and sentiment'.[31]

Crushed by the reception of a book which had meant so much to her (for reviews were sparse as well as frustrating) Marie bought a full page advertisement in the *Morning Post* announcing that Dr Marie Stopes was the 'Marie Carmichael' author of *Love's Creation*. Her blatant and rather pathetic attempt to win popularity and boost sales failed and her novel, published by John Bale & Co., the medical publisher who had published her sociological work, did not go into a second edition.

Marie always took an active part in publicizing her books, and in the summer of 1928, when *Love's Creation* appeared, she was desperate to place advertisments in *The Times*. Convinced that the press, particularly *The Times*, was carrying out a vendetta against her, she 'phoned persistently and her manner was anything but conciliatory. On 26 June a letter was sent to her from the Editor's office stating that he had received complaints both from his secretary and from the telephone operators 'of your attitude on the telephone today'. Marie had demanded an interview with the Editor but was warned that if she neglected the 'ordinary courtesies of business intercourse' her request was unlikely to be granted. She replied with a telegram complaining that she could not get *The Times* to make a note of her telephone number. Although she did eventually meet the Editor, Geoffrey Dawson, and the Advertising Manager, she did not receive the recognition she wanted. She was reminded that *The Times* was a family newspaper and therefore not a proper medium for much of her advertising. Marie never gave up. She had already discovered the names of the directors of *The Times* and, at last, in January 1938, she persuaded a friend, W. Talbot Rice, to buy 300 shares in the paper in his name on her behalf in the hope that she would be able to influence *The Times's* policy indirectly.[32]

In February 1929, Charlotte died at the age of eighty-eight. Despite their terrible rivalries Marie was closely linked to her mother and had supported and helped her in her old age. Family pride in both of them was strong and towards the end Charlotte had derived enormous pleasure from Marie's achievements. When little Harry was born, Charlotte told Marie that she had a beautiful baby, but 'not so beautiful as my baby was'. Marie remembered that all her life. It was, she said, the first time her mother ever paid her a compliment.[33]

The following month Marie took her little boy and the nurse to stay at the Imperial Hotel, Torquay, registering under the name of 'Mrs Carmichael' for fear of Catholic 'enemies'. She was struggling to edit the manuscript of *Mother England*, a short collection of letters from working-class women. 'Oh my darling,' she wrote to Humphrey, 'how lovely life could be if this awful strain of self-sacrificing work didn't blacken it always.' Harry, their son was looking 'celestially beautiful and talking much of God.'[34]

At home Humphrey attended anti-birth control meetings with copies of their own paper, *Birth Control News*, handy to sell to opponents if he could. He also had ambitions to write a book, a history of AVRO, the family aircraft firm, and half jokingly suggested that Marie would have to 'give up yours and help me with mine . . .' Marie, recuperated from the winter's troubles, indicated that she would appreciate contact of a less cerebral kind with her husband. 'I hope you have spring and a young man's fancy when I return . . .'[35]

Marie's great hope for the future, for the Race, now lay with her small son, Harry, known to his fond parents as Buffkins. Marie disapproved of families with only one child and both she and Humphrey would have liked to have more. But the injuries she had suffered after Harry's birth, and her age, made the risk of having other children too great. In 1926, when Harry was two, she wrote asking her solicitors to try to find a little boy to adopt between the age of twenty months and two-and-a-quarter years. The child, she stipulated, must be completely healthy, intelligent and uncircumcised. She would not object to adopting an illegitimate child provided that the parents were free of inherited disease and the child was not born of rape.[36]

The lucky boy would be brought up in the nursery alongside the son and heir and, if his intelligence warranted, would be sent to university and given a suitable start in life. The utmost secrecy was to be observed.

Not until 1928, through acquaintances in Manchester, did Marie hear of a suitable child, Robin, an orphan brought up by two impoverished but adoring aunts, who believed they were giving their nephew a wonderful start in life when they sent him to stay with Marie's family that year. But within two years the five-and-a-half-year-old was in trouble.

The Misses Wilkinson felt Marie was too severe: 'I know you think we didn't know how to treat Robin and are silly, nervy old maids,' and they became definitely agitated when Marie told them that the child needed whipping. On 20 July 1930, Marie replied:[37] 'I have not yet whipped Robin and have no need to as he does not disobey me often,' but added, ominously, that the little boy had imposed on the kindness and gentleness of the governess so that Marie feared a few, probably only three, whippings would be necessary. Marie considered that a child of five-and-a-half should be able to count and recite the alphabet every day without coaxing. Her comments contain a chilling echo of her own mother's attitude to herself when she was Robin's age. Not surprisingly, the Misses Wilkinson asked for their nephew to be returned.

The next candidate came from the National Children's Adoption Society in 1931. Marie was happy to keep Dick – Richard Scott-Foster – for a time but did not want to commit herself to adoption. When the Society pressed for more definite plans for Dick's future, Marie wrote that she feared that he would never 'bloom so as to be a credit to us' and agreed to return him with 'a sigh of relief'. He was, she wrote, in 'much better condition than when I got him'.[38]

Her attitude to the series of little boys who came to live as Harry's companion was cool and appraising. None of the children could, of course, measure up to her adored son and they doubtless felt the difference in treatment. Dick was returned as unsatisfactory in March 1932. Robin was once again offered the opportunity of an upbringing in Marie's care but in less than a year returned to his aunts. They sensed that Marie had tired of the child and felt that their love would make up for any material advantages that she could offer.

In 1933, John Bicknell was taken in with the hope that Marie would adopt him, but he too was rejected for lack of academic ability and literary and artistic sensibility. The little boys must have been terrified of the overpowering lady who offered sweets and treats they had never dreamt of and meted out threats and punishments in awe-inspiring anger.

The next boy Marie took in was Barry Cuddeford, the son of a former Indian Army family struggling to maintain their living standards in South London. Barry (Marie arbitrarily decided to call him Roy, perhaps to distinguish him from Harry) had lacked suitable tuition and was backward in Latin, French, Arithmetic and Algebra. The Cuddefords were delighted when Marie explained that Harry's tutor, Mr Bird, would educate their son up to Matric standard, although he would not be able to take the Public School Entrance Exam. That arrangement too went sour within six months. In May 1935, Marie wrote to Major Cuddeford complaining that 'Roy' had dirty habits. While he was in the bath, she had discovered his underpants in his bedroom 'absolutely soaked with urine and, of course, smelling horribly'. His behaviour, she wrote, rendered him 'unfit to live in a decent household'. Marie suggested that the boy needed thrashing.

Major Cuddeford was prepared to accept the humiliation, prepared to thrash Barry (which Marie considered 'obvious and right') but his wife was not. Marie's phrase about the boy being unfit for a decent household rankled. Two days later she wrote to Marie to tell her that she and her husband had decided to keep Barry at home for good and send him to the local school. Even if they succeeded in curing their son of this particular complaint, another was sure to arise. Therefore they felt that the best course would be for Barry to leave Marie's care.

Marie did not like this turn of events; it was not what she had planned. She sent a telegram to Major Cuddeford: 'Your wife's letter surprising. Consultation with Tutor essential. Keeping Roy here as arranged.'[39] She seemed insensible to other parents' feelings and only after a telegram from Mrs Cuddeford and a letter from Major Cuddeford was Barry finally returned to his parents where he was allowed to be called by his own name.

At forty-five, in the mid–1920s, Marie seemed to have achieved everything that she had ever wanted, an outstandingly successful career, an adoring husband, an adored son, and considerable wealth. By the time she reached fifty, the 1929 Stock Market crash had eroded Humphrey's investments, married life had lost some of its rapture and, although she was more widely known than ever (Low had begun to make cartoons of her in the *Evening Standard*) she was more and more involved in controversy.

Her total involvement in the birth control campaign worried one or two of her more perceptive friends. George Bernard Shaw, who followed her career with amused admiration, believed that her most important contribution to society lay elsewhere:

I think you should insist on the separation in the public mind of your incidental work as a scientific critic of methods of contraception with your main profession as a teacher of matrimonial technique. People do not yet understand that there is such a thing as a technique of marriage, and that a would-be violinist taking up a fiddle and expecting to get music out of it without instruction, is not more absurd than a husband taking a wife, or a wife a husband in the same darkness. You are really a matrimonial expert, which is something much wider and more needed than a specialist in contraception. You should make it clear that you are a doctor, not a Malthusian nor a trader in sterilizing devices.[40]

But his advice came too late.

In November 1928 Marie's anti-Catholic mania was literally inflamed when a thirty-four-year-old Roman Catholic spinster, Elizabeth Ellis, a sweetshop assistant, tried to set fire to her mobile clinic in Bradford, believing she was acting in obedience to God's law. Arrested and brought before the magistrates, Ellis refused to be bound over and a week later poured petrol over the caravan. This time she gutted it completely, causing about £200 worth of damage.

Marie rushed up to the hearing, warning the nurse in charge of the clinic not to inform the police of her presence. She placed advertisements of a meeting in leading provincial papers, the *Leeds Mercury*, the *Yorkshire Post*, the *Bradford Telegraph and Argus* and the *Bradford Observer*. At a large public gathering in Bradford Marie raised enough

ATTEMPTED REVOLUTION IN DUBLIN.

CAPTURE OF DESPERATE PERSON FOUND TO BE IN POSSESSION OF COMPLETE SET OF MARIE STOPES.

OLD LOW'S ALMANACK.

PROPHECIES FOR *1931*

money to buy two more caravans. In the January 1929 issue of *Birth Control News* she wrote a gloating note, attacking Catholics who resorted to 'the good old medieval practice of burning instead of enlightening the enemy . . .'[41] There was also an attack in her newspaper on her old enemy, Dr Halliday Sutherland who had, in the meantime, founded an anti-birth control organization, The League of National Life.

When Halliday Sutherland sued her for libel, Marie claimed to be annoyed at the waste of time, as once again Sutherland *versus* Stopes faced each other in the law courts. This time Sutherland lost his case and his appeal. In August 1929, George Bernard Shaw wrote from Malvern, where his plays were in production, to congratulate her:

Dear Marie,
What a lesson! you lose all the cases in which you are clearly in the right. Then you are fortunate enough to be obviously in the wrong and instantly you have a triumph. Moral: take care to be in the wrong always and to conduct your own case.

Congratulations![42]

By 1930, apart from Marie's Mother's Clinic and the Welfare and Sunlight Centre, opened by Norman Haire in St Pancras in 1926, there were a dozen other voluntary clinics in the country from Aberdeen to Cambridge affiliated to the Walworth Centre. They all decided to unite to form the National Birth Control Council. As elder stateswoman of the movement Marie naturally had to be invited and she proposed the resolution to establish the Council. But co-operation did not come naturally to her and it was not a happy arrangement.

In April 1930 Marie wrote personally to Pope Pius XI, pleading for his help in promoting contraception. They were, she assured him, both on the same side, both opposed to the 'evil practice of murderous abortion' and both dedicated to the service of humanity. If she expected a personal reply she was disappointed, but on the last day of the year, the Pope issued *Casti Conubii*, the first papal encyclical on marriage for fifty years.[43] In a section of the Letter, headed 'False Notions concerning Marriage', the Pope might easily have been referring to the work of Marie Stopes:

> For now, alas, not secretly nor under cover but openly, with all sense of shame put aside, now by word, again by writings, by theatrical productions of every kind, by romantic fiction, by amorous and frivolous novels, by cinematographs portraying in vivid scene, in addresses broadcast by radio telephony, in short, by all the inventions of modern science, the sanctity of marriage is tramped upon and derided; divorce, adultery, all the basest vices either are extolled or at least are depicted in such colours as to appear to be free of all reproach and infamy. Books are not lacking which dare to pronounce themselves as scientific but which, in truth, are merely coated with a veneer of science in order that they may the more easily insinuate their ideas . . . First consideration is due to the offspring, which many have the boldness to call the disagreeable burden of matrimony and which they say is to be carefully avoided by married people not through virtuous continence (which Christian law permits in matrimony when both parties consent) but by frustrating the marriage. Some justify this criminal abuse on the ground that they are weary of children and wish to gratify their desires without their consequent burden. Others say that they cannot, on the one hand, remain continent nor, on the other, can they have children because of the difficulties whether on the part of the mother or on the part of family circumstances.

> But no reason, however grave, may be put forward by which anything intrinsically against nature may become conformable to nature and morally good. Since, therefore, the conjugal act is destined primarily by nature for the begetting of children, those who in exercising it

deliberately frustrate its natural power and purpose sin again nature and commit a deed which is shameful and intrinsically vicious.

Marie thought the Papal Letter was a personal reply to her letter. Perhaps that was not an entirely ludicrous idea, since when Dr Halliday Sutherland visited Rome in 1930, the Pope granted him a personal audience and remarked on his battle against birth control.[44]

Late Blooms

'Don't hypnotize yourself into old age' Marie Stopes advised an American doctor when she herself was forty. 'My husband and I are going to be young until we are eighty.'[1] In her fifties she was as good as her word, at her happiest out-of-doors, walking seven or eight miles a day on a Saturday in the Surrey hills; swimming in the sea from her lighthouse at Portland; sunbathing in a deep-backed, short bathing dress ('no tomfoolery of beach pyjamas for me'); dancing; riding; gardening and romping with her son.

She enjoyed food 'pure and uncontaminated', ate a raw, new-laid egg or two with a weak cup of tea when she was tired, and relished chicken with boiled rice, 'as they do it at the Ritz', raw apples, roast pheasant and curly chips, and rich plum-cake. Her diet included orange juice, fluffy omelettes and whitebait, food she recommended to her readers to stimulate sexual appetite.

In 1928 *Enduring Passion* appeared, a sequel to *Married Love* offering, 'Further new contributions to the solution of Sex Difficulties'. Marie had laboured over it for years, gathering evidence from hundreds of correspondents and writing carefully and earnestly. As idealistic as *Married Love*, her later volume promised serenity, and lifelong and 'enduring monogamic devotion' to those who followed her precepts. The book sold well and went into eight editions.

Marie had achieved Married Love and Radiant Motherhood, not without difficulty. But now her own private life was not quite as confident as the title implied. 'To you, hoping it's true' she wrote in Humphrey's copy of the manual for middle-aged lovers. Her advice in the book included reassurance to wives that sexual fulfilment after the menopause was possible and suggestions to husbands who suffered premature ejaculation, a problem she found particularly widespread among middle-class Englishmen. (Her solution to remedy the condition included a lotion to render the penis less sensitive, advice to attempt intercourse for a second time after a pause, and a suggestion that a husband should rouse his wife to orgasm manually.) In a chapter headed 'Under-Sexed Husbands' Marie specifically pointed out the difficulties that might affect men with spinal injuries (Humphrey had suffered from a jarred spine after his air crash ten years earlier).

> In men blows or other injuries to the spine (such as may be experienced through a fall in the hunting field or wounding in warfare or other form of accident) involving those spinal nerves which control the sex organs, may leave the man not only temporarily, but more or less permanently, incapable of a normal sex life.[2]

Even for Marie that was rather near the bone.

There were clear signs in her marriage that after the first happy years, the glamour was wearing thin. The couple had always slept in separate rooms to preserve 'modesty and romance' as she had recommended in *Married Love*. If they went away together, Humphrey was relegated to the second-best bedroom for more prosaic reasons. 'The trouble with him,' she explained to a Mrs Clayton who had kindly offered to put the couple up after Marie's speech to the Portsmouth British Medical Association, 'is that though we love being together, he fidgets and snores so that neither of us gets any rest unless we have a room alone. If you have a tiny room, just a dressing-room with a camp-bed in it, that will be all we want, otherwise I am going to chase him out to a hotel . . .'[3]

Humphrey had always been adoring and respectful towards his wife; after ten years of marriage he had become almost her shadow. He believed in birth control, had proved it before he met her, but now more than anything else he believed in Marie Stopes. When he spoke to the Hornsea Rotary Club in October 1930, the vote of thanks referred almost exclusively to his wonderful wife. 'I agreed with them,' he told her. Humphrey worked at the Clinic, dealing with administration, and sleeping overnight there if necessary. It was he who registered the trade-mark of her 'Pro-Race' cervical cap.

For two or three years after the Clinic was established, Humphrey was described as co-founder; now he was resigned to being a second string. Sometimes he ventured a criticism, urging Marie not to exaggerate the number of patients who attended, for fear that she would lose credibility. (Her claim, in 1930, that she had a failure rate of only 0.52 per cent in 10,000 cases, led the distinguished eugenist, Dr C. P. Blacker, to write that her assessment 'was not borne out by other clinics' and 'would be received with scepticism by other workers in birth control'.[4]

Usually Marie's tendency to exaggerate did not trouble Humphrey unduly. The difficulty lay not in their work together but in the imbalance of their relationship. As she gained in confidence and stature, he lost his grasp on personal identity. Helena Wright, a doctor who had first met the couple on their honeymoon, visited Marie's clinic after a ten-year absence. She was appalled at the change: Marie had become more dogmatic and opinionated than ever, bitter about her own lack of medical qualifications and distraught at Roman Catholic interference. As for Humphrey, Helena Wright described him as a 'gramophone record'.[5]

Marie spent her fiftieth birthday at the Imperial Palace Hotel, Torquay, with Harry, who was convalescing from scarlet fever, while, in London, Humphrey had to report to a room full of disappointed women at the Society for Constructive Birth Control's Annual Meeting that his wife was away. In Torquay, Harry's nurse was with him and Frisk the peke, too, to cheer him up, but Marie was a possessive and jealous mother, convinced that if she stayed away for even an hour or two, little Buffkins would 'crock up'. She disliked hotel life and chafed at the predominantly elderly residents and the proprietors who were modernizing the establishment: 'damn fools, putting basins with taps and electric fires in the whole of this house.'[6]

In her own home smoking was banned and guests had to go upstairs to a smoking-room or into the garden if they wanted a cigarette. In the hotel she couldn't get away from the smoky atmosphere and stuffy lifts and only stayed on for the hot salt baths which she was convinced helped to make Harry strong.

During 1930 Marie spent three holidays away from her husband – in the spring and autumn at the Imperial Palace Hotel, Torquay, and in the summer at the lighthouse, where Humphrey had come down to visit for a few days. All through October and November she was in Torquay with her son. Humphrey was now writing nine or ten letters to Marie's one. Three times in October he asked her whether he should come to Torquay for a weekend at the beginning of November and whether he needed a dinner jacket, his self-abasement faintly embarrassing, before she finally replied. When she wrote with a list of requirements for her homecoming, he did reply with a tinge of sarcasm: 'We will look round for everything to be in Imperial Palace order and a bell in your room . . .'[7]

In retrospect the reasons for the gradual decline in the marriage seem clear. Marie often emphasized that a woman's first baby 'should be her husband – he really needs just the simple loving and petting that is demanded by a child'.[8] Yet ever since Harry was born, Humphrey had begun to feel excluded. Marie was so possessive of her son that she preferred to have him on her own. Although the old endearments persisted in her letters (now more rarely sent) Humphrey, who had basked in the warmth of her love in their early married life, was now a mere husband – not even a breadwinner.

Despite his promise to Marie in the first year of marriage that he would not invest more than £5,000 without consulting her, Humphrey had invested heavily in Gerrards & Co., a firm that sold garage equipment. The firm had suffered badly in the 1929 slump and by 1932 could not pay Humphrey back his loan of £22,838. No letters exist on the subject between husband and wife but, given their relationship, Humphrey obviously told Marie of his unwise investment.

His financial difficulties were compounded by an even more serious deficiency in a husband: he appeared to have lost his sexual drive. Early in February 1931 Marie persuaded him to visit one of her medical friends who was an active member of the Society for Constructive Birth Control. The doctor's report to Marie was disturbing:

> I saw your husband yesterday and feel convinced that there is trouble in the spine . . . His knee jerks are exaggerated and the difficulty he has with regard to getting up at night, sometimes on several occasions to pass water, all point to a defective enervation of the genito-urinary segment of the body arising in the lumbar region of the spinal cord.[9]

The doctor added his own interpretation:

> There is something quite unusual and puzzling about his whole personality. I can express it best by the term 'arrested development': his youthfulness is not that of vitality but of arrested growth; he seems to me to be living in 'mid-air' as it were skimming life: as if the shock of the 'crash' had partly disassociated his personality from the physical body so that the two are not reacting to each other in usual ways, so that the physical tissues age but the lineaments do not bear the impress of internal struggle which is the usual accompaniment of inner development and which leads one to recognize the existence of a person of matured judgement . . . I have prescribed a strong nerve tonic.

Ignoring medical etiquette her medical friend continued to write letters critical of her husband, telling her that Humphrey's anecdotes were boring, his performance at meetings of the Society for Constructive Birth

Control unsatisfactory when she was away. Her dedication on a new edition of *Contraception* in July 1931: 'To a Proof-Reader, with the gratitude of the author', said it all.

Humphrey was made to feel useless as a husband. Perhaps as a consolation he joined the Surrey gliding club in 1930. He had been one of the few pilots in the First World War who had had earlier experience of flying and he never lost his love of the air. He loved Marie deeply and doggedly and was hurt by her attitude. He wrote to Marie on 9 April 1932:

Dearest Sweetheart,
I am not good at putting my thoughts into words. When a Lancashire lad says, 'I love you,' it means far more than a Poet would get into many verses ... suppose I compared my love in the poetic fashion ·with the sky yesterday evening. It really was a beautiful show.
   The poet would have said his love was like that always changing and each time more beautiful. Floating through the sky smoothly and quietly.
   If I had done that you would have wondered what was the matter and think I had copied it word for word from the 'Girl's Friend' or 'Peg's Weekly' so I must not really burst into verses of rhapsody. You must remember I am a plain spoken and dull Lancashire Lad ... Much love to you and the oddments to Buffkins and Nigger [the dog]. With more kisses to you.
Your loving, dull, stupid
Tiger[10]

The letter did touch Marie for she wrote back on 5 May from the Lighthouse at Portland Bill:

Dearest Tiger,
Please bring a recent 'Who's Who' ...
How I wish we could have a talk that wasn't work.
Yours ever
W.N. [Wood Nymph. She drew a kiss.][11]

That was the last love letter Marie wrote to her husband.

Marie had hated their move from Givons Grove to the smaller, surburban house in Hindhead. Living in a road, 'like other people', her family, she considered, had lost their status as landed gentry. She complained of suffering from 'carbon monoxide poisoning' that year from the inhalation of traffic fumes. In 1932 Norbury Park came up for sale, a handsome eighteenth-century mansion set in forty acres of Surrey hills and woodland. Marie knew the house and the surrounding country well and had attended garden parties in the grounds. From the library there was a view of a magnificent glade of trees; and fuschia, cherry, rhododendron and wisteria which made the house a paradise in summer. The famous 'Painted Drawing-room' was decorated with scenes of sunlit pastures by Cipriani, Gilpen Barret and Pastorini. (Marie, curiously, was to keep the nude statues in the drawing-room covered by the curtains; she found them distinctly unappealing.) In this room, with its splendid views, Fanny Burney, Madame de Staël and her lover, Louis de Narbonne, had sat and conversed. Marie coveted the splendour, the elegance, the magnificent grounds of Norbury Park. Here she could hold a salon, be mistress of the manor. In a last desperate bid to restore the marriage Humphrey agreed to the purchase without letting Marie know that their previous home, Heatherbank, was already heavily mortgaged.

Marie was enchanted with her new setting. She described the winding drive up the hill and then 'we are on top looking like a miniature Buckingham Palace'.[12] This was the home she wanted. At a time of great financial stringency, when Marie was complaining of penury and the funds of the Clinic were shrinking, it was a reckless extravagance. The minimum staff Marie felt she could employ was a cook, nurserymaid, housemaid and two menservants indoors and two full-time gardeners, seven in all to service their little family of three. If anything could restore both Marie's creative power and Humphrey's potency it should have been Norbury Park.

In 1929 Marie had edited a collection of letters from working-class women, *Mother England*[13], revealing the plight of overburdened working-class mothers. Mrs R.G.H. of South Wales said:

... what I would like to know, is how I can save having any more children as I think that I have done my duty to my Country having had thirteen children, nine boys and four girls and I have six boys alive now and a little girl who will be three year old in May. I burried a dear little baby girl three week old who died from the strain of the whooping cough. I cannot look after the little one like I would like to as I am getting very stout and cannot bend to bath them and it do jest kill me to carry them in the shawl ... I was nineteen when I married so you can see by the family I have had that I have not had much time for pleasure and it is telling on me now I suffer very bad with varrecross veines in my legs and my ankles gives out and I jest drops down . . .[14]

Rising unemployment in the 1930s still drove families to desperate poverty but, thanks largely to Marie's initiative, they were now demanding a healthier life.

In her early fifties, her own literary output was less prolific than in the past. The only exception was a Christmas entertainment *Buckie's Bears* produced at the Royalty Theatre in 1931. Marie swore that her six-year-old son 'dictated' the play, the story of two polar bears, Sam and Barbara, who escape from the Zoo into fairyland.

Little Harry was not allowed to read any books, since Marie believed that reading encouraged second-hand minds, but he heard plenty of stories and was prompted to write. Marie told even close friends that Harry Buffkins had done at least 50 per cent of the work. The author today says he cannot remember. In any case, the play was a charming success, produced five times in all. At Christmas 1933 Marie offered a box at the theatre to the Duchess of York: 'My little boy,' she wrote, 'craved the honour of presenting the Princess Elizabeth [now the Queen] with a box to see his play.' The Duchess declined the invitation since the little Princesses were going to spend Christmas in the country. Apart from that flight into fairyland with her son, Marie produced no books of advice or health information and no fiction in the years between 1929 and 1933. She was having trouble with her little son's fostered companions and may well have been going through the menopause, so that even her vitality had flagged. There were also other reasons for discouragement.

Ten years after the publication of *Married Love*, Marie was indisputably a celebrity, known throughout the world for her works on sex. When asked for her autograph or photograph, she now charged five shillings towards the funds of her Society. But by the late 1920s there were signs that control of the movement that had made her famous was slipping from her hands. Political parties, women's groups, doctors and economists had interested themselves in the subject: birth control was 'in'. Marie's methods were so personalized, her opinions so inflexible, that they antagonized medical opinion, just as her opposition to Roman Catholics dismayed other voluntary workers, who felt that her virulent campaign was counter-productive.

She still believed that the small check pessary was the best means of contraception although others now thought the Dutch cap better and no method yet ideal. Although she had appointed her own Medical Research Committee, made up of distinguished doctors, as early as 1923, her opinions predominated. Always it was her obtrusive personal vanity and her exaggerated claims of success that prevented her from being taken as seriously as she deserved. Since 1925 she had not only trained the nurses in her Clinics but set their examinations herself. In one of the questions, candidates were required to write brief essays in reply to objections to contraceptives on the grounds that they were: (a) immoral; (b) led to sterility; and (c) that Dr Stopes's methods are no good.

In 1927 the Medical Committee of the National Birth Rate Commission drew attention to the need for scientific knowledge of the different means of contraception used in the voluntary clinics. The Birth Control Investigation Committee (BCIC) was formed that year to make an impartial and scientific study of the methods, aims and possible effects of contraception, with Sir Humphrey Rolleston as Chairman and Lord Brain and Sir Julian Huxley among the members.

The campaign to persuade Government to offer birth control to all, led by the Labour Party, culminated, in 1930, in a public conference. Health workers, welfare officers, councillors, medical officers of health, women's organizations and birth control organizations all attended, and a resolution was sent from the conference to the Ministry of Health asking for birth control advice to be made available to married people. For years Marie had been writing letters and articles on the subject, even sending deputations. She, of course, wanted all birth control information to be guided by her ideas and channelled through her.

Three months later, in July 1930, the Ministry of Health dribbled out a memorandum, 153/M.C.W. The typewritten document was duplicated and circulated neither to the press nor the Local Authorities generally. Only maternity and child welfare authorities received the memorandum, which squirmed round the subject with obscure wording. First of all, it reaffirmed that it was not the centres' function to provide birth control advice. Only in cases where there were medical grounds, where further pregnancy would be detrimental to health, could such advice be given. And then, as if the very topic were contaminating, the advice had to be given at a separate session. Nevertheless, it represented a triumph. Officialdom had at last conceded that birth control could be used to preserve life.

Marie claimed that a Secretary of State from the Ministry came to her house in Hindhead to hand her a copy of the semi-secret document personally, telling her that the Government had decided not to oppose her work any longer. However she came to possess a copy of the memorandum, Marie was indisputably the first to publish it, triumphantly and in full, in her *Birth Control News* for September 1930. After this public exposure, the Ministry eventually reprinted the document officially. Although local councils were empowered to introduce birth control clinics, opposition, principally from Roman Catholics, delayed their establishment, and Marie Stopes held meetings to back those councils who stood firm against church hostility.

Throughout the 1930s the work of the voluntary clinics was still vital, and in 1930 existing birth control societies decided to amalgamate to form a national birth control organization. The Committee, made up of Labour campaigners, former suffragettes and do-gooders, wanted to exclude Marie Stopes: she was too autocratic and had no medical authority. But Helena Wright, Marie's friend from her early married days, who was by now a prominent doctor in the birth control movement, refused to join unless Marie was included and this was agreed, provided Helena would undertake to 'manage' Marie.[15]

On 17 July, at the home of Lady Denman in Upper Grosvenor Street, Marie Stopes and Ernest Thurtle, Labour MP for Shoreditch and a staunch supporter of the work, proposed the motion that brought the National Birth Control Council into existence. Marie was not happy about the new Association. In her view it was unnecessary to found another society. As they had feared, she tried to dominate the meetings and was 'neither modest nor statesmanlike, nor co-operative on Committee'.[16]

The National Council changed its name in 1931 to the National Birth Control Association (NBCA) to allow new branches to join without representation on the Governing Body. (In 1939 the NBCA changed its name to the FPA, Family Planning Association, because 'in future it would help women to have wanted children in the same spirit as it would help them to avoid having unwanted children', a point Marie had thought of in 1921, when she named her Society for Constructive Birth Control.)

The uneasy co-existence on the Committee of Marie Stopes versus the rest could not last, and in November 1933 she resigned from the Association without stating her reasons. According to Helena Wright, who drove her home, Marie was in a furious temper and told Helena she was the only member of the organization in whom she had any confidence. 'Can you find me a woman doctor who would run my Clinic in my way and according to my instructions?' she asked Dr Wright. 'Dr Stopes, such a woman does not exist,' Helena Wright replied.[17]

In August 1930 it had been Helena Wright, not Marie Stopes, who addressed the Lambeth Conference of Anglican Bishops so persuasively on the subject of birth control that they passed a resolution expressing limited approval for it. Ten years earlier, when Marie had sent what she claimed was a divinely inspired message to the Bishops, they had ignored her. Helena Wright spoke more moderately and rationally of the working-class women who were her patients, who had more children than they could afford. Whether it was her more direct approach or the changed climate in society which Marie had helped to create, it was another sign that she was no longer in sole charge of the movement.

She was to publish four more books on sex and birth control in the 1930s. *Birth Control Today* had the curious sub-title, 'A Practical Handbook for those who want to be their own masters in this vital matter'. That proved popular and went into ten editions. *Marriage in my Time*, one of a series, was not reprinted, while *Change of Life in Men and Women*, published in 1936, also sold well. This book put forward the then startling theory that men as well as women undergo a critical bodily change in middle age. H. G. Wells, who delighted in teasing Marie, denied that possibility.

It's a great and selling idea to write a book on The Change of Life. But I don't find much in the book . . . I am 70 . . . I have never been able to detect any lunar periodicity in my life although I kept a very careful private diary. I don't think there is any male equivalent to menstruation or the menopause.[18]

Marie's war with the Roman Catholics was highly personal. She made one last furious attempt to defeat her old enemies and turn the Protestant press against the infamies of the Roman Catholics. Remembering the spectacular success of *Married Love* and wanting a best-seller, Peter Davies the publisher asked her to write on a subject of her choice. She elected to write on *Roman Catholic Methods of Birth Control*. When it appeared, the book was virtually ignored by the press; Marie was infuriated and frustrated. She tried to bully booksellers who were reluctant to display the book for fear of offending their Catholic customers. When that failed she invited Herbert van Thal from her publishers to Norbury Park to reveal to him a plot she had laid.

His part in the conspiracy was to wait at the main entrance of the

Army and Navy stores in London, with a representative of the Associated Press:

> Dr Stopes was going to demonstrate about her new book, *Roman Catholic Methods of Birth Control* . . . a car suddenly drew up on the other side of the road. A white handkerchief was waved from it – a signal that I was to follow the car. I asked my unwilling conspirator to remain where he was. In a side street I was bundled into the car. Looking as white as a sheet and dressed in green and wearing green sandals, Dr Stopes mysteriously produced a plan. Sweat poured out of me when she told me it was a plan of Westminster Cathedral . . . A copy of *Roman Catholic Methods of Birth Control* was to be chained to the foot of the font of the Cathedral by Dr Stopes herself and I was to play the part of spying out the land . . . I was, to tell the truth, pretty nervous. I had visions of being arrested by the Cathedral authorities for aiding and abetting Dr Stopes. It was indeed hard work getting the Press Association man to come along with me, especially when we confronted a policeman at the Cathedral door.
>
> Eventually, I spied out the place . . . I gave the 'all clear' signal of purchasing a post-card. The 'green ghost' appeared, padded up the aisle, chained the book and went her way again.[19]

A sacristan quickly sawed through the chain. The press-man and her publisher fled. Marie's intricate plot to gain publicity and draw attention to her views on Catholic contraception had flopped. She was still in the thick of the battle, still personally reviled by enemies who tried to imply that any woman interested in such a soiled subject must be a person of loose morals.

The irony was that by the summer of 1933 Marie Stopes was a deeply frustrated woman, not only professionally but personally. The author of *Married Love*, who had done so much to enhance the sex life of couples all over the world, had a husband who could no longer satisfy her. Charged with vitality and health herself, that summer at the Lighthouse in Portland Marie had hoped to revive Humphrey's flagging desire. Humiliated and ashamed, Humphrey had suggested that since he could no longer make love to her, she should take a lover, so long as they could stay together.

At the time she rejected the idea indignantly. She had many men friends, but she was concerned with Harry's welfare, with her birth control work, with maintaining the façade of a marriage. Every Christmas the cards from Norbury Park showed photographs of Humphrey,

Marie and Harry as a happy family. Nevertheless in 1934 she went up to Scotland with Harry; as he grew older he became more and more her escort.

The nature of her work took Marie away from home frequently. Throughout the 1930s she founded new branches of the Mother's Clinic in Cardiff, Aberdeen, Leeds and Belfast. Belfast, with its strong Roman Catholic presence, was a particular triumph for her. The city in the 1930s was by no means a permissive society and the subject of birth control was considered a delicate topic of conversation in polite society there until well after the Second World War. Few medical men outside the University were prepared to support the cause of birth control openly.

To win friends for the new Clinic and introduce Dr Stopes to influential people, a dinner party was arranged by a consultant's wife, with Dr Stopes as guest of honour. The other guests were mainly non-medical people. To the hostess's discomfort, Marie seemed impervious to the usual conventions and social pleasantries and all through dinner 'gave a running lecture on methods of contraception, at one point even producing a Dutch cap from her handbag and passing it round the dinner table'.[20]

The honorary secretary of the Belfast Clinic recalled that Dr Stopes insisted on 'controlling the budget stringently'. No petty cash was available and when items such as crockery, dusters or brushes needed replacing, a detailed request had to be sent to London. Not until written permission was given could replacements be bought.

Funds remained a source of difficulty in the 1930s, with continual rises in costs and although Marie held grand fund-raising balls and dinners she could not raise sufficient money to keep the Clinic bank account always in the black. Since her student days she had made believe that a wealthy man would fund her work, and this time she appealed to Lord Leverhulme, but without success.

Now that birth control clinics were beginning to proliferate at home, Marie turned more of her attention abroad. 'I ought to have a clinic in every country in the world,' she told Earle Balch of Putnams in New York. For years she had concerned herself with India's population problem, written articles about birth control in Indian newspapers, produced a simple pamphlet for oriental countries. She attacked, in print, Gandhi's religious scruples about birth control. (Gandhi contended that birth control led to 'imbecility and nervous prostration'). In South Africa, Australia and New Zealand she had clinics affiliated to hers and longed to see them throughout the Empire. However, she drew the line at helping a Russian professor who asked her for assistance because of her hatred of 'Bolshevism'.

She found the political climate of the 1930s disturbing to her work and remarked to her American publisher on the 'not very cheering' news of the Italian/Abyssinian conflict: 'I shall be glad when the world settles down again, if it does in my lifetime, to let people get on with the things that really matter.'[21]

Always star-struck, Marie tried to inject a little glamour into the world of birth control. She invited Gloria Swanson to be the Guest of Honour at the 1932 A.G.M. of her Society. (She did not come.) In 1934 she sent Gracie Fields copies of her books and she kept hoping that Noël Coward would attend one of her functions.

In the popular press her forthright and extreme views made her an attraction. In 1935 a shrewd editor of the *Guernsey Star and Gazette* asked Marie to write on the theme 'If I had become dictator of England'. Her simplistic recipe:

> Remove existing petty official interferences. Restore independence of character. Stop the dole. Provide work for all healthy people. Fundamentally simplify income tax, releasing stagnation of money. Strengthen and link up the whole British Empire. Plant complete townlets in suitable unpopulated spots in Canada, Australia, Africa etc. Breed for fitness, beauty and a joyous existence.[22]

Although her best work was done, Marie's fame was still increasing: 'your name is better known in the heart of darkest Africa than that of any other writer,' the social anthropologist Professor Malinowski told her in 1934.[23] And in 1935 a group of American academics listed *Married Love* as sixteenth in a list of the twenty-five most influential books of the previous fifty years, ahead of Einstein's *Relativity*, Freud's *Interpretation of Dreams* and Hitler's *Mein Kampf*.[24]

At home, throughout the 1930s, she was canvassed for opinions on Health and Happiness, Love, Marriage, Parenthood, Youth and Middle Age. She was still a striking figure, in woolly, home-made dresses, often in green to bring out the green flecks in her piercing hazel eyes, with no bra or corset, head up, looking out at the world defiantly.

She enjoyed entertaining and gave parties at bluebell time, week-end house parties and children's tea parties that merged into evening dances. Marie's forthright and uninvited views on the right way to feed, educate and generally care for children made her a disconcerting hostess. In

1935 Molly Wallis, wife of the inventor and aeronautical engineer Barnes Wallis, took her daughter Mary, aged eight, to a party given by a mutual friend. Mrs Wallis was struck with the rare beauty and extraordinary dress of one of the young guests, wearing a pleated knitted woollen skirt. Was the child a boy or a girl, she asked Marie. Marie replied that he was her son Harry and she explained candidly that she preferred him to wear kilts to protect his genitals from the risk of wearing ordinary trousers. At eleven Harry either wore loose knitted trousers or kilts. A handsome and intelligent boy, Harry was now a companion for Marie, played chess with her, camped with her and innocently colluded with her to humiliate his father. 'One April Fool's day I pinned a "Kick Me" notice on [Humphrey's] back and he was hurt and angry . . . I was at that time completely identifying with my mother.'[25]

Since she had taken over her new home, the 'Queen' of Norbury Park had become even more imperious in her attitude towards her husband. Marie, of course, appropriated the largest main bedroom, Harry occupied the second main room and Humphrey slept in the third room, facing north. Humphrey, who still looked much younger than Marie, took his meals separately and went his own way. A publishing friend who saw him sometimes at the Society for Birth Control meetings described him as 'a man whipped'.[26]

In 1936 Marie decided to take a cruise for two weeks. For the first time for eighteen years, since Married Love was published, she left home without taking any work or correspondence with her. Her companion on the voyage was Harry, a tall, good-looking lad of twelve. Humphrey remained behind, to answer the telephone and as always to protect Marie Stopes's image.

Now in her mid-fifties, Marie was, in certain respects an outdated figure. Despite the loyal efforts of journalist friends like Mollie Wrench to keep her name in front of the public, Marie's influence was on the wane. Birth control campaigners and one or two Members of Parliament took up the case for Abortion Law Reform in the mid–1930s but Marie Stopes would not countenance it.

Edith Summerskill, a young doctor, later a campaigning Member of Parliament, who admired Marie Stopes, remembered vividly a lunch at Norbury Park. A woman journalist present at the table asked Marie what she thought about the legalization of abortion. 'I do not allow such a matter to be discussed in front of my son,' Marie replied icily and the matter was dropped.[27] She was also vehemently opposed to homosexuality and to any suggestion that unmarried girls, even those who were to be married imminently, should be permitted to obtain birth control advice.

In 1936 Marie Stopes was dreaming of heading a campaign for Beauty in Poetry. She had tired of a world 'that seems to think I was made for its service and would have clawed me to pieces long ago had I not been rooted in rock'.[28] After all her buffeting, all her success and failure, she was still yearning for fairy-tale fame as a writer, a poet, still dreaming of an ideal lover. 'I am going to be a poet of some note before long,' she wrote confidently to her American publisher in June 1937. Reading poetry, writing poetry began to take up more of her time.

In November 1937 Marie read a book about Oxford, *Oxford Limited*, written by a young graduate just down from university with a reputation as editor of Isis and a promising poet. Since Oxford was one of her choices for Harry, she invited the author, Keith Briant, to lunch with her at Norbury Park. Marie felt an instant attraction towards the spirited yet gentle young writer who looked not unlike a younger version of Humphrey. Keith was thirty-three years her junior, sensitive and pliable, and thoughts of him began to intrude in her mind.

In the summer of 1938 Humphrey and Marie were staying at the Lighthouse as usual. On the evening of 23 July Humphrey handed Marie a note. It had no form of personal address and can only be described as a statement:

> Five years ago when here, I told you I wanted no more sex union and that I should not object if you decided to have a lover to replace my deficiency. You were very hurt and answered that it was unthinkable. Now that you have suffered sex deprivation all these years you may feel differently, and I wish to put it on record that, if you did, it would not alter our existing relations, and I should never reproach you or take any steps about it as I have long considered a wife whose husband is incapable of coitus has every right to supplement his deficiency without breaking up the home.

The note was signed 'H. V. Roe'.[29]

The detached style of the communication seems quite uncharacteristic of Humphrey. His tone in his letters to Marie had always been utterly sincere although he could be pompous and stilted as well as tender. This calculated, impersonal note, almost a memorandum, makes it extremely unlikely that Humphrey could have written it. Marie dictated it almost certainly, just as she had formerly dictated notes in which he promised not to waste his money. By 1938, openly despised by both his wife and his son, Humphrey was a broken man. Everything he had tried his hand at had failed. He was, like all Marie's men, extremely sensitive, and he still loved her deeply.

She, however, was now besotted with Keith Briant, inviting him to Norbury or making excuses to meet him in town. As always, she tried to convince herself that she was beyond reproach, her legacy from her mother's stern upbringing demanded that. She had built up such an impregnable image of herself as the people's adviser on love and marriage, that the sanction of her husband for taking a lover was essential.

A month after Humphrey handed her her sexual freedom in a note, another man from her past, Aylmer Maude, died aged eighty. He had spent the week-end of his birthday with her at Norbury Park. For almost a quarter of a century he had remained a loyal and loving friend.

Marie now looked to the future. She had made up her mind to ignore chronological age. At fifty-eight, she was, she said and believed, psychologically twenty-six. To stay healthy she was convinced that she needed sexual intercourse, that the male hormones were vital to her well-being. She began to collect records of men and women who lived to be more than one hundred and to study the reasons for longevity.

The 1930s had been frustrating years for her. She had felt cut off, gagged and unable to speak in public through what she saw as a ban by some of the newspapers, by the cinema (and she considered she had an important future as a script writer) and, most of all, by the evolving BBC. Some of the press, notably *The Times*, ignored her deliberately. Prominent men, priests, economists and doctors all spoke on birth control and population problems on the wireless. Marie wrote endless letters to her supporters asking them to write to the BBC. But despite their loyal letters and her efforts to persuade Lord Reith (who lunched her at Claridges in 1935) she was denied a microphone. The 'gagging' was not imaginary. Marie was a pioneer and had important things to say, but editors and producers were, as she suspected, fearful of offending Roman Catholic readers and listeners, and she did not help her cause by the tone of shrill insistence.

Marie needed an outlet, needed to renew herself and, during 1938, she wrote poetry almost every day and courted the older leading poets assiduously, sending them her work, inviting them to Norbury (the Poet Laureate, John Masefield, declined, very courteously each time), looking not so much for advice as for approval of her work. She gathered round her some strange allies. Marie regarded Lord Alfred Douglas (Oscar Wilde's ageing lover, 'Bosie', now an impoverished man of sixty-eight) as one of the greatest living poets and sent him a batch of her poems signing herself 'Marie Carmichael'. She wanted to keep her identity hidden, since Douglas, a Roman Catholic, had attacked her birth control reforms in print. He replied kindly enough, telling her that many of his own poems had been refused by the press. She took his letter as positive encouragement and decided that her plan must be to have a volume of poetry published. The next question was how.

Alfred Douglas was not too forthcoming. Her work was pleasant, he wrote, but he could not 'hail her as a genius'. She could get a small volume published for about fifty pounds. That was not what she wanted to hear, but she wrote again, and sent more poems. To Alfred Douglas she was taking the whole 'desperate blood and sweat business' of writing a good sonnet too lightly:

> I fear you have a fatal facility. I don't find one of them [her sonnets] which gives me the impression of being a great sonnet . . . All the same I know you won't be discouraged by what I say. It will probably make you angry! And it may egg you on to write a great sonnet. I'll believe it when I see it, but I don't somehow think that great sonnets can be written in a motor car on the way up to London.[30]

Despite the fact that Douglas embodied two of Marie's prejudices, Roman Catholicism and homosexuality, she was delighted with the friendship. She admired his poetry and was attracted by his title. Late in November, Alfred Douglas fell seriously ill and Marie sent a seasonal gift of a cheque and offered to help him with his rent if necessary. He was right about her tenacity. While he was recovering she sent Douglas the typescript of her volume of love poems, with a bottle of the best tonic she knew (Syrup of Hypophosphites, a popular patent medicine at the time). In the New Year, Lord Alfred invited Marie to tea in his rented rooms in Hove, and before that meeting took place Marie revealed her true identity. Alfred Douglas was too taken with the personality revealed in her letters to mind. On 14 February 1939 he wrote:

Dear Mrs Carmichael,
I was astounded to see the signature on your letter received this morning. I had not the remotest idea that you were Marie Stopes . . . I have in the past criticized you rather strongly. Naturally, as a Cath-

olic, I disagree with your views about birth control. But now that you have written one so many kind letters and shown so much interest in me and my poetry and my health and worldly condition, I feel remorseful to think that I have ever had unkind thoughts about you . . .

Marie took tea with Lord Alfred at Hove, thrilled with the 'honour and pleasure' of meeting him. The following month she arranged a literary weekend at Norbury Park. Marie warned Lord Alfred Douglas that her husband was 'very illiterate and laughed at poetry and my son despised it'. Among the guests on the week-end of 18 March were Ernest Shepard, illustrator of A. A. Milne's *Winnie the Pooh*, his son-in-law E. V. Knox, the editor of *Punch* and his wife, and Mrs Munro (presumably the wife of the poet, Harold Munro). Neither Marie nor the majority of her guests had the slightest interest in or understanding of modern poetry. At tea-time Mrs Munro and Douglas had a talk about T. S. Eliot and his poetry which came dangerously near to a fight, with 'Lord Alfred maintaining that Eliot was not a real poet and Mrs Munro violent that he was'. After that Marie managed to steer the conversation away from Eliot and throughout the week-end Lord Alfred reminisced about Wilde. According to Bosie, a number of the jokes in *The Importance of Being Earnest* were part of his own repartee, 'worked up and incorporated in the play'.

In late March beset with money worries, Bosie wrote to Marie confessing his anxieties. With her usual vigour she organized a petition to secure a Civil List pension for him. Among the signatories were James Agate, Edmund Blunden, Sir Arthur Quiller-Couch, John Gielgud, Harold Nicolson, Hugh Walpole, Evelyn Waugh, Virginia Woolf and Marie Stopes.

Meanwhile, Marie worked on her own love poems. Most of them had been written between July and December 1938 and a number, in the manuscript version, were dedicated to 'K'. The thought of Keith began to obsess her. After a dinner at the Ritz, which was to become their haunt, Keith followed her up the stairs. 'I felt his pulsing hand on my arm so softly and insistently and he kissed me so sweetly and softly good night.' Just as years ago she had noted her physical reaction to the desire for Aylmer Maude, now the scientist in her recorded that the thought of Keith, the desire to be with him, was accompanied by definite physical pain in small spasms.[31]

Marie's obsession with Keith had all the intensity and naïvety of adolescence, reflected in her poetry:

THE FIRST WALK

> I feel as though we held each other's hands
> Like babies in a field of daisy chains.
> Did we not run and laugh and sing
> Like children freed from school on sunny day?
> I feel as though we kissed by a sweet briar
> Fond lovers underneath a country moon.
> The foolish outward fact established stands
> We walked on streets remote from country lanes.
> You kept a yard away, said not one thing
> While I could think of nothing more to say.
> No ventured kissing turned our blood to fire,
> Your wordless parting severed us too soon.[32]

At the time she had a passion for 'fire baths'. The heat from a glowing coal fire on a naked body could cure a cold in half-an-hour, she believed, and in her poem 'The Hearth' she paints the scene:

> Primeval forest warms our curtained room
> Primeval energies in hot coals fall
> Into our silence, stir primeval deeps. . .

Like all her lovers, Keith was easily dominated, and in these poems Marie revealed the complexity of her androgynous nature. With Keith, in real life she was the pursuer and, necessarily, the provider. In several of the poems she writes of the love of woman but never more explicitly than in 'Your Moonlit Face' where, in imagination at least, she is the dominant partner in love-making:

> Words have departed
> For your tongue
> Now slip's between caressing lips
> And all my manhood
> Throbs in search of life's
> Deep source within you.[33]

The confusion of her role as a modern superwoman, born out of her time, is reflected in another poem:

HE TO HER

> You tramp in boyish breeches
> You fly in goggled cap
> Toss me your hard-earned riches
> And call a ring a trap.
>
> Spite all your cruel goading
> When we are lone at night
> You shed your modern moding
> Slipping to woman bright.[34]

Marie wrote in the notes to the poems: 'In some of the poems a man is speaking and in others a woman . . .' and she explained that nearly all of them 'sang a first line in my head'. She wrote them down often after waking from sleep, 'with no inkling as to what the poem was to be about'. She warns the too literal reader not to make the mistake of 'assuming only an autobiographic "I" in this book'. Marie explained that a great poet (Lord Alfred Douglas) had found her poems too intimate, 'personal accounts of your own experience with your lover'. 'I state emphatically that they are not so. Many of the most personally worded have no basis in any physical experience of my own, but came swiftly transmitted from the storehouse of human emotion . . .' In a contradictory afterthought, she added: 'Nowadays nothing is too personal for expression in prose, so surely there can be no good reason why the deep pools of the love experience of the human heart should be denied a poet because of the particularity of the radiance that may flash from surface ripples'.[35]

The poem regarded by John Masefield and others as her most successful, 'We Burn', was based not on her amatory experiences but on her knowledge, as a scientist, that the heat of the body depends on the burning of carbon by oxygen within the tissues:

> We speak of fire
> When oxygen leaps swift
> In fierce embrace to carbon,
> Then the lift
> Of heat flicks red-hot tongues
> So fierce they heavenward aspire.
> Eyes that perceive the smoke,
> The glow, the cinder,
> Of swift embrace divalent,

Yet are blind
When the same force plays on a lower scale
Whose ranges lend to man his lissom life,
His power, his love, and all his leaping strife.[36]

Marie claimed that she had tried to deflect comment about her personal passion by the Notes to the poetry. But she could scarcely have been more explicit in her Acknowledgement. First she expressed her thanks to all the eminent men who had helped her: they included John Masefield, George Bernard Shaw, Walter de la Mare, Lord Alfred Douglas and Sir James Jeans, the astronomer. Then, she thanked Keith Briant 'though last, I place first in my gratitude, for he is of the generation for whom the poems are written'. The volume was dedicated to young lovers.

Keith described her as a 'vigorous woman in her fifties, but with clear complexion, vivid, sparkling eyes and chestnut hair, she might have been in her forties.[37] To a young man just down from Oxford Marie had many attractions to offer. She possessed a talent for collecting celebrities at her home and Keith, who was a journalist with the *Sunday Chronicle*, could not fail to make useful contacts through her. Despite her age Marie generated an excitement and a passion for living. Her imagination as well as her body craved the stimulus of a lover and at last, she felt, she had found a man who could satisfy her spiritually, physically and emotionally. At the time, she felt vague spiritual longings, took an interest in theosophy and mysticism, and increasingly she seemed cut off from everyday reality. She invited her young lover to be Guest of Honour to the Society for Constructive Birth Control's Annual Dinner.

Her new *affaire* gave her new fire, new ambition. Now that her collection of poems was complete, she desperately wanted a publisher. Early in January 1939 she went up to see Geoffrey Faber with her poems. He tried to convince her that his firm was committed to publishing *modern* poetry, but on her insistence kept her typescript for ten days and then wrote a letter of rejection which is a model of tact:

Dear Dr Stopes,
When you paid us the compliment of offering us LOVE POEMS FOR YOUNG LOVERS, you set us a more baffling problem than you knew – a problem that has in fact defeated us. It is with very great regret that I find myself obliged to refuse the privilege of publishing them, the more so because it must be most difficult indeed for anybody who is not very familiar indeed with the peculiar position of poetry in the modern publishing world to understand the reasons that we find most

compelling – which is almost as much as to say anybody outside our own office! I tried to indicate the nature of the problem when you came to see me, not – I felt – altogether successfully . . .

When I began to build up this business, my ambition was to give it a universal character. It happened that my principal personal contacts were what are called 'highbrow'; and it followed naturally that our development at first tended in that direction. It is extraordinary how quickly that sort of thing becomes a label – one of those sticky labels which it takes a lot of time and effort to scrape off. Well, I have scraped most of it off by now, and all that is left of it is simply a general sense that we set a high standard – as distinct from a highbrow standard. (Two utterly different things you will agree!)

But in poetry it is different. There we have been confronted by a dichotomy in the world of poetry itself, a phenomenon which belongs to this uneasy transitional post-war age, that is perhaps at the same time a pre-war age. After the war, the publication of poetry became almost impossible – then, by degrees, the distinctively modern school began to gain ground, and through my friendship with T. S. Eliot I and my firm became very specially and closely associated with it as the publishers of Eliot, Spender, Auden and others. I confessed to you when we met that my own earlier ambitions had been in the direction of poetry. But after the war, for whatever reason, my talent, such as it was – began to wither and the reason for that, I think, was not so much a change in me as a change in the world and in the outlook of the younger generations by whose approval poetry must always live when it is first written and published. The direction taken by the representative modern writer was very different from the direction I would have taken. Nevertheless, I have grown to approve it – not absolutely, but in relation to the period; and I suppose publishing it has not only helped me to understand it, but has, in some queer way, satisfied my own frustrated ambition.

That was how our character as the publishers of this modern poetry began. But of course it very soon took on a commercial aspect. It became an important and is indeed now a very important part of our business. And it wasn't long before I discovered that this label was sticking for good. I have made occasional efforts to give our poetical list a more comprehensive character – but never with success. Our public will follow us in the one direction; it will not follow us in the other. And – another danger – our own authors (the poets I mean) watch what we do very closely.

When you brought me your poems I knew that the question for us was not at all 'how good are they?' (for that question has already been authoritatively answered in the way you know) but 'will our list suit them?' And the answer upon which we all agreed, after ten days of discussion is that it will not suit them; that in fact they would as coming from us, make exactly the wrong approach, both to the critics and to the booksellers and through them to the public. That they ought to reach a very large public is not to be doubted. But it would be a mistake (from your point of view) if we published them; and we ourselves, aware of this, should not be as comfortable and confident in our handling of them as a publisher needs to be.

With my cordial good wishes for their great success,

I am
Yours sincerely
GEOFFREY FABER[38]

Marie was out of sympathy politically as well as stylistically with many of the left-wing poets on Faber's list. Although through the influence of Aylmer Maude she had mixed with the Fabians, she was, as she often said herself, a natural Conservative. As she grew older she became more chauvinistic, violently anti-Catholic, of course, and selectively anti-Semitic. One of her rhymes, written in 1942, ran:

> Catholics, Prussians,
> The Jews and the Russians,
> All are a curse
> Or something worse ... .[39]

She disapproved of Mussolini and Hitler for their attempts to raise the birth rate in their countries. But the Nazi policy of breeding for fitness was uncomfortably close to her own. In August 1939, one month before the Second World War broke out, she sent a copy of her volume of poetry *Love Songs for Young Lovers*, which had been published by Heinemann in March that year, to Hitler with a note:

12 August, 1939

Dear Herr Hitler,
Love is the greatest thing in the world: so will you accept from me these *Love Songs for Young Lovers* that you may allow the young people of your nation to have them?

The young must learn love from the particular 'till they are wise enough for the universal.

I hope too that you yourself may find something to enjoy in the book.

Believe me,
Yours faithfully,
Marie C. Stopes[40]

Surviving

During the week-end in which the Second World War broke out, Humphrey, who was living in lodgings in London, wrote to ask Marie if he could come home for two days. 'I can sleep in the Lounge that night if somebody is in my room.'[1] By now he had accommodated himself to being an occasional guest at Norbury Park. He was running Gerrards, the firm in which he had unwisely invested, single-handed.

Humphrey's business Gerrards was close to the Clinic and Humphrey still went in almost every day, visited contraceptive manufacturers when necessary and reported back to Marie.

Harry too, Marie's adored son, was leaving home to start the autumn term at Charterhouse. Marie had decided that the boy needed to gain some formal education before university, although she thought Harry still, at fifteen, usually dressed in brightly coloured knitted trousers or kilts, looked 'horrid' in his school uniform.

At Christmas every year the family presented a united front. They held a large party at Norbury and the Christmas card sent greetings and best wishes from:

Humphrey V. Roe   Marie C. Stopes
and Harry.

But effectively the marriage was over. In her sixtieth year, with her second book of poetry *Love Songs for Young Lovers* published, Marie launched into a new life, her friends and cronies now mainly poets and literary people. Poetry was not a new interest, she had joined the Poetry Society thirty years earlier but now most of her time was devoted to it. That did not preclude her from feeling that she had a mission to save the nation.

Despite her earlier letter to Hitler (and Lord Alfred Douglas and other right-wing friends had persuaded her that Hitler would not invade

Poland), once war was declared she became ferociously patriotic. She offered her home, Norbury Park as a convalescent home for officers – fortunately, perhaps, that offer was declined. She also offered her advice to the Government freely on a multitude of questions. At the end of March 1940 she wrote to Lord Halifax, the Foreign Secretary, for an appointment about a matter that 'Lord Halifax alone can deal with'. Marie assured the Foreign Secretary that it had nothing to do with birth control. She was concerned, she told him, about the urgent need to conserve culture and use the country's graduates wisely and economically in war-time. That was part of Marie's philosophy and perhaps she was also thinking of the future of her lover (who was of military age) and of her own son.

When she came home, she sent the Foreign Secretary a brief summary of her life and career. She had discussed with him the possibility of joining the Cabinet and pointed out that her breadth of contact and variety of expert qualifications might make her 'of real use as a woman statesman . . . I am convinced,' she continued, 'that there ought to be a woman in the Cabinet and very soon she would be of value.' Also the mere presence of Marie Stopes in the Cabinet 'would increase confidence in certain quarters . . .'[2]

From time to time in the past twenty years Marie had considered entering Parliament but her other interests and her lack of footing in any party had prevented her. Intellectually she would have been a great asset, but the vanity which she had never learnt to conceal, and her dogmatism, obscured her judgement. During a debate on birth control in the House of Commons in December 1938, Marie had been present in the Visitors' Gallery. She wrote to Richard Acland, a warm supporter of her cause, grumbling that *The Times* had included the 'cheers' and 'Hear! hear!' when other members spoke but left them out when Dick got up, and omitted the 'absolutely echoing, reverberating "Hear! hear's" from both sides of the House when you mentioned my name'.[3] No Cabinet position was offered but Marie continued to campaign from the sidelines. On 12 July 1940 she sent Winston Churchill a letter marked 'Personal':

Dear Mr Churchill,
May I give you a slogan?
Fight the Battle of Britain in Berlin's air
Lord Beaverbrook has now got the machines – the German's mentality is that of a bully who will squeal if hit between the eyes. Please win

the war in a few weeks by releasing the order to Fight the Battle of Britain in Berlin's air.[4]

It was Mr Attlee who wrote back austerely:

... The question of what targets should be bombed is one primarily for the military authorities.
We will not indulge in indiscriminate bombing of civilians . . .[5]

From the Foreign Office, however, Lord Halifax took her idea more seriously: 'I have read with interest your letter of July 12 [to Churchill] suggesting that the R.A.F. should continuously bomb Berlin. I have also sent a copy to the Secretary of State for Air . . .'[6] That there were some in the Cabinet who held similar views was demonstrated by the bombing of Berlin and other cities.

By 1940 the war began to affect Marie personally. Keith joined the army and became engaged to a girl of his own age. Marie accepted his new attachment (although she tried to avoid meeting his fiancée) but had no intention of giving him up as a lover. She believed that fine young men like Keith should breed fine children.

Humphrey rejoined the Royal Air Force Volunteer Reserve at sixty-two, and Pilot Officer H. V. Roe, on ground duties, regained some of his old self-respect. He wrote to Marie on her sixtieth birthday, sending her a silk cord from a captured German parachute as a present. He sent warm birthday greetings, adding rather sadly, 'I shall be duty officer on that day, so you will be quite safe.'[7]

Like everyone else Marie was short of staff and had to milk her pet cow Daffodil, who was grazing on the front lawn at Norbury Park, and feed the hens. When she could, she shopped for luxuries for Keith, sending him caviar, a lobster and chocolates, and lending him money.

Bombs hit the Mother's Clinic in Whitfield Street in October 1940 during the Blitz, breaking windows and badly damaging the premises. Marie rallied immediately, transferring books, papers, stock and sec-retarial staff to Norbury Park, where she directed operations. Two nurses and an administrative assistant carried on gallantly in London despite the bombs. That November another raid damaged the windows of the Clinic soon after they had been replaced. Marie expected the highest devotion from her nurses, instructing them to ignore air-raid warnings and the wardens and to go on fitting contraceptives until the very last minute: 'only when the sound of actual gunfire or bombs very near is danger point considered to have been reached,' read a notice she pinned up on the walls of Whitfield Street.

At Norbury Park, too, German bombers jettisoned their remaining bombs after raids on London. Two fell on the house, shattering the eighteenth-century plate glass and damaging the Painted Drawing-room, and several more fell in the gardens.

The woods around Norbury Park housed a vast armed camp and the officers' mess was inside the gates of the grounds. Outside camped thousands of soldiers; lorries rumbled past the circular drive incessantly; and officers trooped in and out of the house for hot baths. With fewer staff the upkeep of the house and grounds became a trial to her. She was anxious about Harry, away at Charterhouse, sent him butter and eggs and wanted to send a cake. To reassure her that he was well fed, Harry copied out two days' school menus and told her very charmingly that he did not really need food parcels.[8]

The diet of the whole nation worried her too. She was convinced that the people were suffering from diminished vitality and sex drive due to shortages of good roast beef, eggs and oranges. She was bitterly opposed to the pasteurization of milk. She and her family drank raw milk, fresh from Daffodil her pet cow, and she was convinced that food in its natural form was purest and healthiest. Throughout the war years she wrote endless letters, followed up by visits to the Minister of Health Malcolm MacDonald, and to Lord Woolton, Minister of Food, urging a change of diet.

Throughout the summer of 1940 Marie was working on a long poem in dramatic form, *Oriri*. The He and She in the poem have a background 'aeons long in which they have met repeatedly and loved'. The lovers represent the advance guard of the human race and are protected by Guardian Angels and with choruses of the Spirits of Earth, Air, Trees, Flowers and Elementals. 'Grant power to our wills when we will that human life, instead of fading prematurely in misery and loneliness may, with ever deepening wisdom, attain the understanding of growth as a flower in beauty and peace,' the lovers pray. Marie refused to accept the encroachment of age, and the gulf of over thirty years that divided her from her lover.

The volume which appeared in the autumn of 1940 contained an advertisement for *Love Songs for Young Lovers* published by Heinemann with a recommendation from George Bernard Shaw. He had written to her on 6 March 1939 about the *Love Songs*:

You see, I was right at our first meeting when I laughed at your scientific pretensions and diagnosed you as an ardent dancing girl. Nevertheless the scientific background is interesting as it produces an impersonality that is rare in love poems and gives them a dignity. You are a poet all right. It can't be helped.[9]

The advertisement listed the famous men who had praised her work. In addition to Shaw they included Masefield, Laurence Binyon, Sir Arthur Quiller-Couch – and Dr Havelock Ellis. Literary men admired her for her courage in bringing sexual knowledge to the forefront, and particularly for her work on birth control; they wanted to admire her work. Despite their recommendations however, her poems failed to excite interest.

Llewelyn Powys, the novelist, fatally ill with tuberculosis, was living in Switzerland when he sent her a critique of *Love Songs*, in the autumn of 1939. He would have liked to have been one of her disciples for he admired the 'pluck and independence' of her character, but he was disturbed by 'the kind of idealism that seems characteristic of your mind . . . I often like what is "ugly", you never do'. He disliked the sugar-sweetness of her verse, her use of words like 'noisome' and 'lightsome' and felt that she sometimes played for popular sympathy. 'What I really feel is that your nature has in it a rift. Perhaps you should have been either a poor, neglected poet or a practical philanthropist, either a passionate alchemist or a nice successful, socially ambitious woman.'[10]

Marie wrote back, as always rejecting criticism, 'determined to allow myself at least the pleasure of poetry and therefore it is worthwhile to make it as beautiful as I can'.[11]

Robert Graves was another writer who admired Marie as a radical reformer but was less enthusiastic about her as a poet. After the war, Marie sent him a poem which he did not like and then, without his knowledge, nominated Robert Graves as a Fellow of the Royal Society of Literature. From Deya in Mallorca, he wrote to her explaining his refusal:

I'm one of the very few writers who have continued to keep their independence . . . I write what books I like and where I like and owe no man anything . . . Independence has to be defined by certain rules and one of them is never to join any religious, political, social or literary organization in either an active or honorary capacity or to attend any luncheon, dinner, levée or other function or sign manifestos. This has greatly enlarged my working year nor done any noticeable harm . . . I think that the work you did in the CBC was of extreme importance, it freed people like myself from the degrading sense of being dependent on 'chance' for the birth of children. I have had seven children, well-spaced and healthy and it was of the greatest possible moral help. I have, in fact, the greatest respect for your courage.

About your writing, you and I seem to be following completely different paths. Please, if you like, send me the book, and even if I don't like it, I will still be proud to have it. And let me honourably decline the fellowship.[12]

For Marie, social activities, organizing manifestos, attending dinners was an integral part of the literary life, more important now that war-time restrictions had curtailed her public speaking on birth control. Her poem, *Oriri*, published in 1940, did not bring her the recognition that she craved. Nor did her subsequent volumes of poetry, all but one published at her own expense by Alex Moring Ltd, a small publishing house she took over after the war began. Nothing could shake her conviction that she would be recognized as a great poet after her death.

In her private life with Keith, Marie took the lead, sending him a letter with a box of lilies-of-the-valley to the Savage Club in May 1941, inviting him for dinner at the Ritz Palm Court restaurant. Despite war scars, Norbury Park was still looking beautiful, with the white broom coming up, and lilies out and a cascade of laburnum. Sometimes Marie had to rush back from her idyll in town with Keith to shove Daffodil out of the hen run or cope with the cistern. She was so taken up with manual duties that she had written, she complained, 'not a word of the creative and scientific work for which I was made'.[13]

In her love affair Marie simply ignored those facts about Keith that she did not want to admit. Early in 1942, when Keith was on leave, Marie had invited him to Norbury Park with his parents, who were friends of hers, without mentioning his fiancée. 'I'm afraid we must consider ourselves four now, not three,' replied his mother. 'I do not see how Keith could visit you without Betty. We could not leave her out.'[14]

Humphrey came home, in uniform, for occasional weekends, writing or wiring for permission. Her replies were not always gracious: 'Dear Humphrey,' she wrote in a typed letter, dated 6 February 1942, 'Miss Johns [her secretary] and I have wrestled and struggled with your letter . . . We gather you would like to come home on Wednesday the 18th but as regards returning I cannot and will not have the house waked up at 8 o'clock in the morning . . . you must return the night before.'[15] Humphrey was reminded to bring his coupons or the equivalent in food and to fill up his car with all the food he could get, including vegetables, as a hard frost had prevented them from digging out the vegetables in the garden.

By the end of March 1942, just before his sixty-fourth birthday, Humphrey resigned from the RAF and went back to his small business in London. He was still inordinately fond of Marie. To save petrol, he told her, he wanted to spend two weeks in each month at Norbury Park. He could conduct his business affairs from there and, he promised, he would do his share of the housework:

> I can easily prepare BREAKFAST and cook the porridge and bacon etc. Then you can leave the cleaning and washing up to me. DINNER: I can peel the potatoes, etc., lay the cloth and again clean and wash up.
> The cooking of breakfast, etc., I can easily tackle. But I am a bit uncertain about lunch.
> TEA: That also I can tackle easily so the absence of staff is no reason for me being away from home. My bedroom also I can easily do. Please let me know when I can come to help in the house for a fortnight.[16]

Marie invited him for dinner at Frascati in June 1942, but Humphrey was only 'allowed' to come to Norbury very occasionally.

Her passion for Keith remained fresh and tender: 'Most dear One,' she wrote in May 1942, in the tone she had written to Aylmer Maude thirty years earlier, 'The turmoil, work and heat of the day dies down and I turn to you for a breath of sweet quietness.' The names of her lovers might change but her dream of ideal love remained constant. Her husband was, of course, excluded and by the spring of 1943 he was feeling desolate. He reminded her, as he had done in the past, that they had promised to love each other for ever and at first he had been very, very happy:

> Unfortunately in about seven or eight years you got tired of me and said that the marriage was a great disadvantage, through me you were losing your friends . . . it continued worse and worse. Here I am, sixty-five next month and I have nothing. A husband who writes to his wife for permission to be allowed to come home for a few days and invariably received the answer 'NO'![17]

In his last paragraph Humphrey humiliated himself by asking her if she would allow him three pounds a week out of the interest on money he had given to his son if the day came when he was too old to work. At present he could manage by working and living in fairly cheap lodgings.

> I hope you will allow me to see Harry sometimes. Now, you always appear to want to keep us apart, just as when he was a Baby, you gave reasons why I should not play with him.
>
> Yours, as ever,
> HUMPHREY

As a footnote, he wrote: 'For once answer.'

Marie answered the following day, with a revealing letter: 'My dear Humphrey, You don't realize how day and night I slave beyond my strength.' Marie accused her husband of being selfish and unimaginative. He made a lot of extra work and she was about to lose Ivy, her domestic help. If he would only put his back into finding her a replacement, he could come home for a little while. 'One other detail only,' she added:

> you say after seven or eight years of happiness I tired of you. Do you ever ask yourself what you did about then? When Buffie was eighteen months old – a goldencurled laughing angel. We were sitting in the sunshine of Portland ... with several families ... Buffie tiptoed up behind you and with a gurgle of happy laughter tipped your hat over your eyes. Instead of catching him to you and kissing him, you swore at him and cursed him and swore at me for the 'crime' – and all the people on the beach heard you – and the child was terrified – you seared his soul and mine.

She signed herself: 'Yours affectionately, Marie.'[18]

Morbidly sensitive to criticism, Marie had magnified that tiny incident in her mind and hugged a grudge for fifteen years without speaking of it. Humphrey's outburst against her and her son had been enough to dent the confidence of a woman so outwardly arrogant. In her sixties she was still dogged by the feeling of worthlessness from childhood and it damaged her privately and publicly.

Marie's war-time letters give the impression that, despite her resilience, the deterioration in her professional, marital, maternal and financial status (paper shortage had badly affected the sales of her books) had left her overwrought much of the time. By April 1943 she had found a good, old-fashioned cook, but complained to a friend that she was so constantly overworked that she would soon be ill if she did not have 'somebody to deal with all sorts of varied things, from throwing turnips to my pet cow, dusting the drawing room with me, catching moths in the best bedroom, going in [to the village] shopping, bringing me a hot water bottle when I am nearly fainting . . .'[19]

From 1938 onwards Marie had intended to devote the next twenty years of her life to literature. Certainly throughout the war a cluster of well known literary figures visited and corresponded with her, as well as budding poets whom she liked to cultivate. (Literary women were not so attractive to her; her few close women friends were journalists, who were useful allies.) As early as November 1938 a Lieutenant William Rose rented her lighthouse home in Portland Bill for the modest sum of two pounds ten shillings a week. They were both pleased with the arrangement and Marie paid her winter lodger a visit. Lieutenant Rose (a friend of a young dancer, Margot Fonteyn, who visited the lighthouse) addressed his 'wonderful landlady' as Dr Stopes, Paleontologist and Pioneer.

In war-time the exposed lighthouse was declared a war zone and with Marie's agreement two other naval lieutenants with literary leanings rented it. One of them, Lieutenant Warren Tute, drove up to visit Marie Stopes at Norbury Park, excited at the idea of meeting a world figure. He found her stimulating but unappealing.

She was infatuated with young, creative people . . . Everything appeared very phallic . . . She looked wild, hair all over the place, no bra . . . she was an eccentric – not an attractive woman, absolutely not physically but attractive because she was bursting with ideas.

She had, Tute said, 'all the charm of a viper'.[20]

The setting of the lighthouse stimulated Warren Tute to write a play, *Jack o' Lantern*, with a thinly disguised Marie Stopes as the main character, a spy. When she read the play Marie was appalled; she cut out chunks of the manuscript with scissors and scrawled all over it. If he didn't change the setting she threatened to sue.

Marie was genuinely fond of Lieutenant Rose and when he went down with his ship, HMS *Cossack*, she wrote a long, elaborate elegy, dedicated to the men who died at sea: 'Instead of Tears'. Her eminent friends were sent copies. Walter de la Mare approved of it highly, so did Laurence Binyon, who described it as 'eloquent and noble'. She also showed her creation to a newfound friend, Adam Fox, Professor of Poetry at Magdalen College, Oxford, whom she had cultivated with visits to Norbury, gifts of new-laid eggs and excursions to the opera. Adam Fox was flattering in his comments, interested in her 'Stopesian stanza' with its returning rhymes. Marie gave talks and poetry readings at the Royal Society of Literature and at the Poet's Club during the war. E. M. Forster, a neighbour, came to visit, and in October 1943 Charles Morgan, a well known novelist and playwright at the time, came to stay. Like all prized guests he was regaled with choice old Madeira from Marie's cellar.

In the summer holidays, when Harry was home from school, he and Marie spent the break camping in Cornwall, since the Lighthouse was out of bounds. Marie was still blissfully happy in a tent six feet by four.

Marie's war work, from 1939 to 1945, included fire-watching on her estate and acting as land girl. She saw it as a patriotic duty to bombard Government departments with complaints about their shortcomings and continually harried the Ministry of Food about shortages in the nation's diet. Also, the shortage of rubber directly affected her work. Since the commodity was vital for prosecuting the war, the amount and quality allocated to the manufacturers of contraceptives disturbed her greatly. She feared that the lack of proper preventatives might drive women to turn to abortion. 'Abortion not only causes temporary ill-health but often corrupts the woman's potential motherhood for the rest of her life and is so bad for the race that it is a disaster greater than any German bombing of this country,'[21] she wrote in a disgruntled letter to the Ministry of Supply. Paper was short too and Marie Stopes's books were out of print, although Humphrey was still loyally enquiring for them at local libraries.

She took the war personally, convinced that Goering was gunning for her when his pilots dropped their bombs near Norbury Park. She saw herself as the upholder of standards on every topic: 'I was particulary sorry to read in Hansard the possible vulgarization of our national name of Britons as Britishers,' she wrote to Lord Addison in November 1943. 'Say the two words to yourself – doesn't the sound tell you the difference – Briton – clear, lean, firm, Britisher slush, spread, sloppy – Please, please register your repentance by a vow never to do it again.'[22]

Her self-importance makes it easy to forget that she was still doing valuable work, still crusading in the field of birth control. 'The whole peace of the world depends on my work being available and rightly presented to the backward peoples,' she wrote to Clement Attlee, who was Dominions Secretary as well as Deputy Prime Minister. '. . . do you realize that . . . more Indians have been added to their miserable over-population in the last ten years than our total population?'[23] Her interest in India remained constant and in 1952, Marie Stopes sent a nurse trained at her Mothers' Clinic, Sister Dawson, to Bombay to teach the technique of birth control. To this day there are birth control clinics named after her in the sub-continent.

George Bernard Shaw was ageing now, and Marie maintained her fluctuating, flirtatious friendship with the old man, persuading him to try organic calcium instead of injections for his ailing heart, bringing Keith Briant to see him, sending him her love poems. She was livid when Shaw refused to join the campaign on behalf of Bosie's pension in the spring of 1941 on the grounds that his name would arouse 'furious resentments'. In an undated note she wrote:

Dear G.B.S.
    You are malicious
        misinformed
        mannerless.

In October 1944 Marie wrote ostensibly to congratulate Shaw on his new book, *Everybody's Political What's What*:

My dear G.B.S.
    I bought your new book ...
    It makes grand reading.
    Your pages on religion I feel to be the most vital of all –
BUT – Why no recognition of the fact that I am the only religious teacher of all time who has preached in simple words a life-affecting doctrine which could be accepted by all religions. Enclosed. Please read it ...[24]

(She referred, of course, to her birth control crusade and enclosed a pamphlet.)

She wrote Shaw a poem about their friendship:

BARRIERS DOWN

When I am dead
And you have shed
This clogging clay.
We will reclothe ourselves
Softly and speed away
To realms of joy.

Thank God we leave our skeletons behind!
Those clanking gateways passed
We may at last
Meet in complete embrace,
Frustration free
When bodies interlace.
Now when we try to penetrate our bliss
We find our softness barred
By bones too hard
To melt with fiery anguish of our will.
So I lie still
Straight out with folded hands
Withdrawing soul and spirit from my clay
Thus to enclose you utterly
And wordless every loveliness to say.
Our tender spirits meet in close embrace
Never encompassed when, each face met
Bones baulked the fusion of our dual kiss.[25]

'Surely this is anatomically wrong. Noses perhaps, not bones,' Shaw pencilled in cryptically.

To Churchill she wrote in almost Churchillian language in May 1944, complaining about the dangerous underfeeding of the British people: 'The roast beef of old England has always had a real meaning and is a source of British strength of character, mind and body.'[26] No reply exists.

By August 1945, the war over, Marie was delighted to be back in her Lighthouse at Portland Bill, bathing, drinking seawater, which she believed ensured longevity, and dispatching telegrams of congratulations on the ending of the Second World War to both King George VI and the new Prime Minister Clement Attlee (whose Labour Government she thoroughly disliked).

She was finding the upkeep of Norbury Park increasingly expensive. At the age of sixty-five she seemed to be back in the wilderness again, her marriage in tatters; her home had been damaged seven times, the Clinic four times. By an odd quirk of fate, Humphrey was now involved in a business association with Ethel Barstow (née Burgess) the woman he had jilted for Marie. At one point he lived in a room in her house. Harry was at university, inevitably growing away from his mother's influence. Keith was married, with small children, and her books, no longer sexually startling in the post-war world, were being supplanted by those of a new generation of sexologists.

In 1947, however, she was still interested in and interesting to men. 'Only a few months ago a man of 80 asked me to marry him (forgetting I had a living husband),'[27] she wrote to Sir John Waller, a poet friend. 'You are a gallant girl,' Nancy Astor told her when she was in her seventies.[28] She refused to give in to old age, to failure, to the indifference of the modern world. She believed fervently in her own excellence in every field and was ready to applaud excellence in others. In February 1946 she had been to see the film version of *Henry V* and also the New Theatre's production of *Oedipus Rex* and *The Critic*. She wrote to Laurence Olivier congratulating him vibrantly on his performances: 'it made me feel so delighted that a really first-class actor is alive at the same time as I am, that I owe it to you to thank you warmly for being so splendid.' She had heard that he was born in Dorking and invited him, if he found himself in the district, to her home. Olivier replied with a charming note saying that her letter had made him very happy.[29]

The years had not been kind to her appearance. Marie's face looked heavy, with its strong jaw and prominent nose framed by dyed red hair. Her breasts pendulous and plump, in ill-fitting, low-cut, home-made dresses, beads dangling round her lined neck, only her piercing eyes hinted at the personality behind them. Yet when she spoke, her power, her passion could still thrill an audience. According to her own notes, when she addressed the LSE Student's Union in May 1946 it was the best attended meeting of the year.

Her son Harry, tall and handsome, and now a post-graduate student of twenty-two, was planning his own future, grown to manhood almost without Marie realizing it. She had watched over his development carefully, possessively, made up stories for him, camped with him, shown him how to set up chemical experiments in her laboratory. She enjoyed young company and missed him when he was away. Marie kept a close eye on his health, morbidly afraid of infection and insisted on Harry wiping the cutlery when out for a meal 'even at the Ritz'. When he was eighteen in 1942, staying with Keith's parents, Marie wrote to Mrs Briant insisting that her son must eat a grated raw carrot for breakfast, no lobster, crab or codfish (perhaps because she considered shellfish had aphrodisiac properties and was terrified that Harry might be seduced prematurely) and be sure to take a daily dose of Syrup of Hypophosphites.

For years Harry had been friendly with Mary Wallis and her brother who lived near by. When Harry came home for the holidays they all met and, as they grew older, the young people began to go to golf-club dances together. For Harry's twenty-first birthday, Marie gave a grand party at the Dorchester Hotel. Mary, a seventeen-year-old still at a Protestant boarding school, unwittingly incurred Marie's wrath by asking Harry innocently whether the party could be delayed until after Holy Week so that she could attend. Interference with her arrangements enraged Marie Stopes. Mary did not manage to get to the party but Mrs Stopes harboured a grudge. His mother's antagonism towards Mary merely served to intrigue Harry.

By 1946 Mary was reading history at University College, Marie's alma mater, while Harry was engaged in post-graduate research in meteorological optics at Imperial College. The two students began to gravitate towards each other. They discovered a love of the cinema and went to dances and concerts of classical music. Marie became alarmed when she saw them together, and when they went off to Provence on a group student holiday she was convinced that Mary was plotting to snare her son into marriage. She wrote to Barnes Wallis complaining bitterly of his daughter's scheme; the inventor replied by threatening to sue her. On the morning of 1 October 1947, Harry finally told his mother that he was engaged and intended to marry Mary Wallis. Marie was furious and immediately began to try to sabotage the union.

For an outsider it would be hard to find a rational explanation for Marie's intense objection to the engagement. Though shy and socially inexperienced, Mary Wallis was a charming, intelligent, personable young woman from a family who were on visiting terms with her own. Her besetting sin, or the one that Marie fixed upon, was that she was short-sighted and wore glasses. The morning that Harry broke the news to her she wrote to her son's future father-in-law, voicing forceful objections to marriage – and sent a carbon copy of the letter to Mary.

Harry would have no prospects from her, she pointed out, merely an income settled on him of £300 a year, enough only to free his mind from material worries so that he could 'develop unhampered his special scientific genius'. As an expert on sex she claimed that Harry was physiologically ten years Mary's junior and that the couple were sexually unsuited: 'on Eugenic grounds I should advise against the marriage were they strangers to me. My personal observation of the children makes me sure they cannot give each other lasting happiness . . .'[30] In a letter which was barely courteous, Marie implied that Barnes Wallis had precipitated events by giving his consent to the engagement.

Barnes Wallis had already clashed with Marie Stopes. He had, unfairly, little respect for her ability as a scientist. When she visited his home one evening before the war, the two had argued on every subject they discussed and when Marie, didactic as ever, began to lay down the law on aeronautics, the atmosphere became dangerous. Marie then suggested a game of chess, played by her own rules, 'quick chess' with no pause for thought, but Barnes Wallis still beat her. When Humphrey came to call for her with the car, Marie swept out of the house 'screeching over her shoulder that she had let him win the game only because she had to leave . . .'[31]

Her letter about the engagement angered Barnes Wallis and, although he himself had not been too keen on the match, since he considered Harry a 'young pup', too free in his public attention to Mary, he was concerned for his daughter's happiness and convinced that the pair were in love. He certainly would not allow himself to be bullied by Marie Stopes.

Marie was furious, determined to get her own way and, in February, wrote to a young woman friend telling her that she 'did want Harry to realize how pretty you are and dare I hope that your "new look" is rose pink nails and lipstick . . .'[32] That same month she tried to embroil Humphrey in her crusade, pleading that marriage to Mary would constitute a Eugenic crime against the nation, the family and his children. By marrying Mary, Harry would 'make a mock of our lives' work for Eugenic breeding and the Race'. Mary, she argued, was plain and socially dreary. Marie would not condone the cruelty of burdening children with 'defective sight and the handicap of goggles'.[33]

The single-mindedness that had made Marie such a formidable campaigner refused to allow her to see any point of view but her own in her fanatical disapproval of the marriage. Humphrey, for once, stood firm. He wrote to her sensibly after seeing the pair, saying that Harry was desperately in love, and he personally thought it would be futile to oppose the match and it would make it awkward if Harry did finally marry Mary. He continued to see the engaged couple that spring on friendly terms and they hoped that he, at least, would come to the wedding.

Since the 1930s, when Marie had introduced a series of adopted 'brothers' to his home, Harry had gradually begun to realize how unfair his mother could be and, now disillusioned, he would no longer be persuaded by her blandishments or her anger.

In June, Marie sent on the wedding invitation to Humphrey, claiming that Mrs Wallis had refused to send them (Marie and Humphrey) any invitations for their friends. 'Harry is evidently completely Mary's slave . . .'[34] Marie did not attend the wedding at St Laurence's Church, Effingham on 27 July 1948 and in the marriage announcement the name of 'Stopes' was omitted. Humphrey was present.

In November he went to stay with the young couple in Cambridge. 'They looked after me very well and Mary really is a good cook,' he reported to Marie. 'They are quite happy and everything is all right . . .'[35] By then Marie had taken the tragically blind step of cutting herself off from her son and daughter-in-law. She had not given them a wedding present but later sent Harry a hundred pounds to spend on himself. He bought a piano and Mary took lessons.

All Marie's manoeuvres were, of course, desperate bids to win back Harry's love and devotion exclusively to her. Harry, to his credit, remained loyal to his wife, always hoping that Marie would realize that he and Mary were practising the ideal of 'married love' she had preached for thirty years. Mary, though intimidated by the awe-inspiring spectacle of Marie's disapproval and malice, was a person of integrity who would not be crushed by her mother-in-law. Marie was often invited to stay with the young couple, and when Jonathan, their first son, was born, there was a half-hearted reconciliation. She did visit occasionally but for her daughter-in-law they were chilling occasions. Marie cut Harry out of her will, and believed for the rest of her life that he had betrayed her by his marriage.

The timing of Marie's invitation to Augustus John to make a portrait sketch of her was curious, barely two months before her son's marriage. Both Fellows of University College, London, they had met at the annual dinners. John agreed to her suggestion and was entertained in style in the autumn, staying in Fanny Burney's room and drinking Marie's fine old (1878) Madeira.

'I'm very proud that you have done me the honour to draw me . . .' Marie wrote to him. 'Many of my distinguished friends envy me and say you have made me immortal . . .'[36] Having cut herself off from her son and written off the future of her family, it seems that Marie was making sure that she would live on through art. Four years later, in 1952, considering John's sketch too insubstantial she approached Sir Gerald Kelly, the President of the Royal Academy, to ask him to paint a head and shoulders for an agreed fee of 500 guineas. After all, she concluded, 'it isn't so much for the immortality you give'.[37]

For the first time for years, in 1948, no Christmas party was held at

Norbury Park. Marie went away on a cruise to Madeira, telling Humphrey that the servants were leaving and she could not face Christmas without them. But without Harry, the festive season must have seemed a hollow feast to her. The previous Christmas had been a fiasco, Marie had struck Mary Wallis and her family off the guest list and although Harry helped dutifully with the preparations for the party, when the guests arrived he slipped out by the back door.

Humphrey took the news of her voyage in good part and paid back fifty pounds off the £1,000 loan Marie had made him. He was an ailing man, suffering from kidney trouble, and in the late spring went into a nursing home in Croydon. Marie wrote anxiously to the matron enquiring about his diet, sending eggs and visiting him in the last weeks. He died on 27 July 1949, aged seventy. Keith Briant wrote to her with obvious sincerity, telling her that her husband was: 'one of the gentlest, kindest and most charming men I have had the honour to know . . .'[38]

Throughout their marriage Humphrey had remained loyal to Marie and she realized that she would never find such complete devotion again. For many years, from 1921 to 1948, Humphrey had been Honorary Secretary to the Society for Constructive Birth Control, unflagging in his concern. The Annual Meeting of the CBC was cancelled that year.

At that stage in her life, Marie was deeply interested in the mysteries of the occult, although she wisely kept this interest to herself and refused to be publicly associated with the subject. 'The three sides of me already in public contact – composition of coal, my sociological clinics and poetry are quite enough,' she said.[39]

Nearing seventy, her husband dead, her son and his family alienated, she was by no means ready to fade into old age. When asked by a correspondent to advise whether it was dangerous for a widow of sixty-eight to masturbate occasionally, when unable to sleep, she replied vigorously:

I know of one case in which a woman was over sixty before she had any sex feelings at all and some women still have active sex feelings at eighty . . . That she does have sex feelings is a sign of strength and vitality and she is to be congratulated and encouraged, but I should not advise sex union more than once a month at that age . . .[40]

Friendship, more than sex, served as a solace and encouragement to Marie after Humphrey's death. Nearly all her friends were useful as well as kind to her. Walter de la Mare, whose son Richard was chairman of

Faber, enjoyed the contact, the visits and the little gifts of eggs – and butter from Daffodil the cow.

> Dear Daffodil, I wept to see
> Another gift to me –
> Tears not of injocundity
> But simply gluttonous glee.
> And Oh, how kind your Mistress is:
> I mean, of course Marie.
> Please moo affection's thanks to her
> From Walter d.

And 'Daffodil' replied in felicitous rhyme:

> My mistress sends her love with mine,
> And writes for me a grateful line.
> I bid her say that we both ask
> Your thanks should not become a task,
> For not a ton of the best butter
> Is worth one line that you could utter.[41]

Marie left scores of unpublished poems and limericks in her papers:

> A stoneybroke airman of Shoreham
> Made brownpaper breeches and woreham
> He looked nice and neat
> Till he bent in the street
> To pick up a nut, then he toreham.

Yet recognition as a serious poet eluded her. When reviewers failed to notice her books and literary editors rejected her poems, she put it down to the Catholics stealing the mail before it arrived at the newspaper offices and the reprehensible judgement of the critics.

In the 1950s she disliked the American influence upon Britain intensely, and in a letter, written on 23 February 1951, she accused Attlee, the Prime Minister, of being 'flaccid' in defending the interests of Britain. He had failed to realize the 'passionate intensity of devotion every true Briton feels towards the Navy,' she wrote, horrified at the suggestion that an American might become Supreme Commander of the British Home and Atlantic Fleet.[42]

In the 1920s Marie had been at least thirty years ahead of her time; now, she was out of step in the modern world. When she went out to Germany to visit Keith and talk to the troops about venereal disease in

1950, she realized sadly that the life of the British army officers over there might represent the last of the civilization she valued. Nevertheless, when Keith told her that she would be dining in the Officers' Club at HQ, where there would be music, she brightened visibly: 'Shall I wear my ball dress?' she asked. She stayed with Keith and his wife during June 1950 and saw nothing incongruous in her situation as godmother to her ex-lover's two small sons. She was still immensely fond of him although inevitably their relationship had changed.

In 1952, The Royal Commission on Marriage and Divorce invited her to give evidence, and this time she determined that her remarks would be reported. British women were divided biologically into three types, she asserted in a statement to the press. Some girls of fifteen or sixteen were fully mature and ripe for marriage and child-bearing; the majority were ready for marriage between eighteen and twenty-one; and then there were women who could be married earlier but were not sexually mature and physiologically developed until the ages of twenty-seven to thirty. (She was, of course, drawing on her own experience as a late developer sexually and her 'evidence' had no scientific basis.) The popular press played up her comments that fifteen-year-old girls should marry instead of hanging round street corners causing trouble. Later Marie insisted that she had only meant that very young marriages should be legally possible but socially discouraged. With her remarkable vitality, she was still passionately absorbed in the subject.

Once again, at seventy-two, the stirrings of sex were exciting her. In 1952, Avro Manhattan, a splendid-looking man in his thirties, had written an anti-Catholic book, *The Vatican in World Politics*, which was much talked about. Marie liked successful young men and was delighted to discover an author who mistrusted the Roman Catholics as much as she did. She had already come across Avro Manhattan before the war. A young writer and painter, he was a part of H. G. Wells's socialist set. (Later in life his sympathies swung to the extreme right.) Marie disliked his politics and quarrelled with him over what she regarded as anti-social behaviour. One of Manhattan's woman friends became pregnant and had an abortion and Marie accused Avro Manhattan of 'murdering' the infant. But that was in the past, when she was in love with Keith Briant. Avro was now a published author and Marie was unattached.

In November 1952, perhaps with the gunpowder plot in mind, Marie invited Avro Manhattan to a bonfire where they could bake potatoes and roast chestnuts. The Russians and Americans were exploding atom bombs, she wrote, but the two, solitary, civilized beings would explode chestnuts. The meeting of true minds did not, apparently, take place until the middle of December. On the 6th, Marie wrote:

Dear Avro Manhattan,
I'm looking forward to making a bonfire and dancing with you on the 13th. Could you arrive at 6 prepared with things for staying the night and also for dancing in the house.

It will be good to have a little adult conversation, my world seems to consist of many aged infants mostly. I hope your book will get good reviews, mine has not one yet.[43]

Marie was referring to a collection of her poems, *Joy and Verity*, published, this time, by the Hogarth Press.

Avro was a painter as well as a writer and the following year invited Marie to see his work. Afterwards she wrote to him in an effusion of delight:

Dearest and most precious Avro,
My heart is still beating extra hard with the joyous excitement of all the beauty you showed me ... Truly I was more than a little afraid to see your pictures, case they had in them something I could not find harmonious; and yet I should have had to speak the truth and it would have been terrible for me ... Dearest – the reality was so glorious I am singing with joy ... you are a genius ... Thank you from the depths of my being for such a cascade of fresh beauty ... Make no mistake you are a great artist, with a touch unequalled by any current painter – pictures by you will be treasured hundreds of years hence ... Dearest, most precious one, all the gods and angels guard you.

Marie[44]

That a seventy-two-year-old woman could write with such passionate enthusiasm to a man of thirty-nine reveals how unconscious Marie was of the age difference. Avro Manhattan could scarcely ignore it. Her flattery, her generosity, her adoration (and she was after all immensely distinguished) must have been gratifying to an aspiring artist.

When Harry visited the house and noticed a river scene of Manhattan's hanging in the drawing room, he was unimpressed and asked who the undistinguished artist was. Marie was distinctly piqued. She was completely infatuated and although she no longer poured out love poems, and physical passion was no longer consuming, the two communed in their hatred of Roman Catholicism, their shared interest in mysticism and psychic phenomena (Avro was a member of the Inter-Planetary Society, which Marie joined in 1954), and their disdain for the common people.

Marie was enchanted to discover that they apparently shared an identical taste in painting. When they visited the Royal Academy together in February 1954, they each made a secret note of the work they had found the most impressive. For Marie the fact that she and her twin soul had chosen the same painting left her dizzy with joy: 'as tho' I'd drunk champagne made of bubbles of eternity sparkling through the waters of life . . .'

Almost fifty years earlier, in her twenties, she had written ecstatic letters to Fujii, her first love. Now in her seventies she revelled in the excitement of finding a new hope, a new love. She began work on a play, *Venus and Methuselah*, a battle between the power of love and the supremacy of the intellect in which, of course, love triumphs over 'poisonous thought'.[45] In the same month that she finished her play, which was never published or staged, she fancied she saw Humphrey's ghost appearing in her bedroom at midnight.[46] In her heightened state, she was extremely impressionable. Avro Manhattan, a member of the British Inter-Planetary Society, had conveyed his enthusiasm for the subject to Marie and on December 1, 1953 she spotted a blue light in the sky, she was certain it was a flying saucer travelling from Dorking. Marie joined the Inter-Planetary Society in 1954.

She felt reinvigorated, still battling to get her work published and noticed. The Leatherhead Theatre Club may have turned down *Don't Tell Timothy*, a play she had written more than a quarter of a century earlier; her efforts to get her only published novel, *Love's Creation*, reprinted did not succeed, but in the summer of 1953 the Hogarth Press was advertising the twenty-sixth edition of *Married Love*, the seventh edition of *Enduring Passion* and the tenth edition of *Birth Control Today*. In university circles her fire and eloquence made her a popular speaker. (Sometimes she would throw a clutch of condoms to an audience of medical students, telling them that they ought to become familiar with contraceptive devices.) When she spoke to an enthusiastic audience in the Oxford Union debate on the motion: 'The world would be a better place without the political power and influence of the Roman Catholic Church', in January 1955, the President of the Union, Jeremy Isaacs, described it as 'one of the most enjoyable debates I remember'.[47]

When Marie appeared, decked out in furs and jewels, beads and slippers of brocade, everyone in the audience felt a sense of occasion.

Her enthusiasm remained unquenched. In January 1955 she had written a play for Yvonne Arnaud. The actress politely returned it, the dialogue, she regretted, was 'not professional enough'. Marie visited Sadler's Wells more than once for the production of a light opera *The Immortal Hour* and congratulated the theatre. Nor had she lost her trenchant power to complain. When a plate fell in her kitchen, caused, she claimed, by vibrations from a huge, low-flying aeroplane over Norbury Park, she wrote immediately to Sir John Slessor, Marshal of the Royal Air Force and Chief of Staff.[48]

Very occasionally Harry and Mary and their small children Jonathan, Catherine and Helena, would come to stay for weekends or at Christmas, but the atmosphere was always tense. At one memorable Sunday lunch, Marie piled Harry's plate high with roast beef, potatoes and vegetables. When he could not finish it, Marie looked down the table accusingly at her daughter-in-law and remarked sharply to Harry: 'Your stomach's shrunk.'[49]

She still ran the Annual Meetings of the Society for Constructive Birth Control and now tried to involve her friends from the world of poetry. Adam Fox, whom she had met when he was Professor of Poetry at Magdalen College, Oxford, was Archdeacon of Westminster. A bachelor, he had lived in College for over fifty years. In June 1957 Marie invited him to be the speaker at the Annual Meeting of the SCBC. They would dine him at the Ritz first, she told him, then in a private room of the Criterion they would hold a semi-social evening with five minutes' business, thirty to forty minutes' talk from a distinguished guest and later 'we walk about eating, drinking and talking to each other'. He could, she suggested, 'apply Plato to our problem or Christianity . . . or just speak in general about the importance of love and Christian kindness in a home. You speak so beautifully . . .'[50]

Adam Fox was clearly terrified at the prospect but eager to please. He thanked her for the handsome invitation but 'whatever qualifications can I have for accepting it, who have lived in a place called a College and not in a home since 1897?' He asked her, 'Would he be advising mothers or doctors or what?' He was worried about the publicity. He could not, he said, risk a headline in the *Daily Mail*, 'Bachelor Archdeacon tells mothers what to do'. In the end, Canon Fox wanted so much to oblige Marie that he accepted, but with obvious misgivings. 'My dear Marie,' he wrote on 10 October, 'I shall be there at 6.50 p.m.

at the Ritz on October 17th unless there is an accident on the Railway between Oxford and Paddington . . . I haven't the faintest idea what to say and don't even know what CBC on the leaflet you sent me stands for unless it is Control of Birth Clinics . . .'[51] One must assume that Canon Fox did his duty.

Marie herself had had a miserable summer. Although she had spent some time at the Lighthouse with Avro Manhattan, he had gone off to France without her and, despite his fond letters, she felt abandoned. Back home again she had childishly banished his favourite statue of Diana to the farthest corner of the grounds. She was a lonely figure now in the rambling eighteenth-century house she had loved so much, with Cherry, her ancient black chow as companion, and Elizabeth, her old servant who was growing deafer and dottier. The garden looked neglected and overgrown, Marie rarely entertained and no longer used her Painted Drawing-room. In the evenings she sat by a log fire in the adjacent Morning Room, staring at the flames.

In the spring of 1957, she had felt an unaccustomed weakness and pain and reluctantly consulted physicians and specialists. Results of tests by three different specialists diagnosed cancer of the breast, so far advanced that no operation was recommended. Marie flatly refused to accept the diagnosis. With her usual thoroughness, she investigated all the 'cures' for cancer in the experimental stage all over the world, chemical, homeopathic and other means of treatment, and decided on a homeopathic treatment in Bavaria. The cure involved a cancer-specific salve which shrank and hardened the malignant tumour within five days. After a week to a fortnight, the underlying healthy tissues would begin to grow. However, Marie deliberately concealed from the German doctors the degree of malignancy from which she was suffering and the fatal diagnosis of the English doctors.

Despite her scientific training, Marie's capacity for self-delusion had, in this case, taken on perilous proportions. 'The doctors say I am dying but I refuse to believe it. I am going to Germany to a clinic where I will have an operation,' she confided to Keith Briant in a letter. Keith found it unbearable to think of Marie, so vibrantly alive, as a dying woman. He did not want to accept the fact. 'I am sure the doctors you have seen are mistaken and I am certain that you will come back from Germany fully recovered,' he wrote.[52]

Apart from Keith, her doctors and her devoted secretary Mrs Windley, no one knew of her condition, not even Avro Manhattan or her son. However, she was realistic in one respect.

On 10 October 1957, she made out a final will, leaving the bulk of her estate, her copyrights and her house to the Royal Society of Literature, her Clinic to the Eugenics Society and generous bequests to the British Museum. The personal element in her life was largely neglected. Keith Briant was to receive a rose-embossed silver tankard; his sons (Marie's godsons) Dermot and Shane, £100 each; and her grandson Jonathan the freehold of a house in Richmond, Surrey. Harry received the *Greater Oxford Dictionary* and other small bequests. Avro Manhattan was not mentioned at all. What is most extraordinary in her will is that Marie Stopes, the feminist fighter, virtually ignored her two young granddaughters, Catherine and Helena. They were to receive 'such furs, laces, scarves and trinkets as my son selects for them'.[53] In her later years Marie's life had fragmented; in the anarchy of her old age her sympathy with her own sex had diminished.

On 12 November 1957 Marie flew to Germany in secret. Before she left, she had written to her doctor in her usual conspiratorial style: 'I am now hurrying all arrangements ... I go with hope but also with some trepidation and so I am very glad to have your promise to fly out and rescue me if I send you a telegram with the code word in it "Niagra".' She suffered racking pain and remained in Germany for six weeks. For once *The Times* accepted an advertisement from her on Christmas Eve: 'Dr Marie Stopes has been seriously ill in Germany and regrets that her Christmas greetings to many friends may be delayed.' By mid-January she was back in Norbury Park and she kept up the fiction that she was cured.

In her seventy-eighth year, Marie tilted at a Roman Catholic windmill for the last time. A British naval steward, Brian Rouncefield, had married a Maltese Catholic girl, Beatrice, in a registry office, but on returning to Malta Beatrice had written to him saying that her marriage was invalid under canon law. She was planning to marry again on the island and Brian Rouncefield's money was frozen in Malta. He took ship to Malta to try, without success, to win back his wife and his money. Marie saw him as a Protestant pilgrim and started a fund for him in March 1957, but her crusade foundered. In June, she took a holiday with Avro Manhattan at Eze Plage on the French Riviera.

However, if she had tilted at windmills, she had also slain giants. In July 1958, almost forty years after Marie had first revealed her 'message' to the Anglican Bishops at the Lambeth Conference, the Conference acknowledged the necessity for birth control and vindicated Marie Stopes's 'obscene' ideas in words that might have been dictated by Marie herself. 'The procreation of children is not the sole purpose of Christian marriage; implicit within the bond of husband and wife is the relationship of love with its sacramental expression in physical union . . . the responsibility for deciding upon the number and frequency of children has been laid by God upon the conscience of parents everywhere . . .'[54]

By the time she read those words, Marie realized that she was dying and she could no longer continue her work. She decided to dissolve the Society for Constructive Birth Control. Dr Blacker of the Eugenics Society offered to place a notice in his journal about the Society.

'Dear Dr Blacker,' she wrote in a dignified note on 18 September 1958, 'Thank you for your letter. It is most kind and I appreciate your offer to give us a notice in the EUGENICS REVIEW about the dissolution of the Constructive Birth Control Society.

'For more than 30 years it has been an expensive burden in trust to myself and I would prefer no notice of dissolution to appear'.[55]

Two weeks later, on 2 October 1958, at 2.35 a.m., Marie Stopes died in her bedroom at Norbury Park, thirteen days before her seventy-eighth birthday. At the last she had suffered great pain and a haemorrhage of the brain which semi-paralysed her. She was alone at the end and it was not until Marie was barely conscious that Mrs Windley, her devoted secretary, dared to use her initiative to summon Harry to her bedside. She died as bravely and stubbornly as she had lived.

The funeral arrangements she had made in her will were characteristically forceful. 'I most emphatically wish to be cremated at Golders Green', she wrote, 'and to have my ashes scattered on the sea – as near the Race as a fisherman can safely go at Portland Bill, Dorset.'

A memorial service was held at St Martin-in-the-Fields, London on 15 October 1958, her birthday. Marie would have been gratified by the turn-out. The Deputy Prime Minister, Mr R. A. Butler, read the Lesson from the Revelation of St John the Divine: 'And I saw a new heaven and a new earth . . .' The congregation sang the Eaton Anthem: 'Blest are the pure in heart' and, fittingly, her old friend Dr Adam Fox paid tribute:

. . . It fell to her . . . to espouse a cause which was strange to most and shocking to many, and to see it at last generally accepted without protest and widely adopted as a matter of practice . . . Those who felt the impact of her personality will find themselves missing her ever and anon, believing it impossible so much vitality should be lost or wasted . . .'[56]

Such was the power of that contradictory personality that Marie Stopes was hated and loved with great intensity, always controversial, always in the thick of life. Although she was destined to miss out on the rapture of married love she so longed for herself, her writings helped thousands of others and future generations to enjoy it:

> I feel most bound to thank you for a large share of the happiness of our blissful wedding night and of the many happy unions which have succeeded it . . . Can a man's life hold any experience so sweet as the occasion when he first feels a woman – his beloved wife – in his arms – shaken to the depths of her being in the ecstasy of physical union with him.[57]

At her memorial service, one of her favourite hymns, 'He who would valiant be', was sung. They should have changed the pronoun.

Notes

Marie Stopes left a maze of clues to her complicated life in the mass of letters and papers she bequeathed to the British Museum. After her death in 1958 a three-ton lorry was needed to transport them from her home in Surrey to Great Russell Street. These papers are now divided between the Manuscript Department of the British Library, who hold over 300 boxes, the Contemporary Medical Archives Centre at the Wellcome Institute for the History of Medicine, and Dr Harry Stopes-Roe, who holds a collection of family letters, photographs, unpublished manuscripts, etc.

When I was pursuing my researches the British Library Stopes Collection was not completely catalogued; therefore the only reference given for this collection is BL-S. The Stopes–Roe Collection is referred to as H.S-R Coll., and the Wellcome Institute's papers as CMAC: PP/MCS.

Marie Stopes also wrote of her own life in both fiction and fact, and the two are not always easy to distinguish. Her first two 'authorized' biographies were written during her lifetime and virtually dictated by her to her close friend and biographer Aylmer Maude. Her third, posthumous, biography was written by Keith Briant, an intimate friend of her later years. Ruth Hall's 1977 biography revealed new insights and proved an invaluable guide.

To avoid repetition, the following abbreviations have been used for names of correspondents:

CCS   Charlotte Carmichael Stopes (Marie's mother)
GBS   George Bernard Shaw
HR   Humphrey Roe (Marie's husband)
HS   Harry Stopes (Marie's father)
MS   Marie Stopes
WS   Winnie Stopes

1   Growing Pains

1   Charlotte Carmichael Stopes, *The Sphere of Man in relation to that of Woman in the Constitution*, T. Fisher Unwin, London, 1907.

2   Marie Stopes's Will, 10 October 1957.
3   F. S. Boas, *C. C. Stopes, Some aspects of her life and work*, a paper read to the Royal Society of Literature, 21 May 1930.
4   P. Chalmers Mitchell, *Thomas Henry Huxley*, Methuen, London, 1913.
5   HS to CCS, August 1880, H. S-R Coll.
6   Sydney Smith, *The Enfranchisement of Women*, A. Ireland & Co., Manchester 1879.
7   C. C. Stopes's Diary, 15 November 1880. BL-S.
8   Ibid., 15 March 1882, BL-S.
9   Aylmer Maude, *The Authorized Life of Marie C. Stopes*, Williams & Norgate, London, 1924.
10 Ibid.
11 Dr Harry Stopes-Roe, interview with author, March 1990.
12 C. C. Stopes's Diary, September 1886, BL-S.
13 HS to CCS, 30 July 1886, HS, S-R Coll.
14 HS to MS, 30 July 1886, BL-S.
15 Ibid., 3 September 1886, BL-S.
16 CCS to MS, 31 August 1887, BL-S.
17 Ibid., 10 September 1888, BL-S.
18 MS to HS, 10 July 1892, BL-S.
19 HS to MS, 10 September 1892, BL-S.
20 Marie Stopes's Diary, 4 October 1892, BL-S.
21 CCS to MS, 28 October 1892, BL-S.
22 Ibid., 18 January 1893, BL-S.
23 MS to HS, 12 March 1893, BL-S.
24 HS to MS, 24 January 1894, BL-S.
25 MS to CCS & HS, 14 January 1894, BL-S.
26 Dr A. Anderson to MS, 24 January 1894 BL-S.
27 CCS to MS 24 April 1896, BL-S.
28 Ibid., 14 October 1896, BL-S.
29 HS to MS, 15 October 1896, BL-S.
30 Ibid.
31 M. C. Stopes, *Man, Other Poems and a Preface*, Heinemann, London, 1914.
32 MS to HS, 20 July 1898, BL-S.
33 HS to MS, 9 April 1899, BL-S.
34 MS, Gertrude Colls, Olga Kapteyn, Christine Pugh to Clothilde Von Wyss, undated, BL-S.
35 Clothilde Von Wyss to MS and passim.
36 Ibid.
37 F. M. L. Thompson (ed.) *The University of London and the World of Learning, 1836–1896*, The Hambledon Press, 1990.
38 Ibid.

2 Scholarly Pursuits

1 MS to WS, 24 April 1901, BL-S.
2 Marie Stopes, *Sex and the Young*, Gill, London, 1926.
3 Guy Pilgrim to MS, 3 December 1901, BL-S.
4 MS to Guy Pilgrim, 5 December 1901, BL-S.
5 Clothilde Von Wyss to MS, 10 November 1901, BL-S.
6 University College *Gazette*, March 1902, H.S-R Coll.
7 HS to MS, 20 August 1902, BL-S.
8 MS to HS, 8 October 1902, BL-S.
9 WS to MS, 7 August 1902, BL-S.
10 HS to MS, 14 October 1902, BL-S.
11 MS to CCS, 5 December 1903, BL-S.
12 Marie Stopes, 'A Man and his Mate', unpublished novel, H.S-R Coll.
13 MS to WS, 3 December 1903, BL-S.
14 Ibid., undated (1903–4), BL-S.
15 Ibid., undated (1903–4) BL-S.
16 MS to CCS, 24 October 1903, BL-S.
17 Isadora Duncan, *My Life*, Gollancz, London, 1928.
18 MS to CCS, 13 March 1904, BL-S.
19 Isadora Duncan, op. cit.
20 Marie Stopes, 'Autobiographical Fragment' on visit to see Isadora Duncan dance on 13 March 1904, BL-S.
21 MS to CCS, 24 March 1904, BL-S.
22 MS to WS, undated (1903–4)BL-S.
23 MS to CCS, 24 March 1904, BL-S.
24 MS to WS 20 April 1904, BL-S.
25 MS to WS, 5 June 1904, BL-S.
26 Alvara Humphrey to MS, 18 August 1904, BL-S.
27 Ibid., 23 December 1904, BL-S.
28 MS to Alvara Humphrey, 11 January 1905, BL-S.
29 Kenjiro Fujii to MS, Keith Briant, *Marie Stopes*, Hogarth Press, London, 1962.
30 MS to Kenjiro Fujii, 6 December 1904, BL-S.
31 Ibid.
32 MS to Alvara Humphrey, 3 November 1904, BL-S.
33 Evelyn Weiss to MS, 31 January, 1905, BL-S.
34 G. N. Mortlake (pseudonym of MS) *Love Letters of a Japanese*, Stanley Paul, London, 1911.
35 Ibid.
36 Kenjiro Fujii to MS, 25 April 1905, BL-S.
37 CCS to MS, 30 January 1905, BL-S.
38 CCS to MS, 17 February 1905, BL-S.

39 MS to CCS, 19 February 1905, BL-S.
40 CCS to MS, 19 March 1905, BL-S.
41 MS to Professor Goebel, 6 November 1904, BL-S.
42 CCS to MS, 5 May, 1905, BL-S.
43 M. Stopes to K. Fujii ('The Nutritive Relations of the Surrounding Tissues to the Archegonia in Gymnosperms', *Beihefte zum Botan. Centralblatt*, vol. 20, 1906).
44 MS to K. Fujii, 19 November 1905, BL-S.
45 Marie C. Stopes, *The Study of Plant Life for Young People*, Alexander Moring, London, 1906. (MS quoted from the review in the *New Phytologist*, in a letter to CCS of 4 November 1906.
46 MS to CCS, 25 October 1905, BL-S.
47 Ibid., 15 March 1907, BL-S.
48 Keith Briant, *Marie Stopes*, The Hogarth Press, London, 1962.
49 G. N. Mortlake, op. cit.
50 HS to MS, 15 October 1896, BL-S.

3 Japan

1 Marie Stopes, *A Journal from Japan*, Blackie, London, 1910, dated 11 August 1907.
2 B. H. Chamberlain, *Things Japanese*, Charles E. Tuttle, London 1904.
3 Marie Stopes, *A Journal from Japan*, Blackie, London, 1910, dated 22 August 1907.
4 Ibid., dated 24 August 1907.
5 Ibid., dated 1 September 1907.
6 Ibid., dated 22 September 1907.
7 MS to CCS, 28 February 1908, BL-S.
8 Marie C. Stopes and Joji Sakurai, *Plays of Old Japan the 'No'*, Heinemann, London, 1913.
9 Marie Stopes, *A Journal from Japan*, op. cit., dated 27 November 1907.
10 MS to WS, 27 November 1907, BL-S.
11 MS to CSS, 30 January 1908, BL-S.
12 G. N. Mortlake, *Love Letters of a Japanese*, Stanley Paul, London, 1911; and Marie Stopes, *A Journal from Japan*, Conclusion (p. 267) op. cit.
13 MS to WS, 25 April 1908, BL-S.
14 Marie Stopes, *A Journal from Japan*, op. cit., dated 24 October 1908.
15 MS to CCS, 29 March 1908, BL-S.
16 MS to Charlie Hewitt, 18 April 1908, BL-S.
17 MS to WS, 28 March 1908, BL-S.
18 Ibid.
19 MS to Prof. F. W. Oliver, 29 April 1908, BL-S.
20 MS to Prof. F. E. Weiss, 21 May 1908, BL-S.

21 Olga Kapteyn to Marie Stopes, 28 July 1908, BL-S.
22 Marie Stopes, *A Journal from Japan*, op. cit., dated 19 August 1908.
23 G. N. Mortlake, op. cit.
24 MS to Claude McDonald, 16 November 1908, BL-S.
25 Claude McDonald, to MS, 17 November 1908, BL-S.
26 Kenjiro Fujii to MS, 26 December 1925, BL-S.
27 Marie Stopes, 'The Two Japans', unpublished comedy in verse, undated, H.S-R Coll.

4   Independence

1   Marie Stopes, *A Journal from Japan*, Blackie, London, 1910, dated 25 February 1908.
2   Ibid., entry dated 4–8 November 1907.
3   Helen McMurchy to MS, 18 February 1909, BL-S.
4   'On the Tent-Building Habits of the Ant, Lasius Niger Linn', with Charles Gordon Hewitt, in *Memoirs and Proceedings of the Manchester Literary and Philosophical Society*, Vol. 53, 1909.
5   Charlie Hewitt to MS, 22 August 1909, BL-S.
6   MS to Charlie Hewitt, 26 August 1900, BL-S.
7   Edith Garner to MS, 5 March 1910, BL-S.
8   MS to Edith Garner, 15 March 1910, BL-S.
9   Ibid., 23 March 1910, BL-S.
10 Charlie Hewitt to Edith Garner, 23 March 1910, BL-S.
11 Henry Bassett to MS, 10 May 1910, BL-S.
12 MS to Henry Bassett, 12 May 1910, BL-S.
13 Ray Strachey, *The Cause*, Virago, London, 1978.
14 MS to *The Times*, 16 December 1909.
15 Captain R. Scott to MS, 22 December 1909, BL-S.
16 Marie Stopes, typescript in H.S.-R. Coll.
17 Ibid., later published in *Man, Other Poems and a Preface*, Heinemann, London, 1914.
18 Marie Stopes, ed., *The Sportophyte*, April 1910, CMAC:PPS/MCS.
19 G. N. Mortlake (pseud.) 'A Man and his Mate', unpublished novel, 1910, H.S-R. Coll.
20 MS to WS, 4 February 1911, BL-S.
21 Ibid., 11 February 1911, BL-S.
22 MS to CCS, 8 March 1911, BL-S.
23 Maurice Hewlett to MS, 1911, BL-S.
24 Ruggles Gates, statement, c. 1962, BL-S, Add. M/S.
25 Marie Stopes, Circular letter, July 1911, BL-S.
26 Helen McMurchy to MS, 28 October 1911, H.S-R Coll.
27 MS to Assistant Secretary, Royal Society, 29 April 1911, BL-S.

28 Alfred Gibson (solicitor) to MS, 4 June 1912, BL-S.
29 Isabel P. Evans to MS, 29 November 1912, BL-S.
30 Marie Stopes, *Married Love*, Fifield, London, 1918.
31 MS to Aylmer Maude, 17 December 1912, BL-S.
32 Ibid., 8 March 1913, BL-S.
33 Ibid., 14 August 1913, BL-S.
34 Ibid.
35 Provost of University College, London, to Aylmer Maude, March, 1916, BL-S.
36 Olga Kapteyn to MS, 20 August 1913, BL-S.
37 Marie Stopes, *Vectia: A Banned Play and a Preface on the Censorship*, Bale Sons and Danielsson, London, 1926.
38 F. H. Brewin to MS, 26 October 1911, BL-S.
39 Dr A. Routh to MS, 4 August 1919, BL-S.
40 Dr E. Claude Taylor, Certificate of Marital Status of Marie Stopes, 6 May 1914, BL-S.
41 Ruggles Gates, 1962, BL-S. Add M/S. Keith Briant also described Marie Stopes as 'highly, if not oversexed' in his biography, *Marie Stopes*, Hogarth Press, London, 1962.
42 Ibid.
43 Ibid.
44 MS to Aylmer Maude, 31 December 1913, BL-S.
45 Ibid., 21 February 1914, BL-S.
46 MS to *The Times*, 6 April 1914.
47 MS to Aylmer Maude, 16 May 1914, BL-S.

5 Breaking Out

1 MS to Aylmer Maude, 4 August 1914, BL-S.
2 Ibid., 5 August 1914, BL-S.
3 Ibid.
4 Petition drawn up by Braby & Waller, Solicitors, October 1914, BL-S.
5 Marie Stopes, publication notes for *Married Love*, 1914–1915, BL-S.
6 Dorothy Garley to MS, 19 July 1915, CMAC:PP/MCS:A.98.
7 Marie Stopes, *Enduring Passion* . . . G. P. Putnam & Sons, London, 1928.
8 *Married Love*, G. P. Putnam & Sons (14th edition, London, 1924. pp. 53, 63, Appendix 168.
9 Ernest Starling to MS, 19 July 1915, BL-S.
10 Marie Stopes, *Vectia*, Bale Sons & Danielsson, 1926.
11 MS to Aylmer Maude, 4 July 1915, BL-S.
12 Ibid., 1 September ?1915, BL-S.
13 Ibid., 16 May 1914, BL-S.
14 Ibid., 16 April 1916, BL-S.

15 Walter Blackie to MS, 13 July 1915, BL-S.

16 MS to Walter Blackie, 16 July 1915, BL-S.

17 Marie Stopes, verses, undated, H.S-R Coll.

18 Macmillan's Readers' reports, Sotheby's Catalogue, 19 July 1990.

19 Margaret Sanger to MS, 3 July 1915, PP/MCS: A.304.

20 Margaret Sanger, *My Fight for Birth Control*, Faber and Faber, London, 1932.

21 Margaret Sanger to MS, 6 July 1915, CMAC:PP/MCS:A.304.

22 MS to President Woodrow Wilson, undated, c. September 1915, BL-S.

23 MS to Aylmer Maude, 9 May 1915, BL-S.

24 R. V. Wheeler to MS, 13 July 1916, BL-S.

25 Edward Carpenter to MS, 26 May 1916, BL-S.

26 MS to Aylmer Maude, 16 August 1916, BL-S.

27 R.B. to MS, 1 October 1916, BL-S.

28 Jessie Murray to MS, 16 March 1916, BL-S. See also MS's publication notes for *Married Love*, BL-S.

29 MS to Aylmer Maude, 23 August 1916, BL-S.

30 WS to MS, 23 August 1917, BL-S.

31 GBS to MS, 24 September 1917, BL-S.

32 MS to GBS, 27 September 1917, BL-S.

33 Marie Stopes, Evidence to the Cinema Commission of Inquiry, 1917, BL-S.

34 Ibid.

35 Russell Wakefield to MS, 8 May 1917, BL-S.

36 MS to Russell Wakefield, 8 May 1917, BL-S.

37 Russell Wakefield to MS, 20 August 1917, BL-S.

38 R. V. Wheeler to MS, 20 June 1917, BL-S.

39 Edward Bristow, *Vice and Vigilance: Purity Movements in Britain since 1700*, Gill and Macmillan, Dublin, 1977.

40 Ernest H. Starling to MS, 23 November 1917, BL-S. Reprinted in *Married Love*.

41 Keith Briant, *Marie Stopes*, Hogarth Press, London, 1962.

42 Binnie Dunlop to MS, 15 November 1917, BL-S.

43 HR to MS, 6 February 1918, BL-S.

44 Humphrey Roe's diary, 11 February 1918, H.S-R Coll.

6 Fulfilment

1 HR to MS, 20 February 1918, BL-S.

2 MS to HR, 20 February 1918, BL-S.

3 Ibid., 26 February 1918, BL-S.

4 MS to Aylmer Maude, 1 April 1918, BL-S.

5 MS to C.O., RFC Officers' Hospital, 4 April 1918, BL-S.

6   Humphrey Roe's diary, 14 April 1918, H.S-R Coll.

7   HR to MS, 16 April 1918, BL-S.

8   MS to HR, 20 April 1918, BL-S.

9   Ibid.,

10   Humphrey Roe's diary, 21 April 1918, H.S-R Coll.

11   Ibid., 30 April 1918, H.S-R Coll.

12   MS to HR, 15 April 1918, BL-S.

13   HR to MS, 1 May 1918, BL-S.

14   MS to HR, 8 May 1918, BL-S.

15   MS to to the Department of Scientific & Industrial Research, London, 17 May 1918, BL-S.

16   Aylmer Maude to MS, 3 May 1918, BL-S.

17   MS to Aylmer Maude, 17 May 1918, BL-S.

18   Aylmer Maude to MS, 17 June 1918, BL-S.

19   Havelock Ellis to MS, 9 November 1918, with a copy of a typescript article, 'The Menstrual Curve of Sexual Impulse in Women', BL-S.

20   Lesley Hall, *Hidden Anxieties*, Polity Press, London, 1991.

21   Ibid.

22   Havelock Ellis, *Studies in the Psychology of Sex*, Vols I-VII, F. A. Davis Co., Philadelphia, 1900, 1901, 1903, 1905, 1906, 1910, 1918.

23   Marie Stopes, Obituary of Havelock Ellis, *Literary Guide*, September 1939.

24   Vera Brittain, *Testament of Youth*, Fontana, London, 1979.

25   Marie Stopes, *Married Love*, A. C. Fifield, London, 1918.

26   Ibid.

27   W. N. Willis, *Wedded Love or Married Misery*, London, 1920.

28   C. P. Blacker, *Guy's Hospital Gazette*, 11 October 1924.

29   CMAC:PP/MCS:A.158.

30   CMAC:PP/MCS:A.109.

31   CMAC:PP/MCS:A.42.

32   CMAC:PP/MCS:A.88.

33   CMAC:PP/MCS:A.205, A.87.

34   CMAC:PP/MCS:A.41.

35   CMAC:PP/MCS:A.50.

36   Barbara Evans, *Freedom to Choose: The Life and Work of Helena Wright*, The Bodley Head, London, 1984.

37   CMAC:PP/MCS:A.43.

38   CMAC:PP/MCS:A.123.

39   Marie Stopes, *Married Love*, Fifield, London, 1918.

40   Ibid.

41   MS to unnamed correspondent, 15 March 1918, BL-S.

42   The *Lancet*, 28 December 1918. *The English Review*, August 1918.

43   *Book Monthly*, Autumn Number, 1918.

44   CMAC:PP/MCS:A.197.

45 MS to HR, 24 August 1918, BL-S.
46 HR to MS, 5 July 1918, BL-S.
47 MS to HS, 6 August 1918, BL-S.
48 MS to CCS, 29 August 1918, BL-S.
49 Barbara Evans, op. cit.
50 Ibid.
51 CMAC:PP/MCS:A.49.
52 Marie Stopes, with Dr R. V. Wheeler, *The Constitution of Coal*, for the Department of Scientific and Industrial Research, HMSO, 1918.
53 MS to HR, 24 September 1918, BL-S.
54 HR to MS, 6 July 1918, BL-S.
55 Ibid., 13 October 1918, BL-S.
56 Ibid., 27 October 1918, BL-S.
57 MS to HR, 24 October 1918, BL-S.
58 HR to MS, 24 October 1918, BL-S.
59 The *Practitioner*, July 1923.
60 MS to HR, 27 November 1918, BL-S.
61 Ibid., 11 February 1919, BL-S.
62 MS to the *Leicester Daily Post*, 27 April 1920, CMAC:PP/MCS.
63 MS to C. K. Millard, 27 November 1918, BL-S.
64 Aylmer Maude to MS, 11 November 1918, BL-S.
65 MS to WS, 19 April 1919, BL-S.
66 MS, dictated to her husband, 19 July 1919, BL-S.
67 Keith Briant, *Marie Stopes*, The Hogarth Press, London, 1962.
68 Photograph of dead child with inscription, BL-S.

7   The Turning Point

1   HR to MS, 16 September 1919, BL-S.
2   The *New Witness*, 12 September 1919.
3   S.J.C. to MS, 25 September 1919, BL-S.
4   HR to S.J.C., 28 September 1919, BL-S.
5   HR to MS, 21 December 1919, BL-S.
6   MS to HR, 31 December 1919, BL-S.
7   J. I. Cox to MS, 26 January 1920, BL-S.
8   Aylmer Maude to MS, 6 March 1920, BL-S.
9   Mary Scharleib, *British Medical Journal*, 16 July 1921, & *Medical Views on Birth Control* (ed. Marchant) Putnam, London, 1926.
10 Richard Davenport Hines, *Sex, Death and Punishment*, Collins, London, 1990.
11 Marie Stopes, *Sunday Chronicle*, 15 February 1920.
12 MS to Skilled Employment and Apprentices' Association, 27 May 1920, BL-S.

13 MS to V.A.D., 10 October 1924, BL-S.
14 Marie Stopes, *Radiant Motherhood*, G. P. Putnam, London, 1920.
15 MS to Margaret Sanger, 20 May 1920, BL-S.
16 Marie Stopes, *A New Gospel to All Peoples*, A. L. Humphreys, London, 1922.
17 Lambeth Conference of Bishops, *Report*, 1920.
18 Father F. M. de Zulueta to MS, 12 July 1920, BL-S.
19 Norman Haire, letter to the *Lancet*, 9 September 1922.
20 MS to HM Queen Mary, 21 March 1920, BL-S.
21 Colonel Henry Streatfeild to MS, 23 February 1921, BL-S.
22 Margaret Plymouth to MS, 9 January 1948, BL-S.
23 Mrs G.K. to MS, 23 October 1920, BL-S.
24 Frances Stevenson, *Lloyd George, A Diary*, Hutchinson, London, 1971. (Frances Stevenson noted that in 1914 both she and Lloyd George believed that 'illconditioned women should not be able to get married and have children'.)
25 MS to Frances Stevenson, 30 September 1920, courtesy Ruth Nixon.
26 HR, Circular Letter, 6 May 1919, BL-S.
27 CMAC:PP/MCS:A.138.
28 CMAC:PP/MCS:A.88.
29 Rev. CD to MS, 2 November 1920, BL-S.
30 Rev. JW to MS, undated, BL-S.
31 Anon., undated, BL-S.
32 Rev. C.Y., 29 November 1930, BL-S.
33 Vicar's widow, undated, BL-S.
34 Humphrey Roe's diary, H.S-R Coll.
35 Ibid. in MS papers, H.S-R Coll.
36 Humphrey Roe's notes, 21 October 1917, BL-S.
37 M. Jennings (*Daily Mirror*) to MS, 14 March 1921, BL-S.
38 MS to HR, 31 March 1921, BL-S.
39 MS to Lloyd George, 12 April 1921, BL-S.
40 Frances Stevenson to MS, 14 April 1921, BL-S.
41 Ibid. 10 May 1921, BL-S.
42 *Queen's Hall Meeting*, a collection of speeches, Putnam, London, 1921.
43 Ibid.
44 Ibid.
45 Ibid.
46 Ibid.
47 CCS to MS, 1 June 1921, BL-S.
48 *Queen's Hall Meeting*, op. cit.
49 Mrs Humbert Barclay to Aylmer Maude, 20 June 1921, BL-S.
50 Mary Kidd to Nurse Hebbes, 14 April 1921, BL-S.
51 MS to Nurse Hebbes, 11 June 1921, BL-S.

52 Anon. to MS, 14 September 1921, BL-S.
53 MS to CCS, 9 August 1921, H.S-R Coll.

8 Conflict

1   Harold Cox, *Woman's Leader*, 22 April 1921.
2   Marie Stopes, 6 May 1921, *Woman's Leader*.
3   *Transactions of the Medico-Legal Society*, 1921–2, transcript, BL-S.
4   MS to Margaret Sanger, 21 March 1921, CMAC:PP/MCS.
5   MS to Mary Dennett, 14 June 1921, BL-S.
6   MS to HR, 24 October 1921, BL-S.
7   Ibid., 27 October 1921, BL-S.
8   Ibid., 4 November 1921, BL-S.
9   Ibid., 5 November 1921, BL-S.
10 Noël Coward, *Autobiography*, Methuen, London, 1986.
11 Noël Coward, on board ship, undated (early November), BL-S.
12 *John Bull*, 8 April 1922.
13 Halliday Gibson Sutherland, *Birth Control*, Harding & More, London, 1922.
14 Marie Stopes (ed.) *Birth Control News*, May 1922.
15 Ibid.
16 MS to the Secretary, the Hardwick Society, 18 March 1922, BL-S.
17 MS to J. B. Hance, 18 October 1922, BL-S.
18 J. I. Cox to MS, 29 May 1922, BL-S.
19 Marie Stopes, Political Questionnaire, November 1922, BL-S.
20 MS to CCS, 10 December 1922, BL-S.
21 The *Lancet* 2 (1921).
22 Mr S to MS, 31 October 1922, BL-S.
23 W. Arbuthnot Lane to MS, 22 January 1923, BL-S.
24 Marie Stopes, *Married Love*, Fifield, London, 1918 edition.
25 All extracts from the lawsuit are taken from the transcript in Muriel Box (ed.) *The Trial of Marie Stopes*, Femina Books, London, 1967.
26 Norman Haire to MS, 6 June 1921, BL-S.
27 MS to Norman Haire, 5 June 1921, BL-S.
28 Norman Haire to MS, 8 June 1921, BL-S.
29 Marie Stopes, Autobiographical Fragment, 13 December 1927, BL-S.
30 Mary Abbott to MS, 22/23 February 1923, BL-S.
31 Marie Stopes, Circular Letter, 5 March 1923, BL-S.
32 Ruth Hall, *Marie Stopes*, André Deutsch, London, 1977.
33 *Universe*, 23 May 1924.
34 GBS to MS, 2 December 1924, BL-S.

9 Private Life?

1   MS to CCS, 16 February 1923, BL-S.
2   MS to Dr Robinson, 26 February 1923, BL-S.
3   MS to CCS, 28 February 1923, BL-S.
4   MS to Sister Marjorie, 23 March 1923, BL-S.
5   CMAC:PP/MCS:A.193.
6   J. B. Bunn to G. Thring, (Society of Authors) with circular about Marie Stopes's 'photoplay, Married Love', 28 June 1928, BL-S.
7   Ibid.
8   MS to HR, 11 June 1923, BL-S.
9   Humphrey Roe, election address, 3 October 1923, BL-S.
10 Marie Stopes, *Daily Express*, 16 April 1924.
11 Aylmer Maude to MS, 14 May 1926, BL-S.
12 Lord Cromer to MS, 14 January 1924, BL-S.
13 MS to Lord Cromer, 18 January 1924, BL-S.
14 Lord Cromer to MS, 26 February 1924, BL-S.
15 MS to CCS, 22 March 1924, BL-S.
16 CMAC:PP/MCS:A.225.
17 *Daily Express, Daily Sketch*, 28 March 1924.
18 Marie Stopes, *The First Five Thousand*, Bale Sons and Danielsson, London, 1925.
19 Mrs F. to Mother's Clinic, February 25 1925, BL-S.
20 J. M. Keynes to MS, 20 May 1927, BL-S.
21 MS to Stanley Baldwin, 6 May 1926, BL-S.
22 MS to J. H. Guy, 18 June 1927, BL-S. The letter, in draft, was marked cancelled. She did have a considerable correspondence with the addressee, who was helping her to battle against the Roman Catholics.
23 MS to Cyril Bibby, 24 March 1944, CMAC:PP/MCS:A.30.
24 Mollie Wrench to MS, 2 May 1924, BL-S.
25 *The Road to Fairyland*, Putnam, London, 1926.
26 J. H. Guy to MS, June 1927, BL-S.
27 R. A. Walker, sub ed., *Print Makers' Quarterly*, 26 June 1927.
28 MS to Duke of Northumberland, 24 February 1927, BL-S.
29 MS to Hugh Merriman, solicitor, 16 December 1928, BL-S.
30 H. G. Wells to MS, 14 June 1928, H.S-R Coll.
31 *Morning Post*, 14 August 1928.
32 MS to W. Talbot Rice, 20 January 1938, BL-S.
33 Harry Stopes-Roe to author in interview, March 1990.
34 MS to HR, 11 March 1929, BL-S.
35 Ibid., 17 March 1929, BL-S.
36 MS to Braby & Waller, solicitors, 11 June 1926, BL-S.
37 MS to E. Wilkinson, 20 July 1930, BL-S.

38 MS to Mrs Plummer, National Children's Adoption Society, 25 February 1932, BL-S.

39 MS, telegram to Major Cuddeford, 31 May 1935, BL-S.

40 GBS to MS, 28 October 1928, BL-S.

41 *Birth Control News*, January 1929.

42 GBS to MS, 16 August 1929, BL-S.

43 Pope Pius XI, *Christian Marriage, Selected Papal Encyclical Letters, 1928–31*, Catholic Truth Society, 1931.

44 Halliday Sutherland, *A Time to Keep*, Geoffrey Bles, London, 1934.

10 Late Blooms

1   CMAC:PP/MCS:A.287.

2   Marie Stopes, *Enduring Passion*, Putnam, London, 1928.

3   MS to Mrs Clayton, 29 December 1925, BL-S.

4   C. P. Blacker, *Report of the International Medical Group for the Investigation of Contraception*, London, September 1930.

5   Barbara Evans, *Freedom to Choose: The Life and Work of Helena Wright*, Bodley Head, London, 1984.

6   MS to HR, 8 October 1930, BL-S.

7   HR to MS, 29 November 1930, BL-S.

8   Marie Stopes, *Woman's Pictorial*, 11 March 1952.

9   Dr B.B. to MS, 7 February 1931, BL-S.

10 HR to MS, 9 April 1932, BL-S.

11 MS to HR, 5 May 1932, BL-S.

12 MS to Laura Henderson, 31 May 1933, CMAC:PP/MCS:A.125.

13 Marie Stopes, *Mother England*, Bale Sons and Danielsson, London, 1929.

14 CMAC:PP/MCS:A.211.

15 Barbara Evans, op. cit.

16 Audrey Leathard, *The Fight for Family Planning*, Macmillan, London, 1980.

17 Barbara Evans, op. cit.

18 H. G. Wells to MS, 25 May 1936, BL-S.

19 Keith Briant, *Marie Stopes*, The Hogarth Press, London, 1962.

20 CMAC:PP/S:MCS: GC.39.

21 MS to to Earle H. Balch, 20 October 1935, BL-S.

22 Marie Stopes, *Guernsey Star and Gazette*, 25 January 1935.

23 Professor B. Malinowski to MS, 7 November 1934, BL-S.

24 Edward Weeks, *This Trade of Writing*, 1935.

25 Ruth Hall, *Marie Stopes*, André Deutsch, London, 1977.

26 James McGibbon, Managing Director of Putnams, 1945–9, in interview with author, 1990.

27 Edith Summerskill, *A Woman's World*, Heinemann, London, 1967.

28 MS to Llewellyn Powys, 15 November 1939, BL-S.
29 HR, 25 July 1938, BL-S.
30 Alfred Douglas (Bosie) to MS, 5 November 1938, BL-S.
31 Marie Stopes, Autobiographical Fragment, 4 October 1938, BL-S.
32 Marie Stopes, *Love Songs for Young Lovers*, Heinemann, London, 1939.
33 Ibid.
34 Ibid.
35 Ibid.
36 Ibid.
37 Keith Briant, *Marie Stopes*, The Hogarth Press, London, 1962.
38 Geoffrey Faber to MS, 20 January 1939, BL-S.
39 Marie Stopes, unpublished verse, H.S-R Coll.
40 MS to Adolf Hitler, 12 August 1939, BL-S.

11 Surviving

1   HR to MS, 17 August 1939, BL-S.
2   MS to Lord Halifax, 23 April 1940, BL-S.
3   MS to Richard Acland, 17 December 1938, BL-S.
4   MS to Winston Churchill, 12 July 1940, BL-S.
5   Clement Attlee to MS, 15 July 1940, BL-S.
6   Lord Halifax to MS, 15 July 1940, BL-S.
7   HR to MS, 14 October 1940, BL-S.
8   Harry Stopes-Roe to MS, 1 October 1940, BL-S.
9   GBS to MS, 6 March 1939, BL-S.
10 Llewelyn Powys to MS, 30 October 1939, BL-S.
11 MS to Llewelyn Powys, 15 November 1939, BL-S.
12 Robert Graves to MS, 25 January 1951, BL-S.
13 MS to Keith Briant, 21 November 1941, BL-S.
14 Alice Briant to MS, 13 April 1942, BL-S.
15 MS to HR, 6 February 1942, BL-S.
16 HR to MS, April–May 1942, BL-S.
17 HR to MS, 21 March 1943, BL-S.
18 MS to HR, 22 March 1943, BL-S.
19 MS to Miss Estoe, 29 April 1943, BL-S.
20 Ruth Hall, *Marie Stopes*, André Deutsch, London, 1977.
21 MS to to the Ministry of Supply, 26 May 1944, BL-S.
22 MS to Lord Addison, 14 November 1943, BL-S.
23 MS to Clement Attlee, 18 June 1941, BL-S.
24 MS to GBS, 31 October 1944, BL-S.
25 Marie Stopes, poem, undated, BL-S.
26 MS to Winston Churchill, May 1944, BL-S.
27 MS to to John Waller, 23 May 1947, BL-S.

28 Nancy Astor to MS, 29 July 1953, BL-S.
29 · Laurence Olivier to MS, 6 February 1946, BL-S.
30 MS to Barnes Wallis, 1 October 1947, H.S-R Coll.
31 J. E. Morpurgo, *Barnes Wallis*, Longman, London, 1972.
32 MS to 'My dear June' (no surname) 10 February 1948, BL-S.
33 MS to HR, 14 February 1948, BL-S.
34 MS to HR, 5 June 1948, BL-S.
35 HR to MS, 22 November 1948, BL-S.
36 MS to Augustus John, 17 December 1949, BL-S.
37 MS to Gerald Kelly, 3 July 1952, BL-S.
38 Keith Briant to MS, 3 August 1949, BL-S.
39 MS to H. Moore Pim, 25 March 1949, BL-S.
40 CMAC:PP/MCS:A.200.
41 'Daffodil' to Walter de la Mare, 5 May 1950, BL-S.
42 MS to Clement Attlee, 23 February 1951, BL-S.
43 MS to Avro Manhattan, 6 December 1952, BL-S.
44 Ruth Hall, op. cit.
45 MS to Thomas Moult, 7 October 1953, BL-S.
46 MS, Autobiographical Fragment, 28–29 October 1953, BL-S.
47 Jeremy Isaacs to MS, 20 January 1955, BL-S.
48 MS to John Slessor, 22 December 1952, BL-S.
49 Mary Stopes-Roe, in interview with author, 1990.
50 MS to Adam Fox, 6 June 1957, BL-S.
51 Adam Fox to MS, 10 October 1957, BL-S.
52 Keith Briant, *Marie Stopes*, The Hogarth Press, London, 1962.
53 Marie Stopes's will, 10 October 1957.
54 Lambeth Conference, *Report*, July 1958.
55 MS to C. P. Blacker, 18 September 1958, CMAC:PP/MCS.
56 Keith Briant, op. cit.
57 CMAC:PP/MCS:A.190.

Chronology

1880 Marie Stopes, born 15 October, Edinburgh, to Charlotte Carmichael Stopes, scholar, and Henry Stopes, architect. At six weeks old travelled to permanent family home in south London.

1884 Winifred Stopes, Marie's younger sister, born 13 March.

1885–92 Educated privately by her mother and a governess.

1892 Day pupil at St George's High School, Edinburgh.

1894 Family moves to Hampstead and Marie and Winnie transfer to North London Collegiate.

1900 Enrols in Science Department of London University.

1902 Graduates BSc, with Honours in Botany (1st class) and Geology (3rd class).

1903–4 Post-graduate work at University College. Enters Botanical Institute of Munich University on a travelling scholarship. June 1904 awarded Ph.D. In October appointed lecturer in Botany at Manchester University, the first woman on the Science staff. Forms attachment to a married Japanese professor (Fujii) whom she first met in Munich.

1905 Fujii visits Manchester and tells Marie he is getting a divorce. She considers herself betrothed. She gains her D.Sc., London, the youngest Doctor of Science in Britain.

1906 Publishes papers on the nature of coalballs. Applies to Royal Society to visit Japan in search of paleobotanical material.

1907–8 Attached to Imperial University, Tokyo. Travels widely in search of fossil plants.

1909 Return to England. Appointed lecturer in Paleobotany at Manchester University. Moves to Well Walk, Hampstead with Winnie.

1910 Publication of *Ancient Plants* and *A Journal from Japan*. Two unsatisfactory love affairs with academics. Leaves Manchester on grounds of ill health.

1911 Visits Canada to study flora. Meets and marries Canadian geneticist, Reginald Ruggles Gates. Couple return to England in April.

1912 Beginning of marriage breakdown. Meets Aylmer Maude.

1913 February. Alymer Maude moves in as lodger. By September Marie consults solicitor about divorce.

1914 Ruggles Gates tells Maude to leave the house. In May Marie leaves her husband. In October she files a nullity petition.

1915 Meets Margaret Sanger, American birth control reformer, in London. Organizes petition to President Wilson on Sanger's behalf.

1916 Marriage annulled. Engaged in coal research.

1917 Completes *Married Love*, after years of work.

1918 *Married Love* published to instant acclaim. Second marriage, to H. V. Roe, pilot, and backer of her book.

1919 Birth of first, stillborn child at age of thirty-eight.

1920 *A New Gospel*, claimed by Marie Stopes to have been dictated to her by God, circulated to bishops at Lambeth Conference. Also *Radiant Motherhood* published, followed by a stream of successful sociological works.

1921 Marie Stopes and her husband open Britain's first birth control clinic at Holloway, North London.

1923 Brings libel action against Halliday Sutherland, Roman Catholic doctor who accuses her of 'experimenting on the poor'. She finally loses the case after two appeals. Production of her play, *Our Ostriches*, and her film, *Maisie's Marriage*.

1924 Gives birth to a son, Harry Verdon Stopes-Roe on 27 March.

1928 Series of lawsuits throughout the year. Sued for libel by editor of *Morning Post* and by Halliday Sutherland. Her first novel, *Love's Creation*, published.

1930 Joins National Birth Control Council (later the FPA).

1934–8 Deterioration of her second marriage. In July 1938, she exacts statement from her husband permitting her sexual *carte blanche*.

1939 Publication of *Love Songs for Young Lovers*. Takes over small publisher, Alexander Moring, and publishes several more volumes of her own poetry. Passionate love affair with young writer, Keith Briant.

1949   In July, Humphrey Roe dies.

1952   In love again, with Avro Manhattan, a young writer.

1957   Cancer diagnosed, flies to Germany for secret 'cure'.

1958   Death of Marie Stopes, 2 October. Memorial Service at St Martin-in-the-Fields.

Select Bibliography

Of Marie Stopes's own works, I have listed the principal books which illustrate her development, classified by subject. For a more complete list, readers should consult the bibliography by Peter Eaton and Marilyn Warnick, *Marie Stopes, a preliminary checklist of her writings*, published by Croom Helm in 1976.

Works by Marie Stopes

SOCIOLOGICAL

Married Love, A. C. Fifield, London, 1918. New York, the Critic & Guide Co., 1920

Wise Parent, A. C. Fifield, 1918

A Letter to Working Mothers, published by Marie Stopes, 1919

Radiant Motherhood, G. P. Putnam & Sons, London, 1920, NY 1921

The Truth about Venereal Disease, Putnam, London, 1921

A New Gospel to All Peoples, A. L. Humphreys, London, 1922

Contraception, its Theory, History & Practice, Bale Sons & Danielsson, London, 1923

1925 The First Five Thousand (Report on Mothers' Clinic) Bale & Danielsson, London, 1925

The Human Body and Its Functions, Gill Publishing Company, London, 1926

Sex and the Young, Gill, London, 1926

Enduring Passion, Putnam, London, 1928, Putnam, New York, 1931

Mother England, letters to M.S., Bale & Danielsson, London, 1929

Roman Catholic Methods of Birth Control, Peter Davies, London, 1933

Birth Control Today, William Heinemann, London, 1934

Marriage in My Time, Rich & Cowan, London, 1935

Change of Life in Men and Women, Putnam, London, 1936, Putnam, NY

Your Baby's First Year, Putnam, London, 1939

Sleep, The Hogarth Press, London, 1956

PALEOBOTANY

Ancient Plants, Blackie, London, 1910

'The Four Visible Ingredients in Banded Bituminous Coal: Studies in the Composition of Coal', *Proceedings of the Royal Society*, London, Vol. 90, 1919

POETRY AND PLAYS

Man, other poems and a preface, Heinemann, London, 1913

Plays of Old Japan, the No (With Prof. J. Sakurai), Heinemann, London, 1913

Conquest, a play, Samuel French, London, 1917

Gold in the Wood and *The Race*, two plays, Fifield, London, 1918

Our Ostriches, a play, Putnam, London, 1923.

A Banned Play and a Preface on the Censorship (Vectia), Bale & Danielsson, London, 1926

Love Songs for Young Lovers, Heinemann, London, 1919

Oriri, poem, Heinemann, London, 1939

Wartime Harvest, poems, Alexander Moring, London, 1944

The Bathe, Poem, Alexander Moring, London, 1946

Instead of Tears, poem, Alexander Moring, London, 1947

We Burn, poems, Alexander Moring, London, 1941

Joy and Verity, poems, Heinemann, London, 1952

FICTION

Love Letters of a Japanese (under pseudonym G. N. Mortlake) Stanley Paul, London, 1911

The Road to Fairyland (under pseudonym Erica Fay) Putnam, London, 1926, Putnam, New York, 1927

Love's Creation (under pseudonym Marie Carmichael), Bale & Danielsson, London, 1928

General

BOX, MURIEL, *The Trial of Marie Stopes*, Femina Books, London, 1967

BRANDON, RUTH, *The New Women and the Old Men*, Flamingo, London, 1991

BRIANT, KEITH, *Marie Stopes*, Hogarth Press, London, 1962

CARPENTER, EDWARD, *Love's Coming of Age*, Allen & Unwin, London, 1930

BRITTAIN, VERA, *Testament of Youth*, Gollancz, London, 1933

ELLIS, HAVELOCK, *Studies in the Psychology of Sex*, Vol. I, Random House, New York, omnibus edition, 1936, Vols II, III, IV, Random House omnibus edition, 1937, Vols V, VI, VII, F. A. Davies & Co., Philadelphia, 1906, 1910, 1928

EVANS, B, *Freedom to Choose*, Bodley Head, London, 1984

FRYER, PETER, *The Birth Controllers*, Secker & Warburg, London, 1965

HALL, LESLEY, *Hidden Anxieties, Male Sexuality, 1900–1950*, Polity Press, London, 1991

HALL, RUTH, *Marie Stopes*, André Deutsch, London, 1977

—— (ed.) *Dear Dr Stopes*, Letters to MS, André Deutsch, London, 1978

HYNES, SAMUEL, *A War Imagined*, Bodley Head, London, 1990

LEATHARD, AUDREY, *The Fight for Family Planning*, Macmillan, London, 1980

MAUDE, AYLMER, *The authorized life of Marie C. Stopes*, Williams & Norgate, London, 1924

—— *Marie Stopes, her Work and Play*, Putnam, London, 1933, an expanded version of his earlier book

MORPURGO, J. E., *Barnes Wallis*, Longman, London, 1972.

MORT, FRANK, *Dangerous Sexualities*, Kegan & Paul, London & New York, 1987

SANGER, MARGARET, *My Fight for Birth Control*, Faber and Faber, London, 1932

STOCKS, MARY, *Still More Commonplace*, Peter Davies, London, 1973

STRACHEY, RAY, *The Cause, History of the Woman's Movement*, Virago, London, 1978

SUTHERLAND, H. G., *Birth Control: A Statement of Christian Doctrine against the Neo-Malthusians*, Harding & More, London, 1922

Index

Note: MS = Marie Stopes

Abbot-Anderson, Sir Maurice 180
Acland, Richard 222
Active Birth Centre 128
Aitken, Miss 18, 19
Aldred, Guy 162
Alexandra, Queen 137
Ancient Plants 58, 66
Ancoats Settlement 37
Anderson, Dr A. 14
Arbuthnot Lane, Sir William 133, 163
Arctic Circle 42
Arnaud, Yvonne 242
Astor, Nancy 233
Attempt, The 2
Attlee, Clement 223, 230, 232, 238
Authorised Life of Marie Stopes (Maude)
  180, 186
AVRO (A. V. Roe & Co.) 103, 121–2

Balche, Earle 208
Baldwin, Stanley 184
Bankes, Lord Justice 174
Barclay, Mrs Humbert 149
Barr, Sir James 164
'Barriers Down' 231–2
Bassett, Henry 60, 63
Baylis, Lilian 98
'Beale, Dr Courtenay': *Wise Wedlock* 156
Beale, Dorothea 14
Belfast 208
Bennett, Arnold 91, 130, 147
Besant, Annie 158
Bicknell, John 192
Binyon, Laurence 225, 229
Birkbeck College (London) 21, 24
Birmingham, Bishop of 99, 102, 110, 124
Birth Control Investigation Committee
  204
Birth Control News 159, 194, 205
Birth Control Today 206, 241
Blacker, Dr C. P. 114, 198–9, 245

Blackie, Walter 88
Bourne, Cardinal 174
Bradlaugh, Charles 158
Brewin, F. H. 77
Brian, Lord 204
Briant, Keith 211, 212, 214–17, 223, 226,
  232, 237, 238–9, 243–4
British Association for the Advancement
  of Science 3, 5, 6, 9, 10, 25, 28, 75
British Museum 58, 93
Brittain, Vera 112–13
Broad, F. A. 161
Brora 44
'Brother, The' 17
Brown, Dr 127–8
Bryant, Dr Sophie 15, 19
Buckie's Bears 203
Burgess (*later* Barstow), Ethel 106–9,
  142–3, 232
Buss, Frances Mary 14, 15
Butler, R. A. 245
Butt, Dame Clara 147

Caen University 41
Canada 59–60
Cardiff Naturalist's Society 98–9
Carmichael, Charlotte *see* Stopes,
  Charlotte Carmichael
Carmichael, James Ferrier 1
Carmichael, William 2
Carpenter, Edward 93–4, 112
Catholic Times 157
Change of Life in Men and Women 206
Chappel, Dr Harold 182
Charles, Ernest 163
Cheltenham Ladies' College 2, 14
Chesterton, G. K. 187
Churchill, Winston 222–3, 232
Cinema Commission of Enquiry 98–9, 101
Clynes, J. R. 147
coal 40–1, 121

Collins, V. H. 74
Contagious Diseases Act 100
Contraception: Its Theory, History and Practice 185, 201
Coward, Noël 155–6, 209
Cox, Harold 151
Cox, Dr J. I. 131, 160
Cromer, Lord 181–2
Cuddeford, Barry 192–3
Curie, Marie 75

Daniels, Nurse E. S. 161
Darwin, Charles 3, 134
Davies, Peter 206
Dawson of Penn, Lord 157
Dawson, Geoffrey 190
Dawson, Sister 231
de la Mare, Walter 217, 229, 237–8
Derry, Dr Bromley 147
Don't Tell Timothy 241
Douglas, Lord Alfred 213–14, 217, 221
Drysdale, Dr 102, 154, 156
Duncan, Isadora 31–2
Dunlop, Dr Binnie 102–3, 110, 125

Edinburgh 1–2, 5, 6; MS at school in 11, 12–13, 14
Elizabeth, Princess 137, 203
Ellis, Elizabeth 193
Ellis, Havelock 86, 111, 112, 225
Enduring Passion 86, 197–8, 241
Eskmeals 93, 94, 95, 121
Eskrigge, Edith 152
Eugenics Society 134, 244, 245
Evans, Isobel P. 72–3

Faber, Geoffrey 217–19
Fabian Society 87
Family Planning Association 205
Fay, Erica (pseudonym of MS) 186
Federation of Medical Women 133
Fields, Gracie 209
Fifield & Co. 102, 103, 111, 124–5
'First Walk, The' 215
Fluff (cat) 7, 11
Fonteyn, Margot 229
Forster, E. M. 230
Fox, Adam 229–30, 242–3, 245
Fraser, Sir Hugh 163
Free Church of Scotland 7
Freud, Sigmund 112, 177
Fripp, Sir Alfred 79
Fujii, Kenjiro 32–3, 34, 35–6, 37–9, 41–2, 43, 44–5; with MS in Japan 46–7, 50, 51–6

Galton, Sir Francis 3, 16, 134

Gandhi, Mohandas K. 208
Garner, Edith 61–3
Gates, Reginald Ruggles 68–82 *passim*, 85, 86
Gazette, University College 21, 24
Givons Grove 131, 132, 159, 174, 186
Goebel, Professor 28, 29, 30, 32, 33, 34, 41
Gold in the Wood 124
Granville-Barker, Harley 80
Graves, Robert 225–6
Greenhithe 25
Grey, Sir Edward 44, 83, 84
Guy, J. H. 187
Gwynne, H. A. 187

Haire, Dr Norman 168–9, 194
Halifax, Lord 222, 223
Hance, Dr 159–60
Hapgood, Norman 91
Hardwick Society 159
Harpers 91
Hastings, Patrick 163
Hawthorne, Dr Jane Lorrimer 145, 148, 165
'He to Her' 215–16
Heap, Alice Gertrude 122
'Hearth, The' 215
Heath, Sir Frank 24
Hebbes, Nurse 145, 149, 165
Hedin, Sven 56
Hewart, Lord 171–2
Hewitt, Charles Gordon 53, 60–3, 69
Hewlett, Maurice 70, 75
Hitler, Adolf 219–20, 221–2
Hokkaido 47–9
Home Office Experimental Station 93, 94, 95, 121
Human Body and Its Functions, The 185
Humphrey, Alvara 34–5, 36–7
Huntingdon, Charles 175
Huxley, Sir Julian 204
Huxley, T. H. 3, 6, 101

'Idealist's Love, The' 65
Imperial College (London) 72
India 208, 230–1
Inge, Dean 102
'Instead of Tears' 229–30
Inter-Planetary Society 241
Isaacs, Jeremy 241

Jacobs, Dr Aletta 143
Japan 46–57, 59
Jeans, Sir James 217
John, Augustus 236
John Bull 157

Journal from Japan, A 59
Joy and Verity 240

Kapteyn, Olga 18, 28, 55, 68, 76
'Karezza' 86–7
Keating, Father, SJ 153
Kelly, Gerald 236
Keynes, J. M. 184
Kidd, Dr Mary 149
Killick Millard, Dr Charles, 125, 126, 137, 148

Lawrence, D. H.: *Lady Chatterley's Lover* 112
Lawson, Professor George 2
Leatherhead 95–6, 106
Letter to Working Mothers, A 125–6, 140
Ligner, Professor 41
Linnaean Society 58
Lloyd George, David 138, 146
London County Council 81
Love Songs for Young Lovers 217–20, 221, 224–5
Love-Letters of a Japanese 37–8, 51–2, 56, 66, 70
Love's Creation 188–9, 241
Lytton, Lady Constance 147

McColl, Norman 16
McDonald, Sir Claude 56
MacDonald, Malcolm 224
McIlroy, Professor Anne Louise 152–3, 169–71, 180
McMurchy, Helen 59–60, 69, 71
McNabb, Father Vincent 157
McNichol, Miss 53, 60–1
Mair, Miss 13
Maisie's Marriage 178–9
Malham 25
Malinowski, Professor B. 209
Malthusian League 102–3, 125, 156
'Man and his Mate, A' 66–7
Manchester Guardian 104
Manchester University 35–7, 39, 58, 67–8; and suffragettes 43
Manhattan, Avro 239–41, 243, 244
'Man's Mate, A' 90
Marchant, Reverend James 101
Marriage in My Time 206
Married Love 86–7, 110–14, 209; and court case 163–7, 171, 172; first marriage of MS and 73, 76, 78; genesis of 70, 75, 85; later editions of 139–40, 164, 241; preface to 76, 78; pre-publication history of 88, 93–4, 99–104; publication of 105, 108; reaction to 114–19, 131, 140–1; royal

recipients of 137; sales of 172, 186; in United States 154
Married Women's Tax Reform League 71, 80
Mary, Queen 137
Masefield, John 212, 216, 217, 225
Maude, Aylmer 73–6, 80–2, 83–4, 85, 86, 87–9, 91, 95–6, 132, 149, 152; biography of MS 180, 186; death of 212; and MS's second marriage 106, 109–10, 126
Medico-Legal Society 152–3
Menzies, Miss 13
Metcalfe, Herbert 163
Miners' Federation 145–6
Minneapolis 68
Mitchison, Naomi 116
Morgan, Charles 230
Morning Post 187–8, 189
Mortlake, G. N. (pseudonym of MS) 37–8, 67, 70
Mother England 190, 202–3
Mother How Was I Born? 185
Mother's Clinic 144–5, 156–7, 179, 183, 194, 198–9, 204, 223–4
Munich 28–34, 41
Murray, Gilbert 91
Murray, Dr Jessie 126

National Birth Control Association 205
National Birth Control Council 195, 205
National Birth-Rate Commission 124, 134, 204
National Children's Adoption Society 191
National Council of Public Morals 98–9, 101
National Society for the Prevention of Venereal Disease 132
New Generation League 161
New Gospel to All Peoples, A 136–7
New Statesman and Nation 98
Norbury Park 201–2, 210–11, 214, 221–2, 223, 224, 226–7, 230, 232, 243
North London Collegiate School 2, 14–15, 16, 17–19
Northumberland, Duke of 187
Northumberland 83–5
Norwood 5, 6

O'Connor, Dr Bernard 152
O'Connor, T. P. 178
Old Vic 98
Oliver, Professor F. W. 19–20, 21, 26, 27–8, 35, 43, 44, 54, 57, 72, 82
Olivier, Laurence 233
Oriri 224, 226
Our Ostriches 180–1

Oxford Union 241

Pall Mall Gazette 100
Pankhurst, Christabel 43
Pankhurst, Emmeline 42
Pilgrim, Guy 22–3
Pius IX, Pope 195–6
Poetry Society 58, 221
Powys, Llewelyn 225
Putnams 135, 175

Quaker Meeting House 17
Queen's Hall Meeting (1921) 147–9
Quiller-Couch, Sir Arthur 225

Race, The 96–8, 111, 124
Radiant Motherhood 135, 138, 140
Rational Dress Society 10
Raybould, Clarence 98
Reith, Lord 212
Resvoll, Frau 42–3
Reynolds, C. A. 101
Rhondda Valley Education Authorities
  133
Road to Fairyland, The 186
Roberts, G. H. 147
Robin (orphan) 191, 192
Robinson, Dr W. J. 154
Rockefeller, J. D. 92
Roe, Alliott 103
Roe, Humphrey: and birth control 126,
  135, 142–4, 148, 153, 159, 179, 190,
  198; and correspondence 138–9, 179;
  death of 237; and *Married Love* 102–4;
  marriage to MS 105–10, 119–22,
  123–4, 127–9, 130, 159, 179–80, 186,
  190–1, 197–201, 207, 210, 211–12,
  221, 223, 226–8, 232; and son's
  wedding 235–6
Rolleston, Sir Humphrey 204
Roman Catholic Methods of Birth Control
  206–7
Rose, Lieutenant William 229
Rouncefield, Brian 244
Rout, Ettie 133
Routh, Dr Armand 78
Royal Commission on Marriage and
  Divorce 239
Royal Free Hospital 170–1
Royal Society 41, 42–3, 57, 72, 93
Russell, 2nd Earl 152
Russell, Bertrand 162

St John, Father Stanislaus, SJ 164
St Louis 68, 72
St Thomas's Hospital, 71
Sakurai, J. 66, 98

Sanger, Margaret 90–2, 135, 154; *Family
  Limitation* 162
Saville, Dr Agnes Forbes 171
Scharlieb, Dr Mary 132
Scott, C. P. 104
Scott, Admiral Sir Percy 148
Scott, Captain R. F. 40, 64–5
Scott, Sir Walter 1
Scott-Foster, Richard 191–2
Scrutton, Lord Justice 174
Sex and the Young 22
Shaw, George Bernard 74, 96–8, 134, 152,
  175, 193, 194, 217, 224–5, 231–2
Skilled Employment and Apprentices'
  Association 133–4
Slessor, Sir John 242
Smith, H. 146
Smith, Sydney 5
Society of Antiquaries of Scotland 14
Society of Authors 87, 98
Society for Constructive Birth Control
  153, 158–9, 162, 174, 199, 205, 242–3,
  245
Society for the Provision of Birth Control
  Clinics 184
Society for the University Education of
  Women 2
Sportophyte, The 66
Stanley, Dr Ernest 87
Starling, Professor E. H. 101
Stead, W. T. 100
Stevenson, Frances 138, 146, 147
Stopes, Charlotte Carmichael 1–18
  passim, 25, 26–8, 149, 161; complaints
  of 32, 33, 34, 39–40, 41, 43; death of
  190; financial help for 92; and MS's
  first marriage 69, 71–2, 82
Stopes, Henry 3–18 *passim*, 25–6, 45
Stopes, Marie (*principal biographical
  details only*): American visit 153–6;
  birth 5; childhood and early life 5–10;
  coal research 40–41, 121 early writings
  65–7; education 11–20, 21–2, 24–5,
  26–8; film: *Maisie's Marriage* 178–9;
  first love affair 32–56 *passim*; first
  pregnancy and stillbirth of son 123–4,
  127–9, 130, 160; in Japan 46–57, 59;
  libel case against Sutherland 158,
  163–75; at Manchester University 35–7;
  marriage to Gates 68–82 *passim*, 85,
  86; marriage to Roe 105–10, 119–22,
  123–4, 127–9, 130, 159, 179–80, 186,
  190–91, 197–201, 207, 210, 211–12,
  221, 223, 226–8, 232, 235–6; middle-
  age *affaires* 211–12, 214–17, 223, 226,
  227, 239–41, 243, 244; and miners'
  strike 145–6, 184; and Mother's Clinic

144–5, 151, 156–7, 179, 183, 198–9, 204, 223–4; in Munich 28–34; presented at court 183; proposed adoptions 191–3; retained own name after marriage 71; and Roman Catholics 137, 149, 152–3, 157–8, 163–4, 174–5, 178, 186–8, 193–4, 195–6, 206–7, 244; second pregnancy and son 180, 182–3, 185–6, 199–200, 207–8, 233–6; terminal illness and death 243–6; writings see individual titles

Stopes, Winnie 40, 41, 58, 82, 96; childhood and early life of 6, 7, 9, 10–11, 12–13, 14, 15, 25–6, 27, 28; health of 74, 80, 87, 92, 126, 176–8

Stopes-Roe, Harry Verdon 182–3, 185–6, 190, 191, 199–200, 203, 207–8, 210, 221, 224, 228, 232, 244; marriage of 233–6, 242

Study of Plant Life for Young People, The 42

Suffrage Movement 42–3, 53, 63–4, 80–1, 85

Sumida River, The 98

Summerskill, Edith 210

Sutherland, Dr Halliday Gibson 152, 153, 157–9, 194, 196; court case against 163–75

Swanscombe 13, 15, 25

Swanson, Gloria 209

Talbot-Rice, W. 190

Taylor, Dr E. 78, 82

Thurtle, Ernest 205

Times, The 190, 212, 244

Tokyo 46–7, 49–57

Toronto, University of 63

True Manliness 100

Truth About V.D., The 133

Tute, Lieutenant Warren 229

Two Japans, The 67

University College (London): MS's education at 19–21, 24–5, 26–7; MS's work at 67, 72, 75, 141–2

Unwin, Stanley 93, 101

van Thal, Herbert 206–7

Vectia 76–7, 87

Venus and Methuselah 241

Villars 79–80

Voluntary Birth Control League 153–5

Von Wyss, Clothilde 16, 18–19, 22, 23–4

Wagner, Richard 31

Wakefield, Russell 99, 102, 110, 124

Walker, R. A. 187

Waller, Sir John 233

Wallis, Barnes 234–5

Wallis, Mary 210, 233–6, 242

Wallis, Molly 209–10

Walworth Women's Welfare Centre 184, 194–5

Waugh, Evelyn 174

'We Burn' 216–17

Webb, Beatrice and Sydney 98

Weiss, Evelyn 37

Weiss, Professor 35, 43, 54–5, 58, 68

Welfare and Sunlight Centre 194

Wells, H. G. 91, 134, 153, 189, 206, 239

West London Mission 177

Wheatley, J. 184

Wheeler, Professor R. V. 93, 99–100, 108, 121, 142

Wilde, Constance 10

Wilde, Oscar 10

Wilding-Davidson, Emily 81

Williams & Norgate 180, 186

Willis, Isobel 152

Willis, W. N. 114

Wilson, Woodrow 91–2

'Wine that turned to Vinegar' 66

'Winged Egoism' 90

Wise Parenthood 119, 120–1, 123, 124–5, 130, 140, 151; and court case 163, 167–8, 172; sales of 172

Witcop, Rose 162

Women Rebel 90

Woman's Leader 151, 152

Women's Debating Society: at London University 21; in Tokyo 52–3

Women's Society and Political Union 42, 63

Woolton, Lord 224

Wrench, Molly 185, 210

Wright, Helena 120, 199, 205–6

Wuffles (dog) 188

Younger, Lord Justice 174

'Your Mooonlit Face' 215

Yubari 48

Zulueta, Father F. M. de 137